Revelation

& the Mark of the Beast

by Reed R. Simonsen

Volume 6: The Gospel Feast Series

It's Time to Feast Upon the Word!
It's time to be as a Two-edged Sword!

Thank Yous!

To my parents, whose faithful examples of raising a family in a Mormon home has served as examples for many. I have often reflected on how I, like John had been raised by *royal* goodly parents. They are as Zebedee and Salome to me. I have many people to thank, a few have passed beyond: Joseph Smith, Jr., Jeff A. Benner, Rev. Albert Shamon, Jim Jepson, Fred Jepson, Peter Simonsen, Gaylen & MaryAnne Pedersen, David Sexton and of course my parents, who have always encouraged my flights of obsessive research, digging-and-digging into history until answers are found.

A Note to the Reader: I am occasionally asked, "So, who are these books written for? Sometimes it seems you are writing to Latter-day Saints and sometimes it seems you are writing for Christians-at-Large and sometimes it seems like you don't know." The answer is yes. Enjoy the book.

In order to simplify confusion the following terms mean:

Mormon: The Church of Jesus Christ of Latter-day Saints.

Mormondom: The culture of Mormonism.

Mormonism: The doctrine, beliefs, and worldview of the Latter-day Saints held either officially or unofficially.

Saints: Members of The Church of Jesus Christ of Latter-day Saints.

Latter-day Saints: Members of The Church of Jesus Christ of Latter-day Saints.

Secular-Christianity: Christian philosophies and organizations which are traditionally held but are wrong.

Restored Church: The Church of Jesus Christ of Latter-day Saints.

Restoration: The current dispensation of the Gospel from Jesus Christ into the hands of Joseph Smith and his successors in the Holy priesthood.

B.C.E.: Before the Christian Era. (the same as B.C.)

C.E.: In the Christian Era (the same as A.D.)

Table of Contents

Illustrations

Cover Art: George Frederic Watts's Satan with apologies to his Progress.

pg. viii: John the Evangelist by Vladimir Borovikovsky, Kazan Cathedral St. Petersburg, circa 1804.

pg. 18: The Kingdom Flag.

pg. 28: Coat of Arms of the State of Israel.

pg. 47: Collage of the Thyrsus Staff of Dionysus.

pg. 85: The Kingdom Stone.

pg. 86: The angel on the Isle of Patmos by William Blake.

pg. 92: An artist's depiction of the Great Comet seen over Europe in 1007 A.D. These are the Hosts of Heaven, called the Tsabim in Hebrew.

pg. 109: Lucifer Takes the Pope to Hell by William Blake, 1795.

pg. 125: Satan at the Gates of Hell with Mystery Babylon, Death & Sin by William Blake, 1806.

pg. 126: A souvenir card of the Capstone Ceremony of the Salt Lake Temple by Charles Carter.

pg. 142: Europa riding Zeus, Berlin: Verlag von Neufeld & Henius, 1902.

pg. 178: John Outruns Peter to the Empty Tomb by James Tissot.

pg. 188: John sees the Lord, unknown artist.

pg. 212: God the Father Inviting Christ to Sit on the Throne at His Right Hand by Peter de Grebber, 1645, St. Catherine's Convent Museum, Netherlands.

pg, 222: Pope Francis sitting on his white throne.

pg. 227: Dore's Wandering Jew.

A Book with a Blessing
If ye are prepared ye shall not fear.
— *The Lord Jesus Christ to the Latter-day Saints*

There are two books given to man that have the promise of granting a blessing just for reading them: John's *Apocalypse*, known to us as the *Book of Revelation* and the *Book of Mormon*.

Millions of converts to the *Church of Jesus Christ of Latter-day Saints* gained their personal witness of the Restoration of Christianity by reading the *Book of Mormon* with a sincere heart and then praying to God the Father, in the name of Jesus Christ, for a personal witness. Millions, and since 1830, millions upon millions have done just that and today know for themselves that the *Book of Mormon* is truly the third testament of Jesus Christ.

What is less well known is that *Revelation* is also a book with a promise. In the *King James Bible* it reads:

Revelation 1:3 Blessed is he that readeth, and they that hear the words of this prophecy, and keep those things which are written therein: for the time is at hand.

Joseph Smith the Prophet added, "Blessed is he that readeth *and understands.*" You and I have a distinct advantage over all others who want this blessing. We have both the Spirit and the Restoration to aid us. We are going to read this book *and understand it!* The blessing will come in having the courage and conviction to keep these things, for much of the book has happened already and much more is about to happen. The worst of which is at our very doors.[1] Some parts of this *Apocalypse* are down right scary.

How does one not fear the great and terrible day of the Lord? Secular-christians believe that they will be caught up into the clouds and become eunuch-angels in the arms of Jesus. That is why they don't fear. Mormons see it completely different, and praise God! I don't want to be a eunuch in heaven *or anywhere else for that matter.* I want to participate in God the Father's *Plan of Salvation* made possible through the Atonement of my Lord and Saviour Jesus Christ. I want to fill the full measure of my creation as an eternal man. I know many sisters in Zion who feel the same way. *How glorious to be a son or daughter of the Gods, made in their image, male or female!* We have been blessed to have been sent to this Earth in the *Fullness of Times,* kin to the prophets and the Great Messiah. Here we continue the war against evil, armed with all of the keys, knowledge and power to save, through the blood of Christ, ourselves, our children and our kindred dead. Latter-day Saints, of all people, have reason to shout the loudest Hallelujahs of all. Brigham Young liked to say, "We should shout Hallelujah loud enough for Satan in his hell to hear and be afraid."

In regards to the book of *Revelation*, Joseph Smith illuminated all that was necessary to crack open the book. He also left this annoying statement:

The book of Revelation is one of the plainest books God ever caused to be written. — Joseph Smith the Prophet

Before you remind him that he had a *Urim & Thummim* and you don't, let's be grateful that he left us the means to make this book accessible. He also warned the young missionaries *(and I know you are reading this right now. Don't deny it):*

It is not very essential for [young] elders to have knowledge in relation to the meaning of beasts, and heads and horns, and other figures made use of in the revelations... Oh, ye elders of Israel, hearken to my voice; and when you are

As Saints of the Latter-days we need to be careful when telling all that we know. I have seen it many times. We are so excited to share the height and depth of our increased knowledge that we often give the meat to the baby before the milk, and then wonder why the spiritually childish have choked to death on the Restoration. The first need of our friends and neighbors is to hear the warning that the Lord's return is close, and that they need to be prepared. In our case, the need is to utilize the great opportunity we have to *prepare every needful thing* and *hold on to that which is good.* Part of that need is to educate ourselves by feasting at the table of the Lord. As one who has long fallen in love with the writings of John the Apostle, I know that my fear of the last days has lessened because I am preparing myself in the here and now, both spiritually and physically for what is coming.

The *Book of Revelation* is one of the last great mysteries of the future. Like any book of events yet unexperienced, it is impossible to know how everything will happen precisely. Sometimes the Lord flexes His mighty arm, as at Sinai with Moses. Sometimes He works quietly as He did in Upstate New York with Joseph Smith. Only those with eyes to see can really tell one from the other.

Let us explore this matchless book together by examining what we know, what we hope for, and what we suspect, throwing in a heavy dose of educated speculation but always listening to the Holy Ghost to keep us grounded. Remember, we have nothing to fear from the future. Elder Bruce R. McConkie said:

If you have already fallen in love with John's presentation of the plan of salvation as it is set out in the Apocalypse, you are one of the favored few in the Church. If this choice experience is yet ahead of you, the day and hour is here to launch one of the most intriguing and rewarding studies in gospel scholarship in which any of us ever engage - Elder Bruce R. McConkie.

For us that journey beings today... turn the page!

John the Evangelist by Vladimir Borovikovsky, Kazan Cathedral St. Petersburg, circa 1804. Traditionally each of the writers of the Four Gospels were assigned one of the living creatures that surround the Father's throne. John was given the eagle. Who knows why?

Chapter One

John the Belovéd

Whosoever therefore shall humble himself as this little child, the same is greatest in the kingdom of heaven. — *Jesus Christ*

The name *John* in Hebrew is pronounced *Yo-ha-nan* and it means *Jehovah is gracious*. In the Christian-speaking world, John has consistently been one of the top names for boys for over two thousand years. This is certainly because two of Christianity's most loved prophets were named John — John the Baptist and John called the Belovéd and the Revelator. He was by trade a fisherman. It is this John that we will be studying together.

THE TEENAGE APOSTLE

John was the son of Zebedee and Salome. His mother was the sister of Mary the mother of Jesus.[2] He had an older brother named Jacob whose name would be translated as *James* in the *King James Version* of the Bible. They were an affluent family. His father owned a successful, and lucrative, fishing business on the Sea of Galilee in partnership with two sons of Jonah and Joanna, named Andrew and Simon (Peter). They controlled a fleet of boats and hired many servants.

When John the Baptist returned from the desert wearing the *mantle of Elijah* and calling the people to him, Andrew and John went representing their families to check him out. They were both baptized by the Baptist and became his disciples. There was much excitement in the air at that time. The children of Judah, studying the *Book of Daniel*, knew that the Messiah was due. Many wondered if the Baptist was the Messiah. John the Baptist's birth had been a high profile miracle. The Baptist's father, Zacharias, was the rightful High Priest of Israel, making

1

the Baptist the next rightful High Priest after him. The Jews knew this. Magi from Babylon had come to Judah following a supernatural star[3] searching for the rightful King of the Jews. Hundreds of baby boys had been murdered by King Herod in an attempt to stop the true heir from inheriting the throne. Elderly Zacharias had been killed when he refused to give up his baby son John for slaughter. The people knew all of this. These were facts that were still in living memory for the people. This was a sign of their times. It is entirely possible that Zebedee and Salome named their youngest son John in honor of the new High Priest born to Zacharias and Elisabeth, who had disappeared. You will remember that Elisabeth and Salome were related, although we are not certain how closely.[4] It was a very exciting time and when the rightful High Priest of Israel returned from the desert shouting that "the kingdom of Heaven is at hand," Zebedee let his teenage son go with this older business partner Andrew to check him out.

We know that they were encouraged by all that they saw. Flocks of people from all over Judaea were coming to the Baptist to be immersed in water and hear him proclaim that soon the Messiah would appear. They watched as the Baptist made short work of the snooty Elders of Israel who had come to challenge his wisdom and authority. They saw the fearless courage he had when he refused to kowtow to Herod Antipas. The people knew that Herod and Rome had interfered in their religion by appointing their own High Priests but there was little they could do about it.[5] Here, in John the Baptist, they found a High Priest of God's own choosing; one they could follow and admire.

Soon Andrew and John were assisting the Baptist and were nearby him when he performed the most import act of any High Priest ever: the choosing of the national lamb of sacrifice. The Lamb of God that the Baptist chose was THE LAMB that the Father Himself had chosen and whom we sustained in the great family council in heaven in the beginning before the world was. Among the day's crowd, a solitary figure, Jesus of Nazareth appeared seeking baptism. Here is John the Apostle's eyewitness account:

John 1:35 Again the next day after [the Baptist] stood, and two of his disciples [Andrew and John, the son of Zebedee];

36 And looking upon Jesus as he walked, [John the Baptist] saith, Behold the Lamb of God!

37 And the two disciples heard him speak, and they followed Jesus.

38 Then Jesus turned, and saw them following, and saith unto them, What seek ye? They said unto him, Rabbi, where dwellest thou?

39 He saith unto them, Come and see. They came and saw where he dwelt, and abode with him that day: for it was about the tenth hour.

40 One of the two which heard [the Baptist] speak, and followed him, was Andrew, Simon Peter's brother.

Andrew and young John immediately understood the importance of this. The Baptist had selected the Lamb *and* the Messiah. Andrew and John left the Baptist and followed after Jesus to learn about Him. They were impressed by what they saw and decided to tell their families. Returning home, Andrew told Simon, and a friend named Philip, while John told his brother James that they believed they had found the Messiah! Andrew, Simon, Philip, and John decided to follow Jesus back to Nazareth. Although he was only sixteen years of age, John was allowed to go. He was with trusted friends and, after all, he would be staying with his aunt Mary.

While staying with Jesus's mother, they were invited to accompany Jesus to a wedding at Cana where the Lord performed his first public miracle, turning water into wine.[6]

They continued to follow Him on a preaching tour of Galilee and then to Jerusalem where He cleansed the Temple the first time. Zebedee owned a house in Jerusalem (the same one which later Nicodemus would visit in the night seeking to meet Jesus in private.) After this, the fishermen had to get back to work and so they returned to Galilee and their nets, pondering on all they had witnessed.

We are not sure how much time passed, but one day Jesus returned to Galilee by way of Capernaum and called Simon and Andrew from their fishing nets with the famous call: "Come follow me. I will make you fishers of men." He then went up the shore to where James and John were working and invited them to follow Him as well. Soon after, Jesus called them to go out into the area and proclaim the *Good News* of His ministry.

John went out into the world with the original 12 to declare the Good News that the Messiah had come! He practiced blessing and casting out demons and returned to the Lord even more zealous for the cause. Later, when Jesus chose His "three counselors" from the Twelve, John was named 3rd counselor after Peter and his brother James. As such, he was privy to much of the inner workings of the Lord's ministry, making his testimony an extra special eye-witness account.

John earned the title "son of thunder" when he wanted to call down fire from heaven on a Samaritan town that had refused the Lord hospitality. He was cautioned by the Lord for his rebuking of a man using Jesus's name to cast out devils unofficially. Jesus told him that they were lucky to get any support they could. John's zeal for the Saviour was highlighted when his mother asked Jesus on their behalf, if they might have the chief seats beside Jesus in heaven. All the apostles were aware of the affection Jesus had for His young cousin. John soon earned the nickname, "the Belovéd." He wore it with honor.[7]

At the Last Supper, John was privileged to have the seat next to Jesus. As the dinner progressed and the apostles reclined between courses, John rested on Jesus's chest. It was here that He overheard that Judas would be the one to betray the Lord.

John's family fishing business had made them numerous friends in Jerusalem. It is likely that his father had a sales agent in Jerusalem and their business in the area was the reason they kept a house in the capital city. John's family knew the powerful business leaders, elders and high priests of Jerusalem and so, John was invited to the court proceedings when Jesus was tried. John was also at the cross, which must have been unimaginably difficult. One can only ponder on the deep sorrow he had when Jesus turned to him and asked that he take care of His mother Mary. John was with Peter when Jesus's body was prepared and placed in the tomb. When news reached the Apostles that the Lord's body was missing, John outran Peter to the tomb (although he did wait for Peter to catch up before going inside). Then, John's great faith was manifest. He looked into the empty tomb and knew that the Lord had risen! Where others didn't know what to think, he had no doubt. While others wept, John, in faith, rejoiced!

While the Lord was busy giving His accounting to our universal Father and visiting His other sheep in America and elsewhere, the Apostles went back to their fishing trade. It is likely that with all the miraculous events of the past three and a half years, and the unbelievable brutality they had witnessed at the cross, they were uncertain exactly what to do next. I suspect that the calmness of doing what they knew best served as a time of wonderment and deep reflection.

They had had an unproductive night fishing when on the morning they observed a man walking along the shore. He called out to them, asking how the fishing went. They replied, "Terrible. It was terrible."

The stranger called back that they should cast their nets on the right side of the ship instead. They did and their catch was abundant to over-flowing. John turned to Peter and said, "It's the Lord!"

Peter grabbed his fisherman's coat and jumped overboard, swimming to shore as quickly as he could. The other men secured the catch and then brought in the ships.

They found Jesus making them breakfast on the shore. They had a priesthood conference planning out the future work. John noted that despite the enormous catch, the nets did not break; a sure sign that their coming ministry would be a bountiful catch of humanity from all walks of life.

After the Lord's Ascension into heaven, John would work closely with Peter healing the sick and going on a mission to Samaria. There is a somewhat humorous story that has come down to us about this time. It is said that one day the Apostles were talking among themselves about the many events they had witnessed and perhaps it was about the time that Peter and Matthew were writing their gospel accounts. One of the Apostles asked if anyone understood how the Lord had been conceived. They knew that He was the Only Begotten Son of the Father but the language used always said *by the power of the Holy Ghost*. How did that work? The story goes that the Apostles decided that if anyone could find out the answer it would be John asking Mary directly. It is said that Peter was too shy to ask her, so he talked John into doing it. John did ask and just as Mary was telling him, it is said that the room filled with light and the Lord appeared. He told his mother that some things were private family matters and not for the world to know. So Mary, as before, *kept all these things in her heart,* where it still resides.

John served a mission with Peter to Rome. Tradition says that at one point he was captured and condemned to death by being boiled alive in oil. He was saved by divine intervention and a church was built on the spot. A second attempt was made to poison him but when he took the cup, the venom within suddenly changed into a serpent and slithered away. These stories are included because many early depictions of John include him as either being lowered into oil or holding a cup with a serpent. These stories served as identifications for John at a time when many medieval christians could not read. He is also frequently depicted as a beardless youth since he was a teenager when called to the Apostleship. In modern times, grasping feminists, wanting to prove that Jesus ordained women to the priesthood, have tried to suggest that the youthful beardless John is a woman, but theirs is a modern invention. *It's not true. John was not a woman.*

While at a General Conference of the gathered apostles, they agreed to take three days and fast and pray together. At the end of which, they would tell the rest what they had learned. Andrew, Peter's brother, told the group that it was made known to him that John was to write this eye-witness account of the Gospel under his own name and that all the Apostles were to read it and certify it. This became the *Gospel According to Saint John* in the *New Testament.*

Shortly before the destruction of Jerusalem, John took Mary and moved to Ephesus. His most famous convert of record is probably Polycarp. We know quite a bit about John from Polycarp and others, although it is impossible to distinguish fact from legend (which is true of much of ancient history.) There was a time when men took the historical records of the ancients more on face value than we do today post-Darwin, and so-called higher, illuminated criticism from the faithless.

Bishop Irenaeus, who was converted by Polycarp and knew him well, said that John lived in the Greek city of Ephesus, in modern day Turkey, until the reign of Emperor Trajan.[8]

While he was living at Ephesus, John was exiled to a penal colony on the island of Patmos. He set up house there in a small cave. It was there that he received the visions known as the *Apocalypse*. It is possible to tour many of these sites and hear the local traditions which are still told about John's stay there. John's cave still exists, and like every Christian place of antiquity, it is dominated by an overly gaudy church. Visitors to John's cave can see where he rested his head and the fissures in the rock where it is said that *he heard the voice of God calling out to him.*

When the Emperor Nerva came to power, the Roman Senate officially undid all of Emperor Domitian's executive orders including all unjust banishments. John was free to return to Ephesus and his original home. Despite his advancing age, he wasted no time preaching the gospel, ordaining new bishops, and setting up the church in Asia. He also served a mission to the Parthians, a people living on the borders of modern Russia and Iran. One interesting story has been preserved from this time. While speaking with a particular bishop, John noticed a fine looking young man, graceful and smart. He told the bishop that he was to teach and baptize the youth, raising him up in the ways of the Lord. The bishop promised to do that and John returned home to Ephesus. The bishop did all that John commanded, taking the youth into his own home and there educated, mentored, and cared for him, until at length, he baptized him. Having done his duty, the bishop relaxed his former care and diligence. It was not long before the young man fell in with wicked peers. At first they merely befriended the lad, entertaining him lavishly with seemingly innocent entertainments. Gradually they expanded their amusements, including the young man in their nightly plundering. Sin added to sin and in time the gang formed themselves into a band of robbers with the young man as their captain. It is said that he, *like an unfettered stallion, excelled them all in blood, violence and cruelty.*

In time, John returned to the area on his Apostolic rounds and asked, "Come now Bishop, return me my deposit, which Christ and I left with thee." The bishop was perplexed. He could not remember having taken any money from John and yet he did not want to suggest that the great Apostle was mistaken. Finally, John exasperated that the bishop did not understand him, straight-forwardedly commanded, "Bishop, give me the young man and brother I left in your charge!"

Realizing at last, the bishop cried out in anguish, "He is dead." John couldn't believe it. He asked repeated questions until the whole story came out. John ripped his garment in half and wept bitterly. He called for a horse and a guide and went at once to the mountain lair of the robbers. At the border of their hideout, John was arrested by the lookout. He calmly told the guard, "Take me to your captain." When the captain saw John, he was overcome with shame and ran off on foot but John followed him, calling out, "My son, why would you flee from your defenseless, old father? Have hope in Christ. I will intercede for you, giving my life for yours should it be necessary. Stay and believe that Christ has sent me to you."

The young robber stopped and wept. He embraced John and it is said that he was *baptized a second time in tears.* John brought him back to the bishop and stayed with the young man through his repentance process until he was restored to full fellowship in the church.[9]

Bishop Irenaeus preserved a story which touches on the humor of John. He said that the aged Apostle once entered a bath house to wash himself but soon learned that one of his harshest critics, the apostate Cerinthus, was also inside bathing. Suddenly John jumped from the bath water and yelled loudly for all to hear, "Let us flee from this place, lest the bath house fall in, as long as Cerinthus, the enemy of truth is inside!"

We begin to lose track of John when he reached approximately 101 years of age. It is said that as a very old man, he would insist on being carried to church where he had just enough strength to rise from his litter and give the same message again-and-again, "Little children, love one another!" After multiple hearings, the church members finally asked, "Master, why do you always repeat the same thing?" To which they say, John retorted, "It is the Lord's command. If you do this, it is enough." His last known acts were to appoint bishops in every new congregation in which he was able.

A tomb was prepared for John in Ephesus but herein lies a mystery. Christian historian William Steuart McBirine made an in-depth study of the lives of the original 12 Apostles. He made an interesting observation in regards to the *death* of John the Belovéd:

[No one has any of the relics or remains of St. John.] This is a strange denouement. Some relics of all the other Apostles still exist, but the grave of John, which is perhaps the best attested of any Apostolic tomb by history and archeology, contains no relics, nor are there any historical traces or traditions of what may have become of them! [It appears that the tomb was never used.]

Again, the wonder of the Prophet Joseph Smith who would have known none of that in 1829 when using the Urim & Thummim in the presence of a witness (Oliver Cowdery), he received the following revelation:

Doctrine & Covenants 7:1 And the Lord said unto me: John, my beloved, what desirest thou? For if you shall ask what you will, it shall be granted unto you.

2 And I said unto him: Lord, give unto me power over death, that I may live and bring souls unto thee.

3 And the Lord said unto me: Verily, verily, I say unto thee, because thou desirest this thou shalt tarry until I come in my glory, and shalt prophesy before nations, kindreds, tongues and people.

4 And for this cause the Lord said unto Peter: If I will that he tarry till I come, what is that to thee? For he desired of me that he might bring souls unto me, but thou desiredst that thou mightest speedily come unto me in my kingdom.

5 I say unto thee, Peter, this was a good desire; but my beloved has desired that he might do more, or a greater work yet among men than what he has before done.

6 Yea, he has undertaken a greater work; therefore I will make him as flaming fire and a ministering angel; he shall minister for those who shall be heirs of salvation who dwell on the earth.

7 And I will make thee to minister for him and for thy brother James; and unto you three I will give this power and the keys of this ministry until I come.

8 Verily I say unto you, ye shall both have according to your desires, for ye both joy in that which ye have desired.

In other words, like a handful of the great prophets of old: Enoch, Moses, and Elijah in the old world; and Jeremiah, Zedekiah and Kumenonhi from the Nephite nation,[10] John escaped the laws of death for a season. He was preserved to continue the mission given to him to prepare the nations for the

Second Coming of the Lord. We can add a few more interesting stories which will have to be authenticated at a future day. For now they make for interesting possibilities.

JOHN IN THE AMERICAS

John's commission was specifically to be an Elias to the heirs of salvation. An Elias is one that goes before. You can think of an Elias like the American military thinks of the Marine Corps. When an assignment is given to take a particular piece of land, the Marine Corps is frequently the first one in. They survey the situation, set up bases, and generally prepare an area for the larger offensive. Someone has to till the ground and plant the seed or when the land owner shows up, (or the Army comes rolling in, to keep the metaphor going) there is nothing but a wasteland, where there needs to be a harvest, or at the very least, a base camp.

There is a fascinating story in the whispered annuals of Americana that I can offer as an example of what an Elias can mean. Don't be surprised if in your American History classes you have never heard of the mysterious *Professor*.

On April 19th 1775, the *Battle of Concord* between the British and the 13 Colonies took place. Congress, on September 13th appointed a *Committee of Three* to design a new flag, of which Benjamin Franklin was chairman. They were instructed to *repair immediately to Cambridge, Massachusetts and confer with General George Washington.*

By something more than a brief coincidence, the Committee accepted an invitation to be guests of the same family with whom a mysterious but extremely intelligent Professor was staying. He would not give them his name, only that he liked to be called *the Professor.*

This home was known by a few to also be the *Cambridge Secret Home*, where rebel anti-British planning meetings took place. It was here that the Committee of Three first met the *Professor*, along with their host and hostess. The Professor offered the Committee a new flag designed by himself. It had the Union Jack of England in the upper left hand corner with seven red and six white stripes, representing, as he put it, the Thirteen Colonies. When General Washington arrived, an official meeting was called and Franklin proposed to make the Professor an official, active, committee member. The Professor presented his design and it was fully accepted. After which the Professor gave the committee a second design, removing the Union Jack portion of the flag, replacing it with thirteen stars in a circle, stating that in due time this change would take place. They would know when it would be appropriate. He told them that a 5-pointed star should be used at that time as a symbol of *the promise of greater spiritual power that was yet to come to America.* The committee took the designs back to the Continental Congress.[11]

On June 7th 1776, Richard Henry Lee, a delegate from Virginia, offered in Congress the first resolution declaring that "these united Colonies are, and of right ought to be, free and independent States... absolved from all allegiance to the British Crown." Due to Lee's sickness, the Second Continental Congress on June 11th 1776, appointed Thomas Jefferson, John Adams, Benjamin Franklin, Roger Sherman and Robert R. Livingston, as a Committee to prepare a formal *Declaration of Independence.*

On July 2nd 1776, Lee's resolution, in its original wording, was adopted. On the 3rd & 4th of July it was debated by the Delegates in Congress with Thomas Jefferson acting as chairman. On the 4th of July great suspense and gloom hung over the Colonies. Many did not approve of total separation from Mother England. Others feared the King's vengeance. Many battles had been fought, but no decisive victory had taken place. Many Americans stood with Patrick Henry's call for "Liberty or Death" since the numerous wicked acts of King George III were no longer bearable. Thus the debate on what to do, and how far to go, continued. The old bell-man standing by the rope at the State House in Philadelphia was losing hope. The crowd of bystanders was becoming discouraged. Should they really break from England officially? Some of them said: "They will never do it." Noon passed, then one o'clock came with no decision by the Continental Congress.

Suddenly, in the midst of this confusion, a fierce voice rang through Independence Hall! The debaters stopped, they looked, and behold, the Professor was in the room, although he had not been invited and the doors had not been opened. His voice, his power, his intellect, and his oratory held the gathered men spellbound. His cry for freedom on their behalf, filled their souls. Space prohibits the quoting in full of the Professor's immortal speech but a few lines will speak for themselves. Several times he stated, "We demand no more than our just due; we will accept and be satisfied with nothing less than we demand." The very building itself echoed his closing words as he cried aloud:

"Gibbet! They may stretch our necks on all the gibbets in the land... yet the words of that parchment can never die!... Sign that parchment! Sign ... by all your hopes in life or death, as men, as husbands, as fathers, brothers, sign your names to the parchment, or be accursed forever! Sign, and not only for yourselves, but for all ages, for that parchment will be the textbook of freedom, the bible of the rights of man forever..." [He then dared to quote God the Father's will by saying,] "Let there be light again! Tell my people, the poor and oppressed, to go out from the old world, from oppression and blood and build My altar in the new." As I live my friends, I believe that to be His voice! Yes... with the last wave of that hand with the last gasp of that voice, [I] implore you to remember this truth — God has given America to be free!... millions [will] look up to you for the awful words: "You are free."[12]

The Professor fell into a seat. John Hancock scarcely had time to pen his bold signature before the quill was grasped by another. It was done.[13] The delegates approached to thank their inspirer, but the Professor *was gone.*

The Grand Union flag was formally and unanimously accepted, and the flag was adopted by General Washington as the recognized Standard of the Colonial Army and Navy.

At 2 p.m. the doors were flung open wide and the old bell man received the signal to ring out the notes of freedom to the shouts of joy from the gathered crowd.

Ridpath's History refers to this event, but Robert Allen Campbell gives more in his Treatise on "Our Flag," covering the designing of the Colonial Flag in 1775 and the Mysterious man, called the *Professor.* I briefly quote:

He is uniformly referred to as the "Professor." He was evidently far beyond his three-score years and ten, and he often referred to historical events of more than a century previous as if he had been a living eye-witness... He was erect, vigorous and healthy, active and clear-minded. He was tall, of fine figure... very dignified in his manners, being at once courteous, gracious and commanding... He ate no flesh,... he drank no liquor,... but confined his diet to cereals ... fruits ... nuts... and the sweets of honey... He was well-educated... and very studious. He spent considerable of his time in the perusal of a number of very rare old books and ancient manuscripts... which were never shown to any one... He always locked them up in a large ironbound, heavy oak chest... He was invited to become an active member of the Committee [on flag design.]

The *Grand Union* Flag proved to be necessary to unite the Colonies. It was saluted by both nations. When the British Army saw it being raised they prepared to attack but when they saw the Union Jack in the corner, the British General said, "See, they are British still." Both he and the American Army saluted it with 13 guns.[14]

There has been much speculation as to who this wise and elderly Professor was. My vote is that he was John the Belovéd, fulfilling his mission from the Lord that *thou shalt tarry until I come in my glory, and shalt prophesy before nations, kindreds, tongues and people.*

We know that John the Belovéd met with Joseph Smith a mere 58 years later before going to prepare the Ten Tribes for their return. While "the Camp of Zion" was on their way to Missouri in 1834, Joseph was some ways ahead of the company one day, when he was seen talking with a strange man by the roadside. When the company caught up to them, the Prophet was alone. That night at camp, Heber C. Kimball asked the Prophet who he'd been talking to. Joseph replied it was the belovéd disciple John, who was then on his way to the Ten Tribes in the North. Brother Everett said that he heard Joseph say that John was among the Ten Tribes beyond the North Pole. Hold that thought for *Appendix B: Joseph Smith on the Beasts of Revelation.*

Does it not make sense that if John was to prepare the Ten Tribes that he would first prepare the birthright Tribe of Ephraim? I believe it does. But, either way the glorious message given our Founding Fathers and the Grand and Colonial Flags he designed to unify our nation were truly God inspired events.

True to form, at some point, John was finished being Elias to the gathered tribe of Ephraim and the returning tribe of Judah. It was time to prepare the hearts and minds of the Lost Ten Tribes. The Mormon relief effort known as *Zion's Camp* may have been the last quorum of Ephraim to see John before his current assignment with the Ten Tribes.

John was blessed to have received a fullness of the knowledge of the Lord. We have been promised that at a future day John's complete witness will be given to us. The Lord gave the Prophet Joseph a piece of this as a gift on May 6th 1833 in Kirtland Ohio:

Doctrine & Covenants 93:6 And John saw and bore record of the fulness of my glory, and the fulness of John's record is hereafter to be revealed.

7 And he bore record, saying: I saw his glory, that he was in the beginning, before the world was;

8 Therefore, in the beginning the Word was, for he was the Word, even the messenger of salvation —

9 The light and the Redeemer of the world; the Spirit of truth, who came into the world, because the world was made by him, and in him was the life of men and the light of men.

10 The worlds were made by him; men were made by him; all things were made by him, and through him, and of him.

11 And I, John, bear record that I beheld his glory, as the glory of the Only Begotten of the Father, full of grace and truth, even the Spirit of truth, which came and dwelt in the flesh, and dwelt among us.

12 And I, John, saw that he received not of the fulness at the first, but received grace for grace;

13 And he received not of the fulness at first, but continued from grace to grace, until he received a fulness;

14 And thus he was called the Son of God, because he received not of the fulness at the first.

15 And I, John, bear record, and lo, the heavens were opened, and the Holy Ghost descended upon him in the form of a dove, and sat upon him, and there came a voice out of heaven saying: This is my beloved Son.

16 And I, John, bear record that he received a fulness of the glory of the Father;

17 And he received all power, both in heaven and on earth, and the glory of the Father was with him, for he dwelt in him.

18 And it shall come to pass, that if you are faithful you shall receive the fulness of the record of John.

19 I give unto you these sayings that you may understand and know how to worship, and know what you worship, that you may come unto the Father in my name, and in due time receive of his fulness.

We have been told that when the Lost Ten Tribes of Israel are ready to return, John will lead them from the north country by land and sea, bringing them with their genealogies, histories and treasures *to the princes of Ephraim in the midst of the everlasting hills.* There, at the hand of the children of Father Joseph of Egypt, they will at last receive a fulness and become full partakers of the rights and joys of Zion.[15]

I hope to be able to see John in the flesh and tell him, "John, I read your book. I loved it! Can I have your autograph?"

Let's explore it together. Who's to say? You might want to get his autograph too.

The Kingdom Flag. A constellation of 12 stars for the Twelve Tribes of Israel with the central star being for the Lord. The colors are blue and white, the same as modern Israel's. There is no red in honor of Isaiah's promise to us found in chapter 1:18.

Chapter Two

Eastern Thinking Lesson VI

It is the glory of God to conceal a word
but the glory of kings to search them out. — *King Solomon*

In this lesson on eastern thinking we are going to explore the artistry of Hebraic Poetry. Of all the original apostles of the Lord, none were more literarily adept in eastern mystical thinking and Hebraic poetry than John the son of Zebedee. His *Gospel* and the *Book of Revelation*, also called the *Apocalypse* are as beautiful and poetic as any of the great texts of the *Old Testament*. John approaches the beauty of even Isaiah with poetic moments such as this one, the opening verses of his *Gospel* eye-witness:

John 1:1 In the beginning was the Word, and the Word was with God, and the Word was God.

2 The same was in the beginning with God.

3 All things were made by him; and without him was not any thing made that was made.

4 In him was life; and the life was the light of men.

5 And the light shineth in darkness; and the darkness comprehended it not.

Many have noted how these verses are a play upon the opening verses of *Genesis*. It is as though John's Gospel was to come first in opening the *New Testament,* just as *Genesis* opens the old witness. Moses said, "In the beginning...." John understood that and more by saying, "In the beginning was the Word." The Jews who read the Torah in its original Hebrew know that hidden in Moses's opening phrase is a curiosity. The actual text reads:

Genesis 1:1 In the beginning God AT created the heaven and the earth.

The A is of course the first letter of the Hebrew Alefbeit, the Alef א. The next letter is the last letter the Tav ת. These letters are not read aloud by the Jews because they have no clear meaning. John understood them to say: *In the beginning was the WORD, the first letter through the last one, the entire Word and the letters too.* We are used to hearing Christ referred to as the *Alpha and the Omega*, to use the more common Greek Alphabet. We studied in *Ruth* how the Alef א is the sign of the Father-creator (thus the male priesthood) and that the Tav ת is literally a cross, like the Lord's on Calvary's hill. Genesis is literally saying that *in the beginning was the Lord Jesus Christ and the Plan of God. From the creation of the World under the direction of Jesus Christ to the final act of His atonement on Calvary, it all centered around our Lord.* It's just that John says it with an eastern heart, which sounds so much better.

His *Book of Revelation* is difficult for westerners because he wrote it in the style of the *Old Testament*. It is as rich in eastern knowledge and symbols as *Isaiah, Zechariah* and *Ezekiel*. In fact, John quotes the *Old Testament* Prophets over 500 times in *Revelation*. It is not possible to understand nor make sense of the book without a grounding in the *Old Testament*. In this thing, John is loudly proclaiming that the *Old* and *New Testaments* are not two separate collections, but really only one single witness that Jesus is the Christ. See *Appendix D* for more.

HEBRAIC POETRY

The Hebrews have always been an educated people. Adam knew how to read and write and taught his children. Modern anthropology after Charles Darwin has made its biggest error in assuming that those races of man which rejected the higher knowledge of Adam, came before him because they were more primitive; meaning more animalistic and ape-like. More primitive doesn't mean earlier, it means "stupider." From the account of Job we have his lament about the uneducated masses of humanity during his day, living in caves because they were too lazy to build a house or plant a garden.[16] Today, we call his contemporaries *cavemen,* and say they are pre-historic. Wrong! They have always been with us. Mankind still has those who prefer to live *under a bridge* and catch a squirrel or pan handle as opposed to gaining a college education and joining the rat race for mammon. I'm okay with that. I believe it's a man's right to live his life his way. Ten thousand years from now, our homeless campfires and the graffiti under our bridges might be viewed as man's first written words! *Kilroy was here!* Stupider is not earlier.

Eastern thinking naturally lends itself to poetry. Simile, metaphor, homily and poetics are a natural way of describing one's internal world. Look at King David's beautiful lyric:

Psalm 23:1 The Lord is my shepherd; I shall not want.

2 He maketh me to lie down in green pastures: he leadeth me beside the still waters.

This is beautiful eastern thinking. The Lord is NOT a shepherd. *I can hear the gasps! Stay with me.* The Lord is not a shepherd and you are not *a* sheep. I can use westernisms here to speak the truth to you in a boring western way. The Lord is actually a God, the Son of God to be exact. He is your redeemer and elder brother. On earth, He resembled the family of David with ruddy good looks and was reportedly a little taller than the average man.[17] He was kind to old and young alike. He healed the sick and gave people profound advice. All of this is true. David is saying all of that and more, but somehow, David's is more tender, more spiritually effective. Internally, in terms of emotional value, the Lord really is a shepherd — the best shepherd. *We okay, again?*

Let's take a short examination of Hebrew Poetry in this lesson on thinking more Jewish. We will see as we explore the *Book of Revelation* that having a few tools in this regard will make the experience richer and closer to being read as John intended. I believe that much of the modern confusion over this book comes from attempting to comprehend John from an overly western point of view.

PARALLELS

One of the poetic styles we will be reading in *Revelation* is a form we will call *Parallels*. The idea is a simple one and thus it is often missed by readers. The form takes the shape of two or more clauses that form a deeper — more complete — third meaning when placed together. It's like saying the same thing twice but a little differently. It's the juxtaposition of the two that gives this deeper meaning. I like to think of it as A + B = C. Here are some easy examples:

Isaiah 51:9 Awake, awake, put on strength, O arm of the Lord; awake, as in the ancient days, in the generations of old. Art thou not he that hath cut Rahab, and wounded the dragon?

This verse is structured in parallels. Note:

A: Awake

B: Awake

That's an easy one. How awake should you be? Very Awake! Ancient Hebrew had no real word for *very* as we do in English. When they wanted you to be *very* awake, they would repeat it: Awake, Awake! In English we would say that the Lord is very holy. In Hebrew we hear the angels declaring that He is Holy! Holy! Holy! That's very holy!

A: put on strength

B: O arm of the Lord.

What is supposed to flex its muscle? The arm of the Lord.

A: Awake as in the ancient days.

B: In the generations of old.

How is the mighty strength of the Lord's arm desired to be? Like it was anciently. When? In past generations. Isaiah is calling for the Lord to behave like He did long ago, in the records and legends of his people. He is asking: Where is the God who toppled the Tower of Babel? Who broke the House of Pharaoh? Who called Israel to the burning mountain top of Sinai? Where is <u>that</u> mighty arm?

A: Art thou not he that hath cut Rahab?

B: and wounded the dragon?

Who is Rahab? Rahab is the wounded dragon. How was he wounded? With a cut.

The concept is exactly the same in more complex Biblical poems. Try it on David's *Psalm 23:*

Psalm 23: 1 The Lord is my shepherd; I shall not want.

2 He maketh me to lie down in green pastures: he leadeth me beside the still waters.

3 He restoreth my soul: he leadeth me in the paths of righteousness for his name's sake.

4 Yea, though I walk through the valley of the shadow of death, I will fear no evil: for thou art with me; thy rod and thy staff they comfort me.

5 Thou preparest a table before me in the presence of mine enemies: thou anointest my head with oil; my cup runneth over.

6 Surely goodness and mercy shall follow me all the days of my life: and I will dwell in the house of the Lord for ever.

Try it out and see if it doesn't add some richness.

1A: The Lord is my shepherd;

1B: I shall not want.

Verse 1 Question: Why will David never want? *Answer: Because the Lord is his shepherd.*

2A: He maketh me to lie down in green pastures:

2B: He leadeth me beside the still waters.

Verse 2: What is the A clause? What is the B clause? What do you get by putting them together?

3A: He restoreth my soul:

3B: He leadeth me in the paths of righteousness for his name's sake.

Verse 3: How does being led in the paths of righteousness restore your soul? *By following wherever the Lord leads, we are restored. Why? For the sake of the Lord's good name. He is a good shepherd after all.*

4A: though I walk through the valley of the shadow of death, I fear no evil:

4B: for thou art with me; thy rod and thy staff they comfort me.

Verse 4: Where and how is David comforted? Why does knowing the Lord has a staff and rod protect you from evil? Why is David unafraid despite the terrible place he walks? *Because God is walking with him. God has brought along both His cane to grab David's neck before he gets lost and His staff to help steady the way and maybe even give David a smack on the hind quarters to correct as needed. Thus, fully equipped, there is no reason to fear anything, not even death.*

5A: Thou preparest a table before me in the presence of mine enemies:

5B: thou anointest my head with oil; my cup runneth over.

<u>Verse 5</u>: What are the preparations the Lord has made for David? *He has anointed him and filled him with abundance even in front of those that hate him.*

6A: Surely goodness and mercy shall follow me all the days of my life:

6B: I will dwell in the house of the Lord for ever.

<u>Verse 6</u>: Why will David's days be full and happy? *Because he has a place in the House of the Lord forevermore.*

When dealing with a passage that feels redundant but somehow lacking, just remember that A + B = C. Readers of the *Kings James Bible* have an advantage here. The scholars who worked over that version were well educated in their day. They spoke Hebrew, Greek and Latin. They had access to Martin Luther's translation as well, which is masterful. English, as a language, was particularly rich at the time as many useful and descriptive words were entering the language from classical Greek and Hebrew, to French, Danish and Latin. This is the reason that English today still uses parallel couplets to hammer home a point or add poetic richness. You still hear people say things like: The day is *warm* and *wonderful*; The sun was *bright* and *shiny*; There is nothing like *hearth* and *home*. There are numerous phrases like this in English. *Kith & Kin*; *Safe & Sound*; *Up & Away*; *Just & True*; *Muscular & Strong*; They can be traced explicitly back to the days of Shakespeare and the public reading of the *Bible* in English with all its parallelisms. Why is home so wonderful? *Because that is where the warmth of the hearth is.*

CHIASMUS

Chiasmus is a more complex form of parallelism.[18] Let's look at a very simple example first.

Psalms 124:7 Our soul is escaped as a bird out of the snare of the fowlers: the snare is broken, and we are escaped.

The pattern to notice is this:

A: Our soul is escaped as a bird

    B: out of the snare of the fowlers

    B: the snare is broken

A: we are escaped.

Meaning is taken as one descends into the poem reaching the moral core at the center. One then proceeds back out of the poem reviewing the lessons that led into the core, sometimes with a twist. Here is a longer example from the *Book of Mormon:*

Alma 34:9 For it is expedient that an atonement should be made; for according to the great plan of the Eternal God there must be an atonement made, or else all mankind must unavoidably perish; yea, all are hardened; yea, all are fallen and are lost, and must perish except it be through the atonement which it is expedient should be made.

Notice the pattern with the core moral:

A: For it is expedient that an atonement should be made

    B: for according to the great plan of the Eternal God there must be an atonement made

        C: or else all mankind must unavoidably perish

            D: yea, all are hardened

            D: yea, all are fallen and are lost

        C: and must perish

    B: except it be through the atonement

A: which it is expedient should be made.

So, the point here is that all men are lost. Why? Because they are hard-hearted and fallen. Thus an atonement is needed, stated twice for emphasis (like saying, holy, holy.) This is God's plan. What was the plan? The Atonement. Why was this the only option? Because it was either that or perish.

The *Book of Mormon* is full of chiasmatic sermons and poems. They are also richly peppered throughout the *Old Testament*. The prophets like them because they reinforce important lessons through repetition. In text they clearly state the truth that God works and thinks *in one eternal round.* Even entire books can be written in Chiasmus. Scholars have illustrated that the *Book of Daniel* has an over-arching chiasmatic structure. The *Book of Revelation* can be diagramed chiasmatically. Some have suggested that Milton's *Paradise Lost* is really an epic chiasmus poem. That would not surprise me in the least.

What most scholars miss however, is that the chiasmatic structure is really a living menorah. You will remember that the Menorah was a grand, golden candelabra that stood in the Temple of Solomon. It had seven candlesticks branching out like tree branches from a center shaft, which was called *the servant branch;* the moral. When lighting the Menorah, the priests would first light the center servant branch and from there light all the others. The servant branch was also known as the *Messiah's Branch.* As the Teacher of Righteousness, it was understood that by the light of the Messiah, all other truths would be known. Light is truth because it shows things as they really are. Dispensational christians make note that Jesus came in the meridian (meaning middle) of Earth's heavenly week. The christian custom of labeling all dates before Christ's birth as B.C., and all dates after Him as A.D., harkens back to the same idea. It is chronological chaismasity!

As we study *Revelation* together pay particular attention to Parallels, both simple A + B clauses and larger chiasmus patterns. This will help glean meaning where it might not be clear otherwise.

Revelation by its very definition is illumination. It makes the dark unknowable — known. It is light where before there was only darkness. As such, it is the ultimate menorah. This gives additional beauty to the Lord's call for all of us to be candles on a stand, letting *our light so shine* that others might know the Lord God and thank the Father of us all for the gift of His Only Begotten Son.

This is the perfect segue into the first chapter of the *Book of Revelation.* You will note that it opens with the Lord God surrounded by the light of a great menorah.

Coat of Arms of the State of Israel.

Chapter Three

A Letter to the Seven Churches in Asia

He that hath an ear, let him hear what the Spirit saith unto the churches.

— Jesus the Christ

The *Book of Revelation* opens with a letter addressed to 7 specific churches in Asia which were under the direct responsibility of John. Secular-christians, who are essentially starving for word from the heavens, place a great deal of value in these opening chapters. Their analysis can be at times very clever. Perhaps the most clever is that they are somehow a secret hidden history of the totality of global Christianity's timeline. For them, it is a reason to study the same. Latter-day Saints use them more in the spirit of the Nephites of old who, "did liken all scriptures unto [ourselves], that it might be for our profit and learning."[19] In short, these letters are not a secret code, they are exactly what they claim to be: letters to 7 specific churches with advice and warnings needed for their day. We can benefit from likening them to ourselves but that is their only modern value.

The more enigmatic chapters which come afterward are deeply pertinent to us living in the last wee minutes of the midnight hour. Let's explore these letters with some brief commentary but save the deeper feast for the body of the text.

The first and most important thing to know about this amazing book is its author. We call it the *Revelation of St. John the Devine*, but John says differently, and from chapter 1, verse 1:

Revelation 1:1 The Revelation of Jesus Christ, which God gave unto him, to shew unto his servants things which must shortly come to pass; and he sent and signified it by his angel unto his servant John:

This letter is a letter from Jesus Christ Himself, the head of the church, written to his Senior Apostle. How cool is that! Also, John wants us to understand that many of the things contained within are things which were to happen very soon; many in John's very day. This is important to know. Not everything we are about to read is future to us. Much of this book has already happened.

We are told right in verse one that an angel *signified* it to John. This is important because the word used is actually *semaino* in Greek. It means *to give by indicating with a token*. This is an official communique from God given after the manner of heaven.[20]

The larger book also fulfills a law of heaven which says that God will not undertake to do anything without first making it known to His living prophets.[21] The revelation was delivered to John by an angel. We will make an argument later that this angel was none other than Father Noah,[22] who seems to be the one tasked with overseeing the Spirit of Elias. John will also add his witness to the book as well:

2 [To John] Who bare record of the word of God, and of the testimony of Jesus Christ, and of all things that he saw.

3 Blessed is he that readeth, and they that hear the words of this prophecy, and keep those things which are written therein: for the time is at hand.

John is putting his good name on this revelation, and adding his eye-witness testimony. He adds his apostolic stamp that *blessed will be everyone who reads it* and who hears it read. More than that, blessed will be everyone who harkens to it because what we are about to read will soon happen.

One of the rights of an elder of the church is to send a blessing within the text of a letter to those who read it. John does this and more. As the senior apostle (we would say bonafide President of the Church of Jesus Christ of Former-day Saints), this is also an Apostolic Blessing. That's like a super-elder's blessing. Biblical historians have noted that this is arguably the only book in the *Bible* with such a blessing and promise. Mormons of course are thrice blessed in that we have just such a promise in the *Book of Mormon* and the *Doctrine & Covenants* (as well as many, many Apostolic Blessings given in Conferences annually in the Church). After such a grand introduction, John opens the letter portion of the revelation for the seven specific churches which he presided over in Asia. It starts with a short personal note:

Revelation 1:4 JOHN to the seven churches which are in Asia: Grace be unto you, and peace, from him which is, and which was, and which is to come; and from the seven Spirits which are before his throne;

Afterward, an even more astounding greeting is given:

5 And from Jesus Christ, who is the faithful witness, and the first begotten of the dead, and the prince of the kings of the earth. Unto him that loved us, and washed us from our sins in his own blood,

6 And hath made us kings and priests unto God <u>and</u> his Father; to him be glory and dominion for ever and ever. Amen.

Wait, God has a Father? *I knew that. How beautiful is that!* Latter-day Saints have many such beautiful passages in the *Doctrine & Covenants*, but here it is solemn proof that the Lord is the same, yesterday, today and forever. The Prophet Joseph Smith riffed on this verse as evidence of the Mormon signature doctrine that man was created as God's children in His image so that we might one day be as He is now. He taught:

31

It is altogether correct in the translation... The apostles have discovered that there were Gods above. God was the Father of our Lord Jesus Christ. My object was to preach the scripture and preach the doctrine, there being a God above the Father of our Lord Jesus Christ. I am bold to declare I have taught all the strong doctrines publicly, and always stronger than what I preach in private. John was one of the men and the apostles [to] declare they were made kings and priests unto God the Father of our Lord Jesus Christ. It reads just so, hence the doctrine of a plurality of Gods is as prominent in the Bible as any doctrine. It is all over the face of the Bible. It stands beyond the power of controversy... Paul says, "There are gods many, and lords many" [see 1 Corinthians 8:5]. I want to set it in a plain, simple manner. But to us, there is but one God pertaining to us, in all, through all...

No man can limit the bounds, or the eternal existence, of eternal time. Hath he beheld the eternal world? And is he authorized to say that there is only God? He makes himself a fool, and there is an end of his career in knowledge. He cannot obtain all knowledge, for he has sealed up the gate to [it]... In the very beginning there is a plurality of Gods. [It is] beyond the power of refutation. It is a great subject I am dwelling on... The heads of the Gods appointed one God for us. When you take a view of the subject, it sets one free to see all the beauty, holiness, and perfection of the Gods. All I want is to get the simple truth, [the] naked and the whole truth.

I want to reason. I learned it by translating the papyrus now in my house. I learned a testimony concerning Abraham. He reasoned concerning the God of Heaven. In order to do that, said he, "Suppose we have two facts. That supposes that another fact may exist. Two men on the earth, one wiser than the other, would show that another who is wiser than the wisest may exist. Intelligences exist one above another, that there is no end to it" [see Abraham 3:16-19]. If Abraham reasoned thus, if Jesus Christ was the Son of God and John discovered that God the Father of Jesus Christ had a father, you may suppose that he had a father also. Where was there ever a son without a father? Where ever did [a] tree or anything spring into existence without a progenitor? Everything comes in this way. Paul says, that which is earthly is in likeness of that which is heavenly [see 1 Corinthians 15:46-48]. Hence if Jesus had a father, can we not believe that he had a father also?

When things that are great are passed over without even a thought, I want to see all, in all its bearings, and hug it to my bosom. I believe all that God ever revealed, and I never hear of a man being damned for believing too much, but they are damned for unbelief.[23]

As a quick side note for those who question the Lord's rationale for sending Chandler's mummies to the Prophet Joseph with the papyri now known as the *Book of Abraham*, note the

Prophet's remark above. Joseph would preach on more than one occasion that Mormonism was a restoration of the higher laws *pre*-Moses. This included the laws, good works, covenants and ordinances of Father Abraham. It is also clear that it was from Abraham that the prophet learned a great deal about the proper endowing power of the Temple. Let's get back to John:

Revelation 1:7 Behold, he cometh with clouds; and every eye shall see him, and they also which pierced him: and all kindreds of the earth shall wail because of him. Even so, Amen.

It is a tradition in Judaism that anytime you read "clouds" as being connected to a visitation of the Lord, it is a symbol of the righteous saints who come with Him. Jesus is a Great King and Great Kings have entourages, including mighty angels who stand guard over their holiness. We celebrate this idea on our modern Temples with the Cloud Stones portrayed there. Christ and His holy entourage will yet return and every one worldwide will know it when it happens.[24]

Revelation 1:8 I am Alpha and Omega, the beginning and the ending, saith the Lord, which is, and which was, and which is to come, the Almighty.

It is common for a great king to list his titles and achievements when giving a proclamation. Note the ones that the Lord picked, remembering that He is free to pick any that He wishes. Ultimately these titles all mean the same thing. Jesus is God Almighty. It is comforting to know that our God is Almighty. The vast majority of the pagan gods men worship are not almighty but have flaws and frailties. They are frequently portrayed as having power over one specific thing; such as love, beauty, harvest time or death. Not Jesus Christ, He is God Almighty! The hero-son of the Almighty Father!

John next gives us a little background as to how and when this Revelation was given.

9 I John, who also am your brother, and companion in tribulation, and in the kingdom and patience of Jesus Christ, was in the isle that is called Patmos, for the word of God, and for the testimony of Jesus Christ.

10 I was in the Spirit on the Lord's day, and heard behind me a great voice, as of a trumpet,

The day was Sunday. If you journey to Patmos, the monks will show you the small fissure windows in John's cave from whence he heard the voice of the Lord. This closes the introduction. *On to the letters!* These 7 churches are particularly blessed to have a letter straight from the Saviour Himself. *You are particularly blessed also for having a Patriarchal Blessing straight from the Saviour just for you too:*

Here are the names of the specific congregations of which the Lord has both advice, praise and correction.

11 Saying, I am Alpha and Omega, the first and the last: and, What thou seest, write in a book, and send it unto the seven churches which are in Asia; unto Ephesus, and unto Smyrna, and unto Pergamos, and unto Thyatira, and unto Sardis, and unto Philadelphia, and unto Laodicea.

12 And I [John] turned to see the voice that spake with me. And being turned, I saw seven golden candlesticks;

13 And in the midst of the seven candlesticks one like unto the Son of man, clothed with a garment down to the foot, and girt about the paps with a golden girdle.

Standing in the middle of a great Menorah, John sees one who looked like his beloved Saviour; only this Son of God was more glorious and celestial. You will remember that when John walked and talked with the Lord, He was a God made flesh. He was a man, the son of Mary. Now that He had overcome all things and returned to the Father triumphant, He is still Jesus but Jesus the Almighty Celestial God. He is still Jesus of Nazareth, only now He is Jesus the Almighty conqueror and redeemer. This is what John means here. He is dressed in perfect white with a girdle of gold around his waist just below his pectorals.[25] Next comes a physical description of Him. Use your eastern thinking skills here. While I am sure this is an actual description, it also benefits from an eastern reading.

14 His head and his hairs were white like wool, as white as snow; and his eyes were as a flame of fire;

15 And his feet like unto fine brass, as if they burned in a furnace; and his voice as the sound of many waters.

You can read this thus: His head is pure just like the crown (his hair, the crown designed by the Father). His sight is fire, burning out all corruption that He sees. His fire is His love. His feet walk the path of judgement proven by His worthiness. When He speaks, the planets (the very universe) answer Him.[26]

Revelation 1:16 And he had in his right hand seven stars: and out of his mouth went a sharp twoedged sword: and his countenance was as the sun shineth in his strength.

See, it's eastern logic. I am certain that the Lord doesn't walk around with a sword in His mouth. Seven is the number of completeness. Yes, there are seven churches but note here that what the Lord grasps with His mighty hand, does not escape Him and cannot be taken from Him. A two-edge sword is a particularly dangerous weapon. It has the ability to cut going in and coming out. It cuts both ways, making it chaismic. The word of the Lord is exactly so. It can cleave the marrow from the bones. The Lord's words do not return to Him empty. The light of His glory is so bright that it is like looking directly into the sun. What a marvelous God we worship! John was beloved of this Great God and yet:

17 And when I saw him, I fell at his feet as dead. And he laid his right hand upon me, saying unto me, Fear not; I am the first and the last:

18 I am he that liveth, and was dead; and, behold, I am alive for evermore, Amen; and have the keys of hell and of death.

John could not stand in His presence, even though he was one highly favored; a personal friend on earth. Jesus had a mission for John and after He strengthened him, the Lord said:

19 Write the things which thou hast seen, and the things which are, and the things which shall be hereafter;

20 The mystery of the seven stars which thou sawest in my right hand, and the seven golden candlesticks. The seven stars are the angels of the seven churches: and the seven candlesticks which thou sawest are the seven churches.

Joseph Smith taught that the Lord will always explain the symbolism He uses if He requires man to understand it. Where symbolism and mystery have not been explained, you are not accountable. John is told that the seven stars held in the Lord's mighty grip are the 7 churches. *How wonderful! I would hope to be held onto so tightly!* The seven candlesticks are the 7 guardian angels of these churches who the prophet Joseph would later clarify as being the seven bishops called to watch over these flocks. I can testify that many a fine bishop has been as an angel-guardian to me in my life, censoring, encouraging and blessing me. I know that many in the church feel the same. Another useful thing to know is that very often the Lord pokes at the pride of people that He censors, using their *secret parts* against them openly. This can be a little difficult to explain but here is an example. One of the symbols most dear to Roman Emperors was *seven stars held in their hands.* Rome sat on seven hills and as a city was the pride of her people. Roman astrologers believed that earth sat amongst seven planets.[27] It was common for the Emperor to call himself, "he who holds the seven in his hand." Meaning that the emperor owned the pride of the people, the city Rome, as well as, the very stars themselves. The Lord saying that He was the one who actually held the stars in His hand would be like Him saying to the President of the United States,

"Listen to He who holds the fifty stars in his hand, who causes the 13 stripes to wave or be still; He who tells the eagle when to cry and when to be silent." While some of these things are lost on us today, they were a comfort to the church, and a slap to tyranny in ancient times. The Lord rules even when He is unseen.

We are going to go through these letters more rapidly than many evangelicals would do. Again, while they have many beautiful lessons within, they are as patriarchal blessings to an era long since passed. The reader would gain more by pulling out his or her own patriarchal blessing or studying the *Doctrine & Covenants*, which are *our letters* for the here and now. Still, as lovers of history, and the word of God, wherever we find it, let's begin. Here is John's hometown after Judaea, the City of Ephesus.

THE LETTER TO EPHESUS

Revelation 2:1 Unto the angel of the church of Ephesus write; These things saith he that holdeth the seven stars in his right hand, who walketh in the midst of the seven golden candlesticks;

2 I know thy works, and thy labour, and thy patience, and how thou canst not bear them which are evil: and thou hast tried them which say they are apostles, and are not, and hast found them liars:

3 And hast borne, and hast patience, and for my name's sake hast laboured, and hast not fainted.

4 Nevertheless I have somewhat against thee, because thou hast left thy first love.

5 Remember therefore from whence thou art fallen, and repent, and do the first works; or else I will come unto thee quickly, and will remove thy candlestick out of his place, except thou repent.

6 But this thou hast, that thou hatest the deeds of the Nicolaitans, which I also hate.

7 He that hath an ear, let him hear what the Spirit saith unto the churches; To him that overcometh will I give to eat of the tree of life, which is in the midst of the paradise of God.

Ephesus was the important port city in Asia Minor at this time. It was the crossroads of the East and West and was known as the *light of Asia* by the famous Cicero. The great Temple of Diana (also known as Artemis) was there; called with the Pyramids, the *wonder of the world*. Diana *loved* sacred prostitution in her temples and as such her centers were places of immorality and other crimes. The sitting Roman Emperor was also worshiped. It was here, during the Great Apostasy in the year 431 A.D., that the Catholic *Council of Ephesus* defined Mary adoration as appropriate, making her the *mother of God*. It was easy since Diana was already worshiped by the people. It is a strongly held belief from antiquity that John moved Mary to Ephesus where he cared for her as requested by the Lord. One of the best attested tombs of Mary is in Ephesus.

The Lord praises the congregation of Ephesus for holding fast to the truth and discerning the liars in their midst. He warns them that in all their goodness they have forgotten the first principles of sainthood. This is good advice. We can be very good people, but if we forget the first principles of the Gospel, if we forsake faith, hope and charity are we really Christians? It can be hard when liars and progressive thinkers are telling us how to live and which doctrines they feel we should and should not embrace. It can be easy to close down and let go of the little things in the guise of self preservation. The Lord is interested in the whole package. His reward is a heavenly reward so He thinks in the big picture.

The Nicolaitans believed that since God created humans, He also created *that which comes to them naturally*. Isn't that convenient. Since God made the weaknesses of the flesh, these weaknesses could not be sinful. They believed in free love and that any love between persons was a love to be celebrated sexually. They seem to have also believed in sex magic. Sex magic practitioners believed that there were magical properties to sex and that the natural pleasant feelings associated were analogous to a spiritual experience. This sometimes included temple prostitution both male and female.[28] This was sometimes referred to as *paying the dog's price* or *playing the harlot*. They held to no dietary standards since they held that *religion is in the soul, and not in the body*. They claimed that belief in God (today we would say, faith and grace) was enough to save. Works were fleshy things and all that was needed was to *love God and forget about what the body does*. All love is love they said. The Lord put Himself on the record saying that these were things He hated and were incorrect doctrines.

THE LETTER TO SMYRNA

Revelation 2:8 And unto the angel of the church in Smyrna write; These things saith the first and the last, which was dead, and is alive;

Revelation 2:9 I know thy works, and tribulation, and poverty, (but thou art rich) and I know the blasphemy of them which say they are Jews, and are not, but are the synagogue of Satan.

10 Fear none of those things which thou shalt suffer: behold, the devil shall cast some of you into prison, that ye may be tried; and ye shall have tribulation ten days: be thou faithful unto death, and I will give thee a crown of life.

11 He that hath an ear, let him hear what the Spirit saith unto the churches; He that overcometh shall not be hurt of the second death.

Smyrna is 30 miles north of Ephesus and was called one of the most beautiful cities in Asia Minor. It had a profitable trading center and its hills were crowned with beautiful buildings and temples. It had a highway that ran through its center known anciently as the Golden Street. It was fiercely loyal to Rome and the arts. It claimed to be the birthplace of the poet Homer (although six other cities also claimed that honor.) It was home to a wealthy and powerful Jewish community who were merciless to the young christian church. It would be in Smyrna circa 155 A.D., that Bishop Polycarp, one of John's converts, would be burned alive for refusing to burn incense in honor of the Roman Emperor's divinity. Polycarp is recorded as saying on the day of his death, "Eighty and six years I have served Christ, and He has done me no wrong. How can I then blaspheme my King and Saviour? You threaten me with a fire that burns for a season, and after a little while is quenched; but you are ignorant of the fire of everlasting punishment that is prepared for the wicked." As he was burning he said, "I bless you Father for judging me worthy of this hour, so that in the company of the martyrs I may share the cup of Christ." Then they ran him through with a spear.

To the saints of the church at Smyrna the Lord expressed sympathy for their poverty but reminded them that any who have the Lord are truly rich. He also expressed sorrow for the religious hypocrites who were calling themselves Jews but were acting more like demons. Judaism teaches kindness and patience not hatred and persecution. The Lord foresaw more sorrows to come for them but promised them a crown of eternal life for those who endured it well.

THE LETTER TO PERGAMOS
Revelation 2:12 And to the angel of the church in Pergamos write; These things saith he which hath the sharp sword with two edges;

13 I know thy works, and where thou dwellest, even where Satan's seat is: and thou holdest fast my name, and hast not denied my faith, even in those days wherein Antipas was my faithful martyr, who was slain among you, where Satan dwelleth.[29]

14 But I have a few things against thee, because thou hast there them that hold the doctrine of Balaam, who taught Balac to cast a stumblingblock before the children of Israel, to eat things sacrificed unto idols, and to commit fornication.

15 So hast thou also them that hold the doctrine of the Nicolaitans, which thing I hate.

16 Repent; or else I will come unto thee quickly, and will fight against them with the sword of my mouth.

17 He that hath an ear, let him hear what the Spirit saith unto the churches; To him that overcometh will I give to eat of the hidden manna, and will give him a white stone, and in the stone a new name written, which no man knoweth saving he that receiveth it.

Pergamos was about 44 miles northeast from Smyrna. It was the center of Roman Emperor worship in Asia. Rome had learned the power of emperor deification from Cleopatra when Julius Caesar returned from Egypt and declared himself the *Roman Pharaoh*. Deification of the Emperor brought church and state together and was a later model for the Roman popes. It is one thing to own a man's body in a civil sense but quite another to claim ownership of the eternal soul of a man. It was a powerful means of unifying and controlling the masses of the Roman Empire. It was a law throughout the Empire that once a year every Roman citizen had to go to one of the Emperor's Temples and burn a pinch of incense to his divinity while crying out, "Caesar is Lord and God!" When the christians refused, they were branded as traitors, disloyal to the State. Furthermore the proconsul of Pergamos had the rare power of *jus gladii*, meaning the *power of the sword*. It was a rare power but it meant that any man could be put to death for any reason on the word of the proconsul alone. Many christians lived under the constant threat of being put to death without trial.

Pergamos was also famous for its immense library. The word *parchment* has its root in the term Pergamos paper. During the third century B.C., the king of Pergamos tried to bribe the head librarian of the Great Library of Alexandria to abandon the Ptolemys for him. When Pharaoh Ptolemy found out, he imprisoned the head librarian and ordered that no papyrus paper be send to Pergamos. So, the scholars of Pergamos used animal hides, tanned smooth instead. These skins were called parchment and were yellowish-brown like today's parchment paper.

In Pergamos the saints were struggling with wicked leaders and rough examples on all sides. They too were having problems with Nicolaitans but it seemed that these saints were not as quick to detect the liars among them. The Lord knew who they were however, and only had one thing to say to them, "You had better repent quickly." He also wanted them to remember that while they lived under Rome's power of the sword there, He was the one with the only sword that mattered.

THE LETTER TO THYATIRA

Revelation 2:18 And unto the angel of the church in Thyatira write; These things saith the Son of God, who hath his eyes like unto a flame of fire, and his feet are like fine brass;

19 I know thy works, and charity, and service, and faith, and thy patience, and thy works; and the last to be more than the first.

20 Notwithstanding I have a few things against thee, because thou sufferest that woman Jezebel, which calleth herself a prophetess, to teach and to seduce my servants to commit fornication, and to eat things sacrificed unto idols.

21 And I gave her space to repent of her fornication; and she repented not.

22 Behold, I will cast her into *hell*, and them that commit adultery with her into great tribulation, except they repent of their deeds.

23 And I will kill her children with death; and all the churches shall know that I am he which searcheth the reins [the kidneys] and hearts: and I will give unto every one of you according to your works.[30]

24 But unto you I say, and unto the rest in Thyatira, as many as have not this doctrine, and which have not known the depths of Satan, as they speak; I will put upon you none other burden.

25 But that which ye have already hold fast till I come.

26 And he that overcometh, and keepeth my works unto the end, to him will I give power over the nations:

27 And he shall rule them with a rod of iron; as the vessels of a potter shall they be broken to shivers: even as I received of my Father.

28 And I will give him the morning star.

29 He that hath an ear, let him hear what the Spirit saith unto the churches.

Thyatira was about forty miles southeast of Pergamos. It was in-between Pergamos and Sardis by road. It had a bustling trade in wool, dyeing of wool, and clothes and goods made from wool. You might remember that Paul's first convert was a woman in Thyatira named Lydia who trafficked in purple fabrics.[31] It was the home of many trade guilds, including potters, dyers, bronze workers, lineners and leathermen. This would later prove difficult for Christians. Guilds, like our modern unions, demanded membership or made *making a living* very difficult.[32] Many of these guilds included worship and sacred rites to idols or pagan gods as part of membership. Many christians suffered under these rules. Very often guild meetings included drunkenness, sacrifices and orgies.

The Lord is mostly pleased with the saints of Thyatira. Their biggest problem was a wicked woman who was demanding leadership in the church, wanting the rights of the male priesthood. The Lord had apparently warned her before but she would not listen. He tells her, and all those who followed her, that they have one last chance, then He will kill them and let them stand as examples to everyone else forever. Those who rejected her, or suffered because of her, would be blessed in the end. *Beware of women who channel spirits.*

THE LETTER TO SARDIS
Revelation 3:1 And unto the angel of the church in Sardis write; These things saith he that hath the seven Spirits of God, and the seven stars; I know thy works, that thou hast a name that thou livest, and art dead.

2 Be watchful, and strengthen the things which remain, that are ready to die: for I have not found thy works perfect before God.

3 Remember therefore how thou hast received and heard, and hold fast, and repent. If therefore thou shalt not watch, I will come on thee as a thief, and thou shalt not know what hour I will come upon thee.

4 Thou hast a few names even in Sardis which have not defiled their garments; and they shall walk with me in white: for they are worthy.

5 He that overcometh, the same shall be clothed in white raiment; and I will not blot out his name out of the book of life, but I will confess his name before my Father, and before his angels.

6 He that hath an ear, let him hear what the Spirit saith unto the churches.

Sardis was up the road about 30 miles southeast of Thyatira. It was the ancient capital of Lydia. The river Pactolus which flowed through Sardis was so filled with gold that its king Croesus was known as one of the richest of men. According to Herodotus, the Lydians were the first people to use gold and silver coins, and the first to establish retail shops in permanent locations. Croesus paid for the construction of the temple of Artemis at Ephesus, one of the Seven Wonders of the Ancient World. The city sat on a plateau which deemed so impregnable that it was not even guarded. Hence it was eventually captured for not being *watchful*. In John's day it was known for its wool and dyes as well as its promiscuity and unprincipled sexuality.

The Saints of Sardis had the problem of losing their love of the gospel. They had not fallen into the depths of depravity like some of the other christian churches, nor had they listened to liars or chased after false leaders. They seemed to be suffering from apathy. It can be hard enduring to the end. I have an aunt who says, "the hardest part about enduring to the end is enduring the end." Good people sometimes just get bored with hanging on and let go. Part of the test of this life is won in the long boring plains that must be traveled in-between the spiritual vistas. It's a good thing to remember when you find yourself bored: Get out there and serve someone, bear witness of the Restoration, or start a gospel feast. *I know, I'm preaching to the choir since we are feasting together but... Feast On! You have stuff to do!*

The Prophet Joseph is recorded as giving only one sermon specifically on the *Book of Revelation*. He felt that the book was too easy to understand on its own and that a lot of time could be wasted trying to figure out symbols which he didn't feel helped us complete the work of the Lord in the very short time we have been given. Of the letters to the churches, he basically ignored them with the exception of the letter to Sardis. In that regards he said the following:

We find [a] promise to individuals living in the church at Sardis which will show something of the blessings held out to the ancients who walked worthily before the Lord... The ancients, though persecuted and afflicted by men, obtained from God promises of such weight and glory that our hearts are often filled with gratitude that we are even permitted to look upon them, while we contemplate that there is no respect of persons in his sight and that "in every nation he that feareth him, and worketh righteousness, is acceptable with him" (see Acts 10:34-35). But... we can draw the conclusion that there is to be a day when all will be judged of their works and rewarded according to the same, that those who have kept the faith will be crowned with a crown of righteousness (see 2 Tim. 4:8), be clothed in white raiment (see Rev. 3:5), be admitted to the marriage feast (see Rev. 19:7-8), be free from every affliction, and reign with Christ on the earth (see Rev. 20:4), where, according to the ancient promise, they will partake of the fruit of the vine anew in the glorious kingdom with him (see Matt. 26:29; Mark 14:25).

At least we find that such promises were made to the ancient Saints. And though we cannot claim these promises which were made to the ancients, or that they are our property merely because they were made to them, yet if we are the children of the Most High and are called with the same calling with which they were called and embrace the same covenant that they embraced and are faithful to the testimony of our Lord as they were, we can approach the Father in the name of Christ, as they approached him and for ourselves obtain the same promises. These promises, when obtained if ever by us, will not be because Peter, John, and the other apostles, with the churches at Sardis, Pergamos, Philadelphia, and elsewhere, walked in the fear of God and had power and faith to prevail and obtain them. But it will be because we ourselves have faith and approach God in the name of his Son Jesus Christ, even as they did. And when these promises are obtained, they will be promises directly to us or they will do us no good [if they are not] our own property (through the gift of God), earned by our own diligence in keeping his commandments and walking uprightly before him. If not, to what end serves the gospel of our Lord Jesus Christ, and why was it ever communicated to us?[33]

THE LETTER TO PHILADELPHIA

Revelation 3:7 And to the angel of the church in Philadelphia write; These things saith he that is holy, he that is true, he that hath the key of David, he that openeth, and no man shutteth; and shutteth, and no man openeth;

8 I know thy works: behold, I have set before thee an open door, and no man can shut it: for thou hast a little strength, and hast kept my word, and hast not denied my name.

9 Behold, I will make them of the synagogue of Satan, which say they are Jews, and are not, but do lie; behold, I will make them to come and worship before thy feet, and to know that I have loved thee.

10 Because thou hast kept the word of my patience, I also will keep thee from the hour of temptation, which shall come upon all the world, to try them that dwell upon the earth.

11 Behold, I come quickly: hold that fast which thou hast, that no man take thy crown.

12 Him that overcometh will I make a pillar in the temple of my God, and he shall go no more out: and I will write upon him the name of my God, and the name of the city of my God, which is new Jerusalem, which cometh down out of heaven from my God: and I will write upon him my new name.

13 He that hath an ear, let him hear what the Spirit saith unto the churches.

Philadelphia was 28 miles southeast of Sardis. A greek king named Attalus built the city as a missionary effort to bring Greek culture eastward into Asia. He was extremely close to his brother Eumenes and so the city was named after him. As it turned out, Philadelphia was prone to earthquakes, daily ones. The populous became so concerned about them that they ended up living in tents away from the buildings, *lest the stones fall from above and kill them*. It was said in the streets that the city was *in need of a new*

The Thyrsus Rod of Sodomy Magic. <u>Top Left</u>: Priestess of Bacchus & Dionysus by John Collier. <u>Top Right</u>: The Thyrsus Staff of Dionysus. It is a pine cone atop a rod with a bow tied about it. <u>Bottom Left</u>: Dionysus with the Thyrsus and Nimrod's cat. Note his feminized hips. <u>Bottom Middle</u>: Kissing the beast man with the Thyrsus. <u>Bottom Right</u>: Pope Francis with the papal shepherd's staff which is a Thyrsus topped with a crucifix. The pine cone symbolizes the pineal gland in the brain which the ancients believed is the seat of the soul and the mystical "third eye." The rod is the human spinal column and the male phallus. The bow is the feminine connection or family of the cult. Demonically, it is saying that via sodomy-magic one can open the third eye and be as the gods. Later, these practitioners would use *Revelation 3:7* to mock the Lord, but He foreseeing this countered with *Revelation 3:8-13* as a terrifying wordplay. In the end, the Lord will not be mocked. See the *Gospel Feast* on *Genesis* for more on this topic.

name. Twice the city had changed its name in honor of two different Caesars who sent relief to them when two particularly nasty earthquakes hit.

Philadelphia is a wonderful word that means: *City of Brotherly Love.* Here is a congregation that has exercised great patience in affliction. The Lord has seen all that they have suffered through and will bless them richly for it. The Lord sees all and keeps all His promises.

THE LETTER TO LAODICEA
Revelation 3:14 And unto the angel of the church of the Laodiceans write; These things saith the Amen, the faithful and true witness, the beginning of the creation of God;

15 I know thy works, that thou art neither cold nor hot: I would thou wert cold or hot.

16 So then because thou art lukewarm, and neither cold nor hot, I will spue thee out of my mouth.

17 Because thou sayest, I am rich, and increased with goods, and have need of nothing; and knowest not that thou art wretched, and miserable, and poor, and blind, and naked:

18 I counsel thee to buy of me gold tried in the fire, that thou mayest be rich; and white raiment, that thou mayest be clothed, and that the shame of thy nakedness do not appear; and anoint thine eyes with eyesalve, that thou mayest see.

19 As many as I love, I rebuke and chasten: be zealous therefore, and repent.

20 Behold, I stand at the door, and knock: if any man hear my voice, and open the door, I will come in to him, and will sup with him, and he with me.

21 To him that overcometh will I grant to sit with me in my throne, even as I also overcame, and am set down with my Father in his throne.

22 He that hath an ear, let him hear what the Spirit saith unto the churches.

Laodicea was 40 miles south of Philadelphia. It had been build by Antiochus II and named after his wife Laodice. It was a banking center and had much civil wealth. It was also known for its wool and cloth and housed a world famous medical center for the treatment of ears and eyes. It is the only letter in which the Lord uses His title *the Amen*.[34]

The Saints in Laodicea are like the saints of Sardis. They are neither passionate about living the commandments and being christians nor are they particularly sinful and ugly about it. They are *neither hot nor cold*. The Lord would prefer either one actually because it would give Him an opportunity to either richly bless them or call them to repentance. Since they are neither good christians nor wicked sinners, there is very little He can do for or against them to help them. He tries to encourage them to *experiment upon the word* and try Him out. If they don't step up, He decides to basically *just spit them out*. He is rebuking them out of love however, but like Mormons who drink coffee in the morning and pay their tithing on their casino earnings at night, they are neither fully committed nor apostate. The Lord is basically saying, *"Pick a side! There is a war on, don't you know!"* It is interesting to note that Paul even had trouble with the Laodiceans. He wrote this warning to the bishop there, thirty years previously, "Tell Archippus to pay attention to the ministry you have received in the Lord, so that you can accomplish it."[35] The Lord doesn't need fair-weather christians or selfish, content fence sitters. To the Laodiceans is the reaffirmation that the Lord hates banking, property rental, and other forms of interest and land lordship. It seems too often to make misers of a few and paupers of the many where both had been given dominion over the creations of God by God Himself.

If you want to study these letters a little more, go back and read them again. You will note that each one opens with a beautiful declaration about the Saviour with a deeply eastern twist. Then offers some praise and warning before ending each with the promise that what He says to one, He says to all. Personally I enjoy the rich list of blessings He offers those who overcome the world. The most fabulous promise being the blessing in verse 21. A special note to all the secular-christians from the murder of Joseph Smith to the present day who mock us for believing that one day we might become godlike as our Lord is Godlike. We are only quoting Jesus Christ and the Bible:

Revelation 3:21 To him that overcometh will I grant to sit with me in my throne, even as I also overcame, and am set down with my Father in his throne.

It couldn't be said any plainer. The Lord's ultimate desire for you is to sit with Him in the Father's throne. Only Gods sit in heavenly thrones, mark that well mockers of the *Church of Jesus Christ of Latter-day Saints.*

What comes next is some of the most amazing passages in all of scripture. After the Lord gives His promises and warnings to the Seven Churches of Asia, he invites John into the very Throne Room of Heaven.

There is no more powerful place in all the Universe and we are invited to see what John saw there.

Come and see,

and rejoice…

Chapter Four

The Throne Room of God

That which hath been hidden from before the foundation of the world is revealed to babes and sucklings in the last days. — *Joseph Smith*

These next two chapters may be my most favorite verses in all of scripture. Very few mortals have been permitted to see into the *Throne Room of Almighty God.* Fewer still — perhaps only John — have been permitted to linger there and write what he saw. John sees a door open in heaven, and like a portal into the eternities, John enters. This is what he sees:

Revelation 4:1 After this I looked, and, behold, a door was opened in heaven: and the first voice which I heard was as it were of a trumpet talking with me; which said, Come up hither, and I will shew thee things which must be hereafter.

Notice the invitation is not to "Go" but to "Come." God wants us to be where He is. We are His children after all.

2 And immediately I was in the spirit: and, behold, a throne was set in heaven, and one sat on the throne.

3 And he that sat was to look upon like a jasper and a sardine stone: and there was a rainbow round about the throne, in sight like unto an emerald.

This is God the Father. The most powerful being in all the universe. Words fail to describe Him but John tries anyway.

4 And round about the throne were four and twenty seats: and upon the seats I saw four and twenty elders sitting, clothed in white raiment; and they had on their heads crowns of gold.

Governing with God are the elders of His kingdom. Mormons are frequently mocked by foolish christians for teaching that it is God's ultimate desire that His sons and daughters rule with Him. It is difficult to take these scoffers seriously when the word of God contains verses like this one. Here are 24 men with crowns (rulers) who are serving God in a ruling capacity. *Joseph Smith didn't just make this all up.* Note: Gold is glory in Hebraic thinking, so these elders have obtained glory.

Revelation 4:5 And out of the throne proceeded lightnings and thunderings and voices: and there were seven lamps of fire burning before the throne, which are the seven Spirits of God.

Here again we have the image of the Menorah. Joseph Smith said that these lights were servants of God; witnesses to His actions and goodness. They may have been the same seven Bishops mentioned in the opening letter. The Lord has said that He is in the midst of us but we can't see him.[36] It is also possible that these are the seven arch-angels who stand as heads of each 1,000-year dispensational period. Tradition has given us the names: Michael, Gabriel, Raphael, Sariel, Raguel, Uriel, and Phanuel.[37] Whoever they are in the end, we are being given a glimpse into the most powerful court of the universe.

6 And before the throne there was a sea of glass like unto crystal: and in the midst of the throne, and round about the throne, were four beasts full of eyes before and behind.

This crystal functions like a great Urim & Thummim from which all things are known to the Father at any time. As sons and daughters of God, redeemed on a future day, each of us will receive our *training wheel Urim & Thummim* in the form of a smaller white stone which will aid us as we progress in our knowledge of the things of God.

John sees animals in the court, as well as, glorified humans. Please note secular-christianity does not believe that animals have souls nor that they will be in heaven, but, when they teach their congregations such, they are not teaching them the *Bible*. My

Bible mentions these, and other animals, as being in heaven. I believe the Bible when it's taught in truth.

7 And the first beast was like a lion, and the second beast like a calf, and the third beast had a face as a man, and the fourth beast was like a flying eagle.

These four noble creations of God represent four of His attributes. He is a Royal King. This is manifested by the Lion in His presence. He is a High Priest. This is symbolized by the Ox. He is a Holy Man. This is the shape and form of His being; His humanity; His intimate temple and physical Fatherhood, and He is a Judge. This is shown in the eagle before the throne.

8 And the four beasts had each of them six wings about him; and they were full of eyes within: and they rest not day and night, saying, Holy, holy, holy, Lord God Almighty, which was, and is, and is to come.

The wings are a sign of the beasts' power to act and to move. Action and motion are a sign of the Priesthood, as such, all of these beasts are male. John also observes their form of worship. The beasts cry out their praise and the elders present toss their crowns at the Father's feet. These human elders rule with God but they acknowledge that they too have a God above them, as do we, He is God our Heavenly Father.

Revelation 4:9 And when those beasts give glory and honour and thanks to him that sat on the throne, who liveth for ever and ever,

10 The four and twenty elders fall down before him that sat on the throne, and worship him that liveth for ever and ever, and cast their crowns before the throne, saying,

11 Thou art worthy, O Lord, to receive glory and honour and power: for thou hast created all things, and for thy pleasure they are and were created.

It is here that the scene gets really interesting. John sees the Father. In His hand, He holds a scroll which is written on both sides and sealed tightly with seven seals.

Revelation 5:1 And I saw in the right hand of him that sat on the throne a book written within and on the backside, sealed with seven seals.

What is not so clear is that this scroll is really an old style eastern deed. In ancient times, if a man needed to leverage his property for some debt he owed, he would write up the deed with his creditor and then roll it up and seal it. On the outside of the scroll, the terms of redemption were written and then anyone willing to fulfill the terms written there, could break the seal and redeem the land. This is the scroll that John observes, but there is a serious problem in our case. Observe:

2 And I saw a strong angel proclaiming with a loud voice, Who is worthy to open the book, and to loose the seals thereof?

3 And no man in heaven, nor in earth, neither under the earth, was able to open the book, neither to look thereon.

John makes a point of telling us that a strong muscular angel with a loud voice makes the challenge to the court and all the universe, "Who is worthy to redeem this debt?" This is a very serious challenge. This deed, as we will see, is the deed to the Earth and all the souls upon it. This deed and debt contains the very soul of you and me! John understood the awful dilemma immediately! His eternal soul was at stake, so is yours. Pay close attention:

4 And I wept much, because no man was found worthy to open and to read the book, neither to look thereon.

No man, in all of God's creation was able to walk past the mighty angel. There was not a soul capable of stepping up to the highest throne and taking the deed out of the fist of Almighty God! Was there no one strong enough to redeem the debt of creation? One of the elders saw John's tears and said to him:

Revelation 5:5 And one of the elders saith unto me, Weep not: behold, the Lion of the tribe of Judah, the Root of David, hath prevailed to open the book, and to loose the seven seals thereof.[38]

Yes, in the Garden of Gethsemane, and later on a Roman Cross, Jesus Christ did it! He alone was worthy enough and strong enough to walk up to the throne and take the deed out of the hand of God Most High!

6 And I beheld, and, lo, in the midst of the throne and of the four beasts, and in the midst of the elders, stood a Lamb as it had been slain, having seven horns and seven eyes, which are the seven Spirits of God sent forth into all the earth.[39]

7 And he came and took the book out of the right hand of him that sat upon the throne.

And out of God's right hand no less! That is real power!

8 And when he had taken the book, the four beasts and four and twenty elders fell down before the Lamb, having every one of them harps, and golden vials full of odours, which are the prayers of saints.

9 And they sung a new song, saying, Thou art worthy to take the book, and to open the seals thereof: for thou wast slain, and hast redeemed us to God by thy blood out of every kindred, and tongue, and people, and nation;

10 And hast made us unto our God kings and priests: and we shall reign on the earth.

The Lord walked the wrath of the wine press of God alone. At that terrible moment it was the prayers of hope and gratitude offered through the ages that was most likely the only thing He could hold on to. When even God forsook Him to fulfill all righteousness, the prayers that we needed Him was all that was left. Because of Him, we have conquered.[40]

Joseph Smith saw in these verses proof of man's future destiny. Mormons believe that when the Lord says it is His desire that we be one with Him, He is not just saying nice words:

You have got to learn how to be a God yourself and be a king and priest to God, the same as all have done before you; by going from a small capacity to another, from grace to grace, from exaltation to exaltation, until the resurrection and sit in everlasting power, and dwell in everlasting burnings as they who have gone before, until you are able to sit in glory with those who are enthroned.[41]

It is astounding to Latter-day Saints that this doctrine is mocked, but it is God's word that is mocked. Mormons take the Lord at His word.

Revelation 5:11 And I beheld, and I heard the voice of many angels round about the throne and the beasts and the elders: and the number of them was ten thousand times ten thousand, and thousands of thousands;

12 Saying with a loud voice, Worthy is the Lamb that was slain to receive power, and riches, and wisdom, and strength, and honour, and glory, and blessing.

13 And every creature which is in heaven, and on the earth, and under the earth, and such as are in the sea, and all that are in them, heard I saying, Blessing, and honour, and glory, and power, be unto him that sitteth upon the throne, and unto the Lamb for ever and ever.

All of God's creation: children, animal, land life, sea life and the planetary hosts of heaven which have joy in their creation, echoed back the song of gratitude: "Worthy, worthy, worthy is the Lamb! Our Lord and Saviour, Jesus Christ!" Joseph Smith gave us this insight into salvation and glory:

John learned that God glorified Himself by saving all that His hands had made, whether beasts, fowls, fishes or men; and He will glorify Himself with them.[42]

These creations also speak:

14 And the four beasts said, Amen. And the four and twenty elders fell down and worshipped him that liveth for ever and ever.

We have already noted that secular-christianity teaches that animals do not have souls and are therefore not capable of salvation. I have personally heard many a minister say that there are no animals in heaven. In this they deny their own Bibles. John saw animals in heaven. Joseph Smith went on to say:

John saw the actual beasts in heaven, to show to John that they did actually exist there. When the prophets speak of seeing beasts in their visions, they saw the images-types to represent certain things. And at the same time they received the interpretation as to what those images or types were designed to represent. I make this broad declaration, that where God ever gives a vision of an image, or beast, or figure of any kind, he always holds himself responsible to give a revelation or interpretation of the meaning thereof, otherwise we are not responsible or accountable for our belief in it. Don't be afraid of being damned for not knowing the meaning of a vision or figure where God has not given a revelation or interpretation on the subject.

John saw curious-looking beasts in heaven. He saw every creature that was in heaven: all the beasts, fowls, and fish in heaven, actually there, giving glory to God. I suppose John saw beings there that had been saved from ten thousand times ten thousand earths like this, strange beasts of which we have no conception. All might be seen in heaven. John learned that God glorified himself by saving all that his hands had made, whether beasts, fowl, fishes, or man. Any man who would tell you that this could not be would tell you that the revelations are not true. John heard the words of the beasts giving glory to God and understood them. God, who made the beasts, could understand every language spoken by them. The beasts were intelligent beings and were seen and heard by John praising and glorifying God. The popular religionists of the day say that the beasts spoken of in the revelations represent kingdoms. Very well, on the same principle we can say that the twenty-four elders spoken of represent beasts, for they are all spoken of at the same time and [are] represented as all uniting in the same acts of praise and devotion...

Read Revelation 5:13 it proves that John saw beasts in heaven and heard them speak praises to God. [I] do not know what language they speak.[43]

Joseph Smith, who had seen into the eternal worlds himself, added his witness:

The angels do not reside on a planet like this earth, but they reside in the presence of God, on a globe like a sea of glass and fire, [a] sea of glass before the throne, where all things are manifest-past, present, and to come. The place where God resides is a great Urim & Thummim. This earth, in its sanctified and immortal state, will be a Urim & Thummim for all things below it in the scale of creation, but not above it.[44]

There is no angel [who] ministers to this earth [but who] either does belong or has belonged to this earth. And the angels do not reside on a planet like our earth, but they dwell with God, and the planet where he dwells is like crystal, and like a sea of glass before the throne. This is the great urim and thummim whereon all things are manifest-both things past, present, and future-and are continually before the Lord. The urim and thummim is a small representation of this globe. The earth, when it is purified, will be made like unto crystal and will be a urim and thummim whereby all things pertaining to an inferior kingdom, or all kingdoms of a lower order, will be manifest to those who dwell on it. And this earth will be with Christ. Then, the white stone mentioned in Revelation 2:17 is the urim and thummim whereby all things pertaining to a higher order of kingdoms, even all kingdoms, will be made known. And a white stone is given to each of those who come into this celestial kingdom, whereon is a new name written which no man knoweth save he that receiveth it. The new name is the key word.[45]

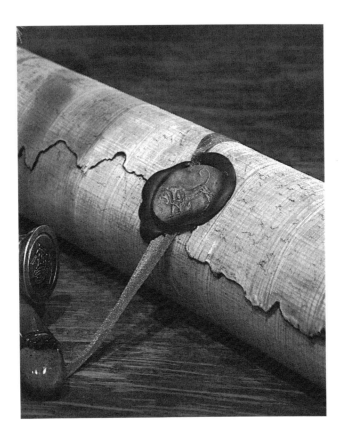

Chapter Five

The Deed in Hand!

The book of Revelation is one of the plainest books
God ever caused to be written. — Joseph Smith the Prophet

It is with gratitude to Joseph Smith that we understand Chapter 6. Secular-christianity believes that *Revelation* is a book that is to be read in order, with each foretold event happening in succession. This has led to a great deal of confusion about the latter-days. Using the *Urim & Thummim*, Joseph was able to inquire of the Lord and learned the correct interpretation of the following events. Ownership of the Planet Earth was divided into 7 sections, each representing a thousand year period. As the Lord became the goel (the kinsman redeemer)[46] for each section, He snapped the seal and took upon Himself the obligation to pay for the sins of that generation.[47] Is it any wonder then that viewing this, all creation, man and beast, found himself in open praise, Holy, Holy, Holy and Worthy, Worthy, Worthy is the Lamb! It is an astounding accomplishment! Let's relive the moment with John as he takes us through it step-by-step.

Having proven worthy of redeeming the Earth and every thing that lives on it, children of God and animal creation, the Lord then reads and fulfills all of the terms on the outside of the scroll. As such, He is free to claim ownership by snapping off each of the seven seals. As He does, the events pertaining to each of those seals comes to life before John's eyes. John discovers that each of the seals contains the sins and horrors of a Celestial day in the life of the Earth. Each seal contains 1,000 years of earth history. John sees the Lord snap the first seal.

THE FIRST SEAL
Revelation 6:1 And I saw when the Lamb opened one of the seals, and I heard, as it were the noise of thunder, one of the four beasts saying, Come and see.

2 And I saw, and behold a white horse: and he that sat on him had a bow; and a crown was given unto him: and he went forth conquering, and to conquer.

The first seal to be snapped and claimed was the period from Father Adam thru the administration of Righteous Enoch to Lamech, Noah's father. One of the beasts at the throne cried like thunder and invited John to witness the history contained under that seal. It is my supposition that John is saying that it was the Lion who first roared.

John saw a white horse being ridden by a conqueror with a bow and a crown. He rode out to subdue and claim the Earth. Here was the glory of the planet as designed by the Lord, and man given dominion to tend it and to tame it. Here also was the vainglory of humanity from Cain, the first murderous Mahan to all the sins he taught his children. By contrast we have Enoch, the only prophet ever to found a city (called Zion) so perfect that its continuance on the planet would actually have hindered the great lessons of agency. It was a period of great crowns and weapons, used for both good and evil. Traditionally, this horseman has been called "Pride." Today we still call a *gang* of lions, a *pride*.

THE SECOND SEAL
Then the Lord snapped the second thousand year seal, the Man offered his invitation to John to witness.

Revelation 6:3 And when he had opened the second seal, I heard the second beast say, Come and see.

4 And there went out another horse that was red: and power was given to him that sat thereon to take peace from the earth, and that they should kill one another: and there was given unto him a great sword.

Another horse and rider appeared, this one red and fierce with a great sword. Here was all the blood shed upon the earth in the days before the great flood. Horrible times that caused God to weep while viewing it. The scriptures say that these were times of blood-on-blood. It become so bad, that at last, God could only justify saving 8 people out of potential millions.[48] Noah, with his wife Emzarah, Shem and his wife Sedeqetelebab, Japheth and his wife Adataneses, and Ham with his wife Egypt were all that were saved. This horseman is known as "War." Only man can truly declare war with God.

THE THIRD SEAL

The third thousand years is next. The events of this seal have the call to witness coming from the living creature with a face like an eagle.

Revelation 6:5 And when he had opened the third seal, I heard the third beast say, Come and see. And I beheld, and lo a black horse; and he that sat on him had a pair of balances in his hand.

6 And I heard a voice in the midst of the four beasts say, A measure of wheat for a penny, and three measures of barley for a penny; and see thou hurt not the oil and the wine.

Now a black horse and rider appear carrying a scale as his weapon. Gone are the days of excess and abundance. The earth has been ruined from the flood. It no longer gives fruit and grain in abundance, but now there are winters and summers, ice ages and rolling arid deserts. Man has to ration and barter to live. Famines are frequent and terrible. This is the age of Father Abraham and pharaonic Joseph, gathering grain to save the people. Through it all, the emblems of truth, the sacred oil and the sacramental wine yet survive. The measurement here is called the *choenix*. It was almost a quart by today's standards. It was considered a daily ration for a soldier or slave. It was enough to sustain life but was not considered a gracious or goodly amount of food. These were also the years of the Israelite bondage to Pharaoh. This horseman is known as "Famine." Like an eagle, famine spreads its wings over the earth lifting some up with upturned wing and condemning others with downturned.

THE FOURTH SEAL

The final horseman comes next. He is introduced by the bellowing Ox when the Lord snaps the fourth thousand year seal. The ox is the sign of God's masculine priesthood.

Revelation 6:7 And when he had opened the fourth seal, I heard the voice of the fourth beast say, Come and see.

8 And I looked, and behold a pale horse: and his name that sat on him was Death, and Hell followed with him. And power was given unto them over the fourth part of the earth, to kill with sword, and with hunger, and with death, and with the beasts of the earth.

All the horsemen are upon the earth now reaping the results of Pride, War, and Famine. The result of all their wrath is Death, the name of our fourth horseman. He has a companion whose name is Hell. These were the years of Moses and the re-claiming of the Land of Israel. These are the years of Nebuchadnezzar and Darius, Alexander the Great, and Julius Caesar. These are the years of the outrages of Edom, Tyre, Phoenicia and Syria. These are the years of the loss of the Temple when Isaiah lamented that Hell *hath greatly enlarged herself* because the people "died without God's gifts of knowledge." It was a time when Satan claimed many souls and reigned with blood and horror through his many false priesthoods and mystery cults. All of the prophet-writers of the *Old Testament* lived during this time and many had given their blood as witness.

It was these slain and weary prophets who cry at the opening of the fifth thousand years. Now the throne beasts are silent. Why? Because the Lord was about to enter His tabernacle of flesh. He is the Prince of Peace and all flesh was to keep silent before Him. There was even silence in the former chaos of heaven. This was the seal that held the ministry of the Lord Jesus Christ and the establishment of His church and kingdom.

Revelation 6:9 And when he had opened the fifth seal, I saw under the altar the souls of them that were slain for the word of God, and for the testimony which they held:

10 And they cried with a loud voice, saying, How long, O Lord, holy and true, dost thou not judge and avenge our blood on them that dwell on the earth?

11 And white robes were given unto every one of them; and it was said unto them, that they should rest yet for a little season, until their fellowservants also and their brethren, that should be killed as they were, should be fulfilled.

The Father had sent many servants into the vineyard and many had been killed. Isaiah had warned them that the owner of the vineyard would next send His heir. Surely they would listen to His son, right? Of course, this seal saw the murder and sacrifice of the Lord Jesus Christ, the murder of most of the 12 apostles as well as numerous christian martyrs in Imperial Rome and all around the world. Here all this blood from righteous Abel to Zacharias, from John the Baptist to General Mormon had turned the altar red with outrage. "How long?!" was the righteous lament! These were given comfort. They were dressed in holiness as fellow servants of Jesus Christ and told to rest a short time until all who would yet witness in blood had been given their chance.[49] Christ had broken the power of death and hell, but there was yet something more to do.

European christianity today owes its exclusive heritage to the martyrs of the west who triumphed over Imperial Rome and would later triumph over Papal Rome. What is less well known to the christian west is the terrible persecution in the east. During this same thousand years, missionaries and apostles established churches in Africa, the Middle East, India and China. History records upwards of 40 million Christians living in the east during this era. They were eventually murdered off by Muslims, Buddhists and the political leaders of the time. Many of the oldest mosques in Iran, Iraq, and Turkey are built on the ruins of conquered Christian churches. There is even evidence that the famous *Dome of the Rock* might have been a Jewish synagogue before being captured and refurbished into the house of Muslim prayer it is today.[50] Either way, the amount of human blood shed on the altar of Christ during this period is vastly greater than westerners are taught to believe.

THE SIXTH SEAL

At the opening of the sixth thousand years, Nature spoke. The earth (the Father's vineyard) was deeply upset over the murder of her creator. The legal heir to the Father had been rejected and killed; and His holy blood had soaked into her skin. Horrible vengeance was warranted.

Revelation 6:12 And I beheld when he had opened the sixth seal, and, lo, there was a great earthquake; and the sun became black as sackcloth of hair, and the moon became as blood;

13 And the stars of heaven fell unto the earth, even as a fig tree casteth her untimely figs, when she is shaken of a mighty wind.

14 And the heaven departed as a scroll when it is rolled together; and every mountain and island were moved out of their places.

15 And the kings of the earth, and the great men, and the rich men, and the chief captains, and the mighty men, and every bondman, and every free man, hid themselves in the dens and in the rocks of the mountains;

16 And said to the mountains and rocks, Fall on us, and hide us from the face of him that sitteth on the throne, and from the wrath of the Lamb:

17 For the great day of his wrath is come; and who shall be able to stand?

In *Book 1: Daniel & the Last Days*, we explored several of the many natural disasters and signs that rattled the nations during the days of earth's six thousand years. Many of the early ones are only remembered in the dusty pages of history. Geologists studying coral in the South China Sea believe they have evidence of an enormous earthquake that caused a massive tsunami in the area circa 1024 A.D.[51] Al-Suyuti in Western Syria lived through a massive earthquake that hit the area on November 10th 1002 A.D. Historical seismologists have cataloged over forty >6.5 magnitude earthquakes and this time from the many record depositories of Syria and Europe. Numerous original documents in Arabic, Latin, Byzantine and Assyrian have allowed details to emerge showing in some cases as many as 100,000 known residents of a city were killed, whole villages disappeared, some quakes lasted for days.[52] All this opened the 6th seal.

Other amazing phenomenon, like the *Night the Stars Fell* on November 13th 1833 and *America's Day of Darkness* when the sun refused to shine on May 19th 1780, are only barely remembered now. More modern ones like the *Great Chicago Fire of 1871*[53], *Great San Francisco Earthquake* of April 18th 1906, the *Eruption of Mount Saint Helens* on May 18th 1980 and the continual *Blood Red Moons* are hardly mentioned. A thousand years is a long period when men's lifetimes are as short as ours. Man's collective memory is even shorter. No child born after the year 2,000 A.D., knows anything about Mount Saint Helens and yet ash from that explosion fell onto cars parked as far away as Salt Lake City.

The panic created by these events did cause many to repent, for a short while, in case the Lord's return was eminent.

Near Y2K and beyond the news continually spouted headlines like: *Billionaires Building State of the Art Bomb Shelters With Pools and Bowling Alleys.* On-and-off men have hid themselves under the rocks to some degree or another to escape *the wrath of the Lamb.* But you will note that the Second Coming doesn't happen in the six seal. Something much more important does.

Follow the logic here: After the murder of Jesus Christ and the blood drenched altar of the Fifth Seal, the angelic hosts are ready to end wickedness on the earth. Indeed for an entire Sixth Seal duration, nature groans back, but these groans are to be a sign from the Lord. A sign that something amazing is about to happen.

Revelation 7:1 And after these things I saw four angels standing on the four corners of the earth, holding the four winds of the earth, that the wind should not blow on the earth, nor on the sea, nor on any tree.

In eastern thinking, land is symbolic of the realm of the living. The sea is the realm of the dead and trees are human bloodlines. These angels are ready to loose the wrath of God on the living, those in Spirit Prison, and all the races of man, but...

2 And I saw another angel ascending from the east, having the seal of the living God: and he cried with a loud voice to the four angels, to whom it was given to hurt the earth and the sea,

This is a very mighty angel. One who is carrying the *seal of the living God.* We know that the sealing powers were given to Elijah to oversee and so it is fair to speculate that this is him. He yells, "Wait! Wait, don't hurt the earth until....[54]

3 Saying, Hurt not the earth, neither the sea, nor the trees, till we have sealed the servants of our God in their foreheads.

This is extremely important. From a righteous indignation point of view, the angels, the Father, and all the murdered righteous from Abel to John the Baptist, and from Jesus Christ through the Christian Church, demand vengeance! The only action is to do as the Lord warned Israel in the Parable of the Husbandman:

Matthew 21:40-14 When the lord therefore of the vineyard cometh, what will he do unto those husbandmen? ...He will miserably destroy those wicked men, and will let out his vineyard unto other husbandmen, which shall render him the fruits in their seasons.

This is what the world, the wicked, and the hosts of hell deserve. But then, where would be the future promises? Where would be the promise to Father Adam & Mother Eve that their children would inherit the earth? Where would be the promise to the people of Enoch that they would return again to the New Zion and rejoice? Where would be the promise to Noah and Shem that their children would live at last in peace? Where would be the new and everlasting covenant, declared unbreakable by God Almighty to Abraham and his children as numerous as the stars? Where would be the promises to the children of Israel wrestled from God by Father Jacob? The promises Joseph of Egypt secured for his Latter-day children? What of Moses and Elijah? What of the eternal throne of the House of David? What of the promises to Isaiah, Daniel, Ezekiel and Zachariah? What of the promised Wedding Feast of the Lamb? And all of the promises made to the fathers by their children and the children to their fathers?

"No!" the great angel cries, "We need one last commission. One more chance. We need to seal the servants of God in everlasting power. We need to separate the wheat from the tares. We need to mark the sheep from the goats. We need one more dispensation of the Gospel!" I can only add to that, "Hallelujah!" What we need is a sure promise. We need one last sealing.

SEALING

In terms of sealing, Joseph Smith wanted to make sure we understood its importance. Today we understand these things clearly, but in the early days of the Restoration, all the world had was the tattered remnants of fallen christianity. These ideas were new and groundbreaking. Satan had so corrupted some of them that the people needed preparation to understand them.

[What is the meaning of a sealing given to saints in former days?] It means to seal the blessing on their heads, meaning the everlasting covenant, thereby making their calling and election sure. When a seal is put upon the father and mother, it secures their posterity so that they cannot be lost but will be saved by virtue of the covenant of their father.

Now I would ask, Who knows the seal of the living God? Behold the ignorance of the world! A measure of this sealing is to confirm upon their head in common with Elijah the doctrine of election, or the covenant with Abraham, which when a father and mother of a family have entered into, their children who have not transgressed are secured by the seal wherewith the parents have been sealed. And this is the oath of God unto our father Abraham, and this doctrine shall stand forever.

What is the seal spoken of in Revelation 7:3? Find it out if you can. I will not reveal it now but will drop an idea that I have never revealed concerning election connected with the sealing of the servants of God in the fore or top of the head .... Covenants, either there or here, must be made in view of eternity. And the covenant sealed on the foreheads of the parents secures the children from falling, that they shall all sit upon thrones as one with the Godhead, joint heirs of God with Jesus Christ. This principle is revealed also through the covenant of Abraham and his children.[55]

John will next see the work progressing in the Latter-days as a symbolic roll count is taken.[56] We have studied numbers together already, put on your Eastern Thinking Cap, here we go:

Revelation 7:4 And I heard the number of them which were sealed: and there were sealed an hundred and forty and four thousand of all the tribes of the children of Israel.

5 Of the tribe of Judah were sealed twelve thousand. Of the tribe of Reuben were sealed twelve thousand. Of the tribe of Gad were sealed twelve thousand.

6 Of the tribe of Aser were sealed twelve thousand. Of the tribe of Nepthalim were sealed twelve thousand. Of the tribe of Manasseh were sealed twelve thousand.

7 Of the tribe of Simeon were sealed twelve thousand. Of the tribe of Levi were sealed twelve thousand. Of the tribe of Issachar were sealed twelve thousand.

Revelation 7:8 Of the tribe of Zebulon were sealed twelve thousand. Of the tribe of Joseph were sealed twelve thousand. Of the tribe of Benjamin were sealed twelve thousand.

Ah, the dreaded 144,000! Whole secular-christian denominations have suffered over this number trying to understand what it means. What is going on here? Is this number literal or symbolic? Your first clue is to look at the tribal names. First count the number of tribes. Yes, there are 12 listed. There are 12 Tribes of Israel, but check the names. Anything seem odd? Anyone missing? Yes, Ephraim and Dan. How can there be 12 Tribes and two are missing? This is your clue that the numbers are not to be read literally but have a more important symbolic meaning.

13 TRIBES OF ISRAEL? WELL,... YES & NO

In terms of the number there are really 13 Tribes of Israel. It happened like this. When Father Jacob (renamed Israel by the Lord) was very old, he called his children together and blessed them. As a gift to Joseph for the many trials he suffered at the hands of his brothers, Israel blessed him with 2 portions of inheritance. Joseph was also legally Israel's firstborn heir.[57] It was common for the firstborn son to get a double portion of his father's inheritance since it was expected that he would take care of his mother, any other women in his father's house, as well as be a support to his younger brothers. Joseph had done all of this and more in Egypt. At the blessing, Israel spilt the Tribe of Joseph into the Tribes of Ephraim and Manasseh. This makes 13

Tribes. So why does the Lord always refer to 12, and why are names missing from John's list in verses 4-8 of chapter 7?

When the Lord is past patience with a people, He will not own them until they repent. You can find examples of this in scripture. When the Lord is angry with Israel, He will sometimes call them the "Children of Jacob." Jacob means *the supplanter* in Hebrew. When they repent, or are at least listening, He calls them the "Children of Israel." Israel means, "he has prevailed with God." Thus the wordplay as we are at times merely the children of the supplanter but when we take God's hand and listen to Him, we become the children who have prevailed. Now you can better understand the Lord's parable of the sower. The great supplanter in the field of the Lord is our enemy Lucifer. Therefore, when the Lord calls His chosen Israel, *children of the supplanter,* He is saying that they are following Satan and not Him. This same thing is happening here in John. The Tribe of Dan is missing from the list because Dan was the Tribe who first brought idolatry into Israel. In heavenly terms, idolatry is the same as adultery. You will remember that the ceremony at Mount Sinai in the days of Moses was an eastern wedding engagement. Thus any god embraced by Israel afterwards was seen as adultery. After the debacle of the Golden Calf, the Lord chose Levi to be His more intimate bride, so to speak.[58] He had wanted all of Israel to be High Priests like Moses was and like Abraham and Melchizedek (aka Father Shem) had been. The drunken orgy at the foot of God's holy mountain, just after the engagement, brought about the probationary priesthood of Aaron. Levi would be disseminated into the tribes and function as the priesthood-bride for the whole family until the arrival of the Messiah, called the *Teacher of Righteousness.* Moses was selected as symbolic chief-bride and via the *Law of Vicariousity*, all Israel would be blessed.[59]

That was a long way of saying this: When Israel acts like an harlot, *she* is acting like the Tribe of Dan. When *she* is acting with devotion to Jehovah, *she* is like Moses and Aaron, or Levi. In order to make the Tribes always come out to 12, since 12 is a heavenly number, God will contract or expand Joseph when the message is symbolic. That is how we know the number 144,000 is not to be read literally here. Dan cannot be listed because this group being *sealed to God* contains no adulterers. In this instance, all worship only the one true God and so are sealed His. Levi thus is added leaving no room for Dan. Joseph is spilt into two, returning the number to a perfect 12. Note here one more curiosity before we address the numbers. The Lord could have spilt Joseph into Ephraim and Manasseh, which would seem more appropriate to the reading, but He does not. In these Latter-days He gives the honor of Ephraim to Joseph. Who was the greatest of all the sons of Joseph of Egypt, the Latter-day Messiah Ben-Joseph, the chief prince of Ephraim and Head of the Sixth Dispensation? He was a farm boy made prophet, Joseph Smith, Jr. I propose to you that this verse is a prophetic wordplay from one great revelator to another. *Hail to the Prophets!* Now to the numbers.

How much do you remember from our feast on *Zechariah*? Numbers in eastern thought have meaning. Twelve is the symbol of God's Government Expanded. Twelve is an interesting number for the combinations that can be pondered from it. 12 = 3 x 4 or the Godhead (the highest governing body) given to the world. 2 x 6 or the testimony of God to fallen man. The Twelve Tribes of Israel served this purpose in *Old Testament* times whereas the 12 Apostles of the Lord have fulfilled it in the *New Testament* and in the Restoration. The symbolic sign of this can be seen surrounding the baptismal fonts of the Holy Temples today. There, 12 marble oxen, symbolic of the masculine force or priesthood through Ephraim, hold up the ordinance of vicarious baptism for the dead. 12 x 12 = 144. So it is all the above symbols of 12 doubled! A double portion for the first born, legal heirs. The number 1,000 is an intensifier to any number. Now can you see it? This number is a symbolic way of saying that all the blessings of Abraham, Isaac and Israel are given to those who are sealed as God's in the Latter-days; posterity as the stars of heaven and the sands of the sea, a multitude without number! We are doing this very thing now in family history work and temple ordinances all around the world. Isn't eastern thinking cool? If you need further proof of this, John clarifies it himself in the next verse.

Revelation 7:9 After this I beheld, and, lo, a great multitude, which no man could number, of all nations, and kindreds, and people, and tongues, stood before the throne, and before the Lamb, clothed with white robes, and palms in their hands;

10 And cried with a loud voice, saying, Salvation to our God which sitteth upon the throne, and unto the Lamb.

11 And all the angels stood round about the throne, and about the elders and the four beasts, and fell before the throne on their faces, and worshipped God,

12 Saying, Amen: Blessing, and glory, and wisdom, and thanksgiving, and honour, and power, and might, be unto our God for ever and ever. Amen.

So our symbolic journey was correct as John sees a "great multitude, which no man could number" from every bloodline of Adam, all worshiping God. They are all dressed alike in white with palms; the ancient hosanna handkerchiefs of their day. They praise God and the Lamb for their kindness, power and perfect justice. All of us, so saved through the *Plan of Salvation*, which is the *Atonement of Jesus Christ*, join our voices in this chorus. In chapels, temples and homes across the globe, Saints of the Latter-days are serving the needs of Christ's Kingdom on earth. The very many engaged in this work on both sides of the veil are a wonder. That is exactly what both John, and one of the elders he sees, declares:

Revelation 7:13 And one of the elders answered, saying unto me, What are these which are arrayed in white robes? and whence came they?

14 And I said unto him, Sir, thou knowest. And he said to me, These are they which came out of great tribulation, and have washed their robes, and made them white in the blood of the Lamb.

15 Therefore are they before the throne of God, and serve him day and night in his temple: and he that sitteth on the throne shall dwell among them.

16 They shall hunger no more, neither thirst any more; neither shall the sun light on them, nor any heat.

17 For the Lamb which is in the midst of the throne shall feed them, and shall lead them unto living fountains of waters: and God shall wipe away all tears from their eyes.

When life in these end of times gets hard, it is useful to remember that all of us wanted to come here. We came to Earth having chosen our gender and having fought Lucifer to become free agents. Life is also short and what we choose and do here will determine the reward we receive in the hereafter. The prize for a good fight, well won, is here again stated: The Bread of Life, the Fountains of Living Water, and the beautiful promise that "God shall wipe away all your tears." God knows you cry. Here is also a chance to use your new eastern poetry skills. Verses 16 & 17 are chiastic. Do you see it?

A: They shall hunger no more

  B: neither thirst any more

    C: neither shall the sun light on them

    C: nor any heat

B: For the Lamb which is in the midst of the throne shall feed them

A: and shall lead them unto living fountains of waters

All of these result in "and God shall wipe away all tears from their eyes."

John wants you to know this because next comes the 7th Seal. We have seen in this overview of Earth's history many terrible struggles and trials. We have seen men's pride, wars, famines and death. We saw all the blood of the martyred prophets, men and women, drenching the altar of heaven as a witness against Lucifer and his followers. We saw the angels ready to do mighty justice in the name of God and punish the earth. We saw nature giving sign after sign that God was nearly done with all of this. We also saw God granting one last commission to glean the field of those who would hear, seal His saints with His name, and prepare Himself a people who would be ready to receive Him in righteousness at His coming. All of this has happened and belongs to the six seals. The Millennial Reign of Jesus Christ is next. It is a 7th seal event; the capstone of the Earth's first week of existence, and what a week it has been!

Chronologically, the Seventh Seal should have opened in the Autumn of 2001 A.D. Mathematically, it should have happened around the 2nd week of September of that year. If that is true, we are living in the 7th Seal right now! So...

How would we know? Where is the Lord?

Chapter Six

The 7th Seal

The Lord is in his holy temple: let all the earth keep silence before him.

— Habakkuk

All of the seals have opened with a noise; a shout, a quake, a lament. The Seventh Seal is different. It opens with...

Revelation 8:1 And when he had opened the seventh seal, there was silence in heaven about the space of half an hour.

Silence...

Why? First of all, silence can only be juxtaposed with noise. The best silence can only happen after a very noisy event. I am going to offer, by way of speculation, that the noise heard around the world on September 11th 2001 was the closing of the Sixth Seal. The great poet-prophet Isaiah may have had this exact event in mind when he foresaw:

Isaiah 33:18 Thine heart shall meditate terror. Where is the scribe? where is the receiver? where is he that counted the towers?

At the following General Conference of the Church, just weeks later, our prophet President Gordon B. Hinckley opened the conference by saying: "The vision of Joel has been fulfilled..." Since the Vision of Joel was a recapitulation of the Sixth Seal, it is logical to assume that the prophet was saying that we had lived to witness the opening of the Seventh Seal. How would we know?

The very sign of the seal's opening was silence. Except for a great noise, due to the half hour of silence, the 6th Thousand

Year block would close and the 7th would open but it would appear to men as if nothing had occurred in terms of heaven.[60]

For wise men on earth, this additional period of time is a gift of mercy. Anytime the Lord extends His judgement is a time for us to repent and improve. It is a time to lay up more treasures in heaven through good works on earth and thereby present to God a much better resumé. The sheer number of new Temples and young missionaries serving speaks with gratitude to God for the extra time we have been allotted. A half hour of heavenly time equals approximately 21 years earth time. During this brief silence on earth, heaven is getting busy.

Revelation 8:2 And I saw the seven angels which stood before God; and to them were given seven trumpets.

3 And another angel came and stood at the altar, having a golden censer; and there was given unto him much incense, that he should offer it with the prayers of all saints upon the golden altar which was before the throne.

4 And the smoke of the incense, which came with the prayers of the saints, ascended up before God out of the angel's hand.

5 And the angel took the censer, and filled it with fire of the altar, and cast it into the earth: and there were voices, and thunderings, and lightnings, and an earthquake.

6 And the seven angels which had the seven trumpets prepared themselves to sound.

At the end of the 1/2 hour of silence, voices, thunderings, lightings and a great earthquake will signal the end of silence. If our speculation is right, we should expect this to happen on or around the Fall of 2022 A.D. Either way, once it begins, it will be woe upon woe. The Lord called this period *the testimony of nature* when missionary work would end and nature, including the hosts of heaven, would preach instead. With the preparations ready, the Lord will in a sense, un-make the world. Here is the first trumpet:

7 The first angel sounded, and there followed hail and fire mingled with blood, and they were cast upon the earth: and the third part of trees was burnt up, and all green grass was burnt up.

God made the earth is seven days, six to work and one to rest. Here we see Him pull the world apart with seven blasts of the trumpet. The first call to arms kills 1/3 of the Earth's foliage and apparently all the grass. *Get your food storage sorted out.*

8 And the second angel sounded, and as it were a great mountain burning with fire was cast into the sea: and the third part of the sea became blood;

9 And the third part of the creatures which were in the sea, and had life, died; and the third part of the ships were destroyed.

The second trumpet sounds! Something like a mountainous comet hits the seas. It kills 1/3 of all the life in the ocean as well as devastates the navies and merchant ships of all nations. Joseph Smith taught that a comet, or something like it, would hail the return of the Lost Ten Tribes as well as the City of Enoch. It is possible that this event *is* also their return.[61]

10 And the third angel sounded, and there fell a great star from heaven, burning as it were a lamp, and it fell upon the third part of the rivers, and upon the fountains of waters;

11 And the name of the star is called Wormwood: and the third part of the waters became wormwood; and many men died of the waters, because they were made bitter.

The third trumpet sounds and this time a comet does strike the fresh water of the planet. This "burning star" has a name: Wormwood. If you want to experience a truly nasty bitterness, you can go to a health food store and buy a tincture made from the herb wormwood. It is used to kill intestinal worms. I tried it once, let's just say that now I can eat raw lemons without issue.

Once you have tasted the bitterness of wormwood, lemons are delicious! Most biblical scholars agree that the burning comet is not covered in wormwood but rather that its effect is something like the herb. It is fascinating to note that scientists have discovered large amounts of cyanogen in the tails of comets. Apparently Halley's Comet contains enough cyanogen in its tail to poison a continent except that Earth's dense atmosphere protects us from it.[62] The comet Wormwood is different. It hits us head on. Men have to drink water to live and so this woe is disastrous to human life.[63]

Revelation 8:12 And the fourth angel sounded, and the third part of the sun was smitten, and the third part of the moon, and the third part of the stars; so as the third part of them was darkened, and the day shone not for a third part of it, and the night likewise.

With the blast of the fourth trumpet, the sun is injured in some manner. One third of the moon and stars are also wounded. This apparently alters the number of daylight hours by 1/3 and deeply darkens the night too.[64] Assuming for argument's sake 12 hours of daylight to 12 hours of night. This woe brings us only 8 hours of daylight to 16 hours of night. Four of these hours to be exceptionally darker and oppressive. With death and darkness all around us, a horrible cry is heard:

13 And I beheld, and heard an angel flying through the midst of heaven, saying with a loud voice, Woe, woe, woe, to the inhabiters of the earth by reason of the other voices of the trumpet of the three angels, which are yet to sound!

There is no word for *very* in the ancient tongue. If you want to say that something is going to bring *very much* woe, you simply repeat the woes. This time there are three, so it's going to be bad.

THE FIRST WOE
Revelation 9:1 And the fifth angel sounded, and I saw a star fall from heaven unto the earth: and to him was given the key of the bottomless pit.

2 And he opened the bottomless pit; and there arose a smoke out of the pit, as the smoke of a great furnace; and the sun and the air were darkened by reason of the smoke of the pit.

3 And there came out of the smoke locusts upon the earth: and unto them was given power, as the scorpions of the earth have power.

4 And it was commanded them that they should not hurt the grass of the earth, neither any green thing, neither any tree; but only those men which have not the seal of God in their foreheads.

5 And to them it was given that they should not kill them, but that they should be tormented five months: and their torment was as the torment of a scorpion, when he striketh a man.

There has been a lot of speculation as to what these creatures are. None of which, is satisfying. The answer seems to be that they are demonic. We know that a star falls to earth from heaven. A star is a point of light. In Mormon thinking it is telestial light or glory that is neither paradisiacal nor celestial. This fallen light in Hebrew is *Hel* (one "l"). We would say *Lucifer* in Latin. In Greek his name is ἐωσφόρος or *the morning star*.[65] He is given the key to open the pit. He has no power to do it until it is given to him. In other words, "his bounds are set." Hell has been called a bottomless pit since it is the lowest point one can fall. Any movement out of the pit can therefore only be up. You can't fall any lower than a pit without a bottom.

Once the pit is opened, a filthy darkness rises out. It dims the already injured sun and oppresses the very air. It is followed by the indescribable — demon-locusts. John does his best to describe them but in the end he settles on telling more about what they do. They are like scorpions in that they go wherever they like and inflict woe and pain on everyone in their way.

Again, we are told the incomprehensible. These are locusts that don't hurt grass or trees, only human beings. More specifically they only hurt those who have not been sealed with the gift of God. There have been many clever explanations of these locusts from Arabic hordes to zombies. The difficulty with it all arises from the next verses. What do you make of this:

Revelation 9:6 And in those days shall men seek death, and shall not find it; and shall desire to die, and death shall flee from them.

I had an uncle who contracted the West Nile Virus years ago and lived through it. I asked him about it and he said, "I wanted to die but didn't. If I could have died, I would have." All from a tiny insect bite. I have never been so sick that I welcomed death, but he has. Still, has there ever been a time on earth when men *wanted* to die but were *unable*? What can this mean? It gets stranger than that:

7 And the shapes of the locusts were like unto horses prepared unto battle; and on their heads were as it were crowns like gold, and their faces were as the faces of men.

8 And they had hair as the hair of women, and their teeth were as the teeth of lions.

9 And they had breastplates, as it were breastplates of iron; and the sound of their wings was as the sound of chariots of many horses running to battle.

10 And they had tails like unto scorpions, and there were stings in their tails: and their power was to hurt men five months.

I remember being in the third grade (public school) when an assembly was called in the lunch room / gymnasium. The speaker was the local T.V. weatherman who was the closest thing I knew to a celebrity. I chuckle today at his brazenness. He was supposed to give a lecture on science and the weather but instead spoke on these verses. It is my first memory of pondering on the ponderous. *Today I doubt that even the Golden Rule is mentioned in public school. So much for In God We Trust.* The weatherman's explanation was that these creatures were Arabian F16 fighter pilots. Re-read the description above again. It does work. You can see the men in their cockpits covered in expensive modern gear. The idea of a modern army as locusts is strengthened by four additional words found only in the Greek Translation of the *Old Testament*, specifically the Book of the Prophet Amos.

Septuagint Amos 7:1-2 Thus has the Lord God shewed me; and, behold, a swarm of locusts coming from the east, and behold, one caterpillar, king Gog. And it came to pass when he had finished devouring the grass of the land, that I said, Lord God, be merciful; who shall raise up Jacob? for he is small of number.

The *Septuagint* is the only version of *Amos* which reads this way. No other version mentions Gog as being king of the locusts. *Amos 7:3-4* goes on to speak of the Lord punishing the oceans too in ways that echo John. Unfortunately the four versions of *Amos* found in the *Dead Sea Scrolls* are damaged in this area and can give us no additional clue as to which version of Amos's locusts were originally intended. John, however, gives us a different name for the locust king — *Apollyon* meaning the *Destroyer* in Greek.[66]

Revelation 9:11 And they had a king over them, which is the angel of the bottomless pit, whose name in the Hebrew tongue is Abaddon, but in the Greek tongue hath his name Apollyon.

The easiest explanation to all of this is to just pin the whole thing on Satan. Ultimately that is true but we are feasters on the word, unafraid to speculate but determined to hold fast to only revealed truth. We will just have to wait and see.

Let's speculate gently for a moment. The Prophet Ezekiel foretold an attack on Jerusalem[67] which appears to be an attack prior to the Second Coming. If this is true it means that there will be two terrible attacks on the Holy City. This makes some sense. All of the early Christian fathers taught that the Jews would rebuild Solomon's Temple before the Second Coming.

The Lord at His return is supposed to be ushered into the Temple once He appears as Messiah. Joseph Smith appears to have taught this as well. Darwinists and later evangelicals berated the Mormons for teaching the return of the Jews to Israel in the 1800s right up to May 14th 1948 when the Jews fulfilled prophecy and claimed Independence in Israel. Today these same mockers are silent and unapologetic. They act as if they knew the truth all along. But their mockery and Joseph Smith's prophetic words are locked in history. They were wrong and our prophet was right. The Jews knew the truth of it. Their first great modern leader, David Ben Gurion[68] said, "You know, there are no people in the world who understand the Jews like the Mormons." One of their chief rabbis, whose name I do not have permission to print, said, "We are not too worried about the particulars of rebuilding our temple, when the time is right, the Mormons will help us figure out anything that we are missing." I'm not exactly sure what he meant, but I liked the sentiment anyway.

All this means that some event will allow the Jews the freedom to rebuild the temple on land that the children of Esau currently claim for themselves. Ezekiel's war appears to suggest that a colossal nuclear defeat of the enemies of Israel will grant the Jews a period of time in which to do it. It also seems to be the case that some amazing protective event (like divine deliverance from a nuclear attack) will rally the Jewish people in faith to rebuild the temple. Again, we are speculating here but the facts fit nicely. If two attacks are correct it would also explain the second woe which seems to be another attack after a short break.

I have laid out all of the theories here because I wanted to sum up this plague with my opinion. I suspect that this woe has its answer in a gentle combination of all of these summations. The Lord has warned us that at a certain point He would withdraw His Spirit from the world leaving only the Gift of the Holy Ghost in place. Mormons know that this gift can only be given by the laying on of hands by one having authority to do so. When the Lord withdraws His Spirit (here also called the Light of Christ), the devil will then have full power over his own. I suspect that what we are seeing here in terms of demon-locusts is in fact the human army of Gog possessed by demonic hordes unleashed by Satan. I believe this is why men and women will be in a frenzy, longing to die but also wanting to destroy. The demonic sons of perdition have no bodies and never will have, this will be their only chance. Feelings of pleasure and pain, rage beyond measure, all of this focused through a stolen physical body. Once possessed with it, they will not easily let it go.[69] In sorrow, one of the three woes is passed, sadly, there are two more.

Revelation 9:12 One woe is past; and, behold, there come two woes more hereafter.

THE SECOND WOE

The second woe contains some strange imagery.

Revelation 9:13 And the sixth angel sounded, and I heard a voice from the four horns of the golden altar which is before God,

14 Saying to the sixth angel which had the trumpet, Loose the four angels which are bound in the great river Euphrates.

15 And the four angels were loosed, which were prepared for an hour, and a day, and a month, and a year, for to slay the third part of men.

The angels bound in the Euphrates? This is not a simple image. John acts like he knows exactly who these are. *You know the angels bound in the Euphrates?* But which Euphrates? The New World one or the Old World one? There is even talk of the heavenly one.[70] If the heavenly Euphrates is meant, then John is here speaking about the "Tsabim" or the planetary hosts of heaven. Modern man does not truly appreciate that the planets are alive and respond to the Lord's call to battle. There was once a heavenly Euphrates in the sky. We will explore this when we study *Genesis* together. For now know that this is a heavenly army. Note the number of soldiers:

Revelation 9:16 And the number of the army of the horsemen were two hundred thousand thousand: and I heard the number of them.

200,000,000 has to be the largest army ever assembled for one earthly battle. Meteors and asteroids were considered heavenly horses by our ancestors. When the Lord spoke to Job about Mars, He used equestrian imagery, even comparing that host of heaven to an impetuous stallion in need of strong reins and a stern rider. These screaming through the atmosphere have been likened to lions with fiery gaping jaws. We have already stated that NASA has discovered a high concentration of cyanide gas in the burning tails of many of these flying astro-hosts.

17 And thus I saw the horses in the vision, and them that sat on them, having breastplates of fire, and of jacinth, and brimstone: and the heads of the horses were as the heads of lions; and out of their mouths issued fire and smoke and brimstone.

18 By these three was the third part of men killed, by the fire, and by the smoke, and by the brimstone, which issued out of their mouths.

19 For their power is in their mouth, and in their tails: for their tails were like unto serpents, and had heads, and with them they do hurt.

20 And the rest of the men which were not killed by these plagues yet repented not of the works of their hands, that they should not worship devils, and idols of gold, and silver, and brass, and stone, and of wood: which neither can see, nor hear, nor walk:

21 Neither repented they of their murders, nor of their sorceries, nor of their fornication, nor of their thefts.

They still would not stop their "murders, sorceries, fornications and thefts!?" What is God supposed to do with such people as this? How much more can mortal humans take and still not acknowledge God's sovereignty and/or repent?

It is at this point in the experience that the vision stops for a moment. We are still in the grasps of the second woe and have the third woe yet to come. We are not finished, not by a long shot, but we pause… It is here that John is called on a mission to to be an Elias. An Elias calling is one of sowing seed for another to harvest. These callings always seem to be connected to Father Noah in some way. Just as Noah *prepped the New Earth* so that another might harvest later.

We will come back to the last woe soon, but let's enjoy the break that's given. See if you can figure out who this angel is at the start of the chapter.

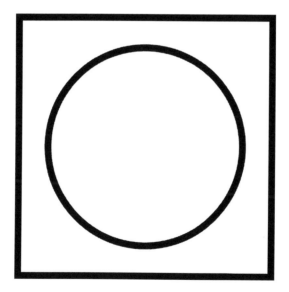

The Kingdom Stone. The square here represents our fallen Earth. The circle represents heaven. Together they are a symbol of the Lord's prayer. "Thy Kingdom Come. Thy Will be done. On earth as it is in heaven." We establish the Lord's kingdom in the same manner that we make these symbols, with a compass and a square.

The angel on the Isle of Patmos by William Blake.

Chapter Seven

A New Mission Call

Take this calling and eat it up; and it shall make thy belly bitter, but it shall be in thy mouth sweet as honey. — *The Angel of the Lord to John*

While working on a new translation of the *Bible* at the Lord's command, the Prophet Joseph used the *Urim & Thummim* to inquire about some of the more enigmatic symbols and their correct interpretation in *Revelation*. The answers are interesting for what they say, and for what they don't say. The Lord is often cautious when giving future events. I believe He is vague on details sometimes for three important reasons. First, our Lord is a lover of man's agency. It was the Father's will, and the Lord's terrible sacrifice, that made men free agents. Agency is precious to Him and He is careful not to undermine it. Since the Lord's word cannot return to Him unfulfilled, any pronouncement He makes must come to pass. Things that *must* come to pass could interfere with agency, thus He is careful in what He proclaims. Second, the total future is not yet written in terms of man, even though it is known to God. Parts are flexible due to repentance. Mortal man has a terrible time understanding how these two truths can exist together. How can God know the future but not have written it? Einstein probably came closest to a simple, mortal answer when he said that time is a dimension. The Lord said that human time was *one big now* to Him. I believe that these are saying the same thing, but the ramifications of such are enormous and beyond the scope of this book. Because time is a big now, some things are locked in place at God's command and other things are fluid, allowing man honest room to repent and change the course of his destiny and future events. No other possibility would be truly fair. Third, it frustrates the attempts of

Satan to destroy every good thing that God is trying to do. Joseph Smith learned this lesson and began hiding some information from the Church's enemies merely to protect the innocent who always got caught in the cross fire. He chastised the brethren for telling our enemies way *too many details* of our plans and warned the Saints directly:

The devil cannot tell a Saint's thoughts, but the moment you speak he knows your mind; he can hear, and if you do not tell your plans, the devil cannot lay plans to counteract yours.[71]

The entire *Bible* can be read as an attempt by Satan to undermine the plans of God and thwart His will. For this reason men must live by faith in every word that comes from the mouth of God and His prophets. Correct faith is the safest option since the Holy Ghost can lead the faithful over any obstacle course (even as it changes) to the destination of safety.

I am mentioning this here because it is entirely possible that the Lord is interrupting *Revelation* in this manner for more than just eastern poetics (which I am fine with anyway). From our position much of the book makes sense, but in John's day there was much that hadn't happened yet.

John is next visited by a mighty angel. One with a special mission call for him. See if you can guess who he is:

Revelation 10:1 And I saw another mighty angel come down from heaven, clothed with a cloud: and a rainbow was upon his head, and his face was as it were the sun, and his feet as pillars of fire:

This is Father Noah, the one charged with restoring all things to the Earth after the Great Flood. The Jews say that clouds, when connected with angels, are the spirits of the redeemed; like the wings of the Lord, these make this angel a Patriarch. The rainbow about his head is the sign of God's covenant safeguarded through the 7 Noahite Laws.[72] He is a being of celestial glory having successfully walked the journey of faith through trial and was found worthy.[73]

2 And he had in his hand a little book open: and he set his right foot upon the sea, and his left foot on the earth,

The little book is John's mission call and the Word of God that he is going to need. Noah straddles land and sea because his decree is going to affect both the living and the dead.

3 And cried with a loud voice, as when a lion roareth: and when he had cried, seven thunders uttered their voices.

4 And when the seven thunders had uttered their voices, I was about to write: and I heard a voice from heaven saying unto me, Seal up those things which the seven thunders uttered, and write them not.

Amen! And Darn it! Thus we don't know what the thunders said. I wish Joseph Smith had asked that one in *D&C 77*, although somehow I'm sure the conversation would have gone like this:

Question: What did the seven thunders say in verse 4, chapter 10.

Answer: The seven thunders spoke words that John was not permitted to write.

I would have tried anyway.

Revelation 10:5 And the angel which I saw stand upon the sea and upon the earth lifted up his hand to heaven,

6 And sware by him that liveth for ever and ever, who created heaven, and the things that therein are, and the earth, and the things that therein are, and the sea, and the things which are therein, that there should be time no longer:

7 But in the days of the voice of the seventh angel, when he shall begin to sound, the mystery of God should be finished, as he hath declared to his servants the prophets.

Here we get the gist of it nonetheless. It has something to do with the Mysteries of God and raising up the hands to heaven. We will let it be until the seventh angel sounds it at a future day. Whatever God wants is right and since He doesn't want it known publicly at this time,[74] "Okay... and darn it!"

Revelation 10:8 And the voice which I heard from heaven spake unto me again, and said, Go and take the little book which is open in the hand of the angel which standeth upon the sea and upon the earth.

9 And I went unto the angel, and said unto him, Give me the little book. And he said unto me, Take it, and eat it up; and it shall make thy belly bitter, but it shall be in thy mouth sweet as honey.

10 And I took the little book out of the angel's hand, and ate it up; and it was in my mouth sweet as honey: and as soon as I had eaten it, my belly was bitter.

All mission calls are thus. They are sweet to the taste but full of nervousness and woe within. Many a young elder and sister knows the joy of preaching the word and bearing testimony, and the pain in the gut that comes when all your attempts to preach are rejected. Nothing hurts more than offering your pearls and discovering only *dogs and pigs* nipping at your open hand. John knows this, but he takes the call anyway.

11 And he said unto me, Thou must prophesy again before many peoples, and nations, and tongues, and kings.

In chapter 1 we speculated on how John may have done exactly that as the mysterious *Professor* who mentored the founding fathers of the United States. It is fascinating to note that there are tales of a mysterious *Wandering Jew* who witnessed the very crucifixion of Christ and then journeyed about the earth unable to die until the Second Coming.[75] He appears in stories as far away from Jewry as China! It will be very exciting to sit at John's feet at a future day and hear tales of his missionary adventures among our various *nations, tongues, kings and brethren.*

We have now come through the left side of the great menorah to the center branch,[76] in other words things are about to get confusing in term of our western concept of prose, poetics and chronological time. In preparing for the last woe, John is going to take us backward from where we sit, in terms of the past. We'll work through it together, but remember that the pattern in a western sense is this:

The Deed of the Earth which Christ Claimed & Repurchased

Seal One: The Years of Adam & Enoch thru Lamech

Seal Two: The Years of Noah & Shem post flood thru Terah

Seal Three: The Years of Abraham's Administration thru Amram

Seal Four: The Years of Moses's Dispensation thru John the Baptist

Seal Five: The Gospel of Jesus Christ thru the Anti-Christ

Seal Six: The Restoration under Joseph Smith the Prophet

Seal Seven: The Millennial Reign of Jesus Christ (under Adam's watch)

> 1/2 hour of silence (about 21 years) when it appears as if nothing has changed from the Sixth Seal

Priesthood Conference at Adam-ondi-Ahman *(suspected position)*

> First Trumpet with First Bowl
>
> Second Trumpet with Second Bowl
>
> Third Trumpet with Third Bowl
>
> Fourth Trumpet with Fourth Bowl
>
> Fifth Trumpet / First Woe with Fifth Bowl
>
> Sixth Trumpet / Second Woe with Sixth Bowl
>
> Seventh Trumpet / Third Woe with Seventh Bowl

The Second Coming of Jesus Christ - The Millennial Reign

> The Binding of Satan for 1,000 years
>
> The Call of the Nations to acknowledge the Rightful King

The Saints Reign with the Lord for 1,000 Years.

Annoying Postscript, Satan is loosed for a short season to gather whatever forces he can before he, and they, are cast into Outer Darkness at last. It is speculated that this short season will be less than 350 years. We will just have to wait and see. No more than that has been openly given.

An artist's depiction of the Great Comet seen over Europe in 1007 A.D. This one, as well as other signs in the heavens, announced the opening of the Sixth Seal or the Dispensation of Joseph Smith, Jr. These are the Hosts of Heaven, called the Tsabim in Hebrew.

Chapter Eight

Armageddon

John saw many strange monsters..., but he saw no monsters stranger than the scholars who've tried to explain his vision. — G.K. Chesterton

With mission call in hand, John is now going to take us back to what is probably the second woe, or the sixth trumpet of the Seventh Seal. Our speculation that some battle (probably the same one Ezekiel saw) allowed the Jews to rebuild their Temple after the fifth trumpet finds validation here, since John is told to measure the Temple. Note also what he is told *not* to measure.

Revelation 11:1 And there was given me a reed like unto a rod: and the angel stood, saying, Rise, and measure the temple of God, and the altar, and them that worship therein.

2 But the court which is without the temple leave out, and measure it not; for it is given unto the Gentiles: and the holy city shall they tread under foot forty and two months.

Here John is being asked to measure the Temple Mount just as "a young man" was asked to do in Zechariah's vision. [77] While it is certainly not earth shattering, it is fascinating to speculate that the young man Zechariah saw was John the Belovéd doing that very thing here. It does make one wonder.[78]

Forty and two months is 3½ years or 1260 days. These are the same numbers given to Daniel.

3 And I will give power unto my two witnesses, and they shall prophesy a thousand two hundred and threescore days, clothed in sackcloth.

4 These are the two olive trees, and the two candlesticks standing before the God of the earth.

John here is referring directly to *Zechariah 4*. We have already explored in Vol 4: *Zechariah & the Teachers of Righteousness* that an obscure Jewish tradition says that these two are Moses and Elijah,[79] the same who performed the Lord's endowment in the same spirit that John the Baptist performed His baptism.

Revelation 11:5 And if any man will hurt them, fire proceedeth out of their mouth, and devoureth their enemies: and if any man will hurt them, he must in this manner be killed.

6 These have power to shut heaven, that it rain not in the days of their prophecy: and have power over waters to turn them to blood, and to smite the earth with all plagues, as often as they will.

These are powers which both Moses and Elijah already have and have already used. Years ago I was extremely surprised to learn that there was an obscure Israeli tradition which stated that Moses[80] and Elijah had both actually been taken into heaven alive *(called dying in the Lord)* so as to be able to witness in blood when needed later. When I first learned this the logic of it hit me profoundly, which is why I lean to this scenario and wanted to make you aware of it. The forces of Gog and Magog will be made up primarily of descendants of Japheth and Edom, both groups who believe in the satanic concept of *Replacement Theology*, a fancy term that means they believe that Israel lost her right to the promises of God with the murder of the prophets and the crucifixion of Jesus Christ. They openly say that all of the promises made to Israel now belong to them. This is not true.

One can find many counters to this false belief in the scriptures and Mormons absolutely denounce it. Replacement Theologists are namely: Catholic, Christian Orthodoxy and Muslim believers. Note that all of these hold Moses and Elijah in great esteem as true prophets of God. It is perfectly within the keeping of my understanding of God's justice that he would send these two revered prophets to try and dissuade Israel's enemies from their damnable actions. It's as if to say, *if Moses and Elijah come down from heaven can't change your wicked plans, no one can.* Our God frequently plays His hand in such a matter so as to leave absolutely no excuse for a terrible punishment, particularly a punishment as severe as total destruction and damnation. Please don't misunderstand, if this logic turns out to be wrong, I'm okay with that. I have heard many Latter-day Saints say that they believe these two prophets will be men from our quorums, meaning members of the modern Seventy or the Twelve. They could be. I rather hope not. I really like our Seventy and the Twelve and the above assignment will be far from a pleasant one. Here is what John says about the mission of these two prophets:

Revelation 11:7 And when they shall have finished their testimony, the beast that ascendeth out of the bottomless pit shall make war against them, and shall overcome them, and kill them.

This is tragic beyond words. However, their conquerors will not be satisfied with their defeat. The corpses of these two witnesses will be mutilated and celebrated over. Like beasts filled with bloodlust after a successful kill, these horrible butchers will be in a frenzy of hellish joy! It will be as though they and their gods have beaten Jehovah-Adonai at last! So evil will the scene be that Jerusalem will appear as Sodom or Egypt[81]. Here is what John has to say about it:

8 And their dead bodies shall lie in the street of the great city, which spiritually is called Sodom and Egypt, where also our Lord was crucified.

9 And they of the people and kindreds and tongues and nations shall see their dead bodies three days and an half, and shall not suffer their dead bodies to be put in graves.

10 And they that dwell upon the earth shall rejoice over them, and make merry, and shall send gifts one to another; because these two prophets tormented them that dwelt on the earth.

But, in the midst of their demonic rejoicing, the Lord will speak to the corpses...

11 And after three days and an half the Spirit of life from God entered into them, and they stood upon their feet; and great fear fell upon them which saw them.

12 And they heard a great voice from heaven saying unto them, Come up hither. And they ascended up to heaven in a cloud; and their enemies beheld them.

13 And the same hour was there a great earthquake, and the tenth part of the city fell, and in the earthquake were slain of men seven thousand: and the remnant were affrighted, and gave glory to the God of heaven.

14 The second woe is past; and, behold, the third woe cometh quickly.

The space between the 2nd woe and the 3rd one seems to be much shorter. The Prophet Joseph said that it would be very much like a woman in labor. As the time of birth draws near, her contractions get closer and closer. It will be the same in our day. The moments of peace between tragedy will be less and less. The good news is that we have been promised that the same joy a new mother has when she holds her newborn will be the same joy the faithful will have when the kingdom finally comes. We, like she, will not remember the pain but rejoice in the new gift of life.

THE THIRD WOE • THE SEVENTH TRUMPET

We have survived some terrible things together, but there is one last woe. This one brings the return of our Lord.

Revelation 11:15 And the seventh angel sounded; and there were great voices in heaven, saying, The kingdoms of this world are become the kingdoms of our Lord, and of his Christ; and he shall reign for ever and ever.

At last! At last! How long have the saints through all ages prayed, "Thy Kingdom Come!" Men have prayed for peace on every altar, but now through these trials their prayers have changed to prayers for the return of the Prince of Peace. There will never be real peace without Him anyway. Why pray for peace when the Lord has said, *"Peace, Peace, but there will be no peace!"*? Today I pray instead for the Prince of Peace and that His will – not mine – be done. Here, finally, He is coming!

Revelation 11:16 And the four and twenty elders, which sat before God on their seats, fell upon their faces, and worshipped God,

17 Saying, We give thee thanks, O Lord God Almighty, which art, and wast, and art to come; because thou hast taken to thee thy great power, and hast reigned.

Men have suffered Cains and Mahans, Nimrods and Pharaohs, Basileis[82] and Emperors, Kings and Queens, Presidents and Magistrates, false Popes and phony Prophets, Mammon and Tyrants, Mahdis and Führers, Social Engineers and greed, Bureaucrats and the Beast System, the self righteous Elites and the self entitled sheep, Minority Oppression and the Radical Religious, Demons and Lucifer — but at last the Lord God Almighty has picked up His own scepter, taken the Great Power that was always His and claimed the inheritance that is His by birthright! Having been through all others, we have come to learn whose way is best and we unitedly want Him. Finally, there is enough blood on the altar.

Pay particular attention to what the Lord has to say of the Saints who fear His name.

18 And the nations were angry, and thy wrath is come, and the time of the dead, that they should be judged, and that thou shouldest give reward unto thy servants the prophets, and to the saints, and them that fear thy name, small and great; and shouldest destroy them which destroy the earth.

To all of those who labour in the kingdom in the many, many small capacities: from mothers at home, who wonder if they are doing enough, to good men who ponder if there might be some reason they were never called into a bishopric or some such higher service, the Lord does not care. Small and great will receive the same reward. How wonderful to be small and tucked beneath the wing of the Almighty on that day when small and great receive the same reward. "Do not despise the small things," the Lord has said. He also said where much is given, much is expected (and required). Since the reward is the same, it's nice to have less to answer for in the end.

19 And the temple of God was opened in heaven, and there was seen in his temple the ark of his testament: and there were lightnings, and voices, and thunderings, and an earthquake, and great hail.

I believe that the ark of His testament, here mentioned, is His personage, His Holy tabernacle, marked with the scars and wounds of His infinite sacrifice; His hands, His feet and His side prove it. He has conquered sin and death and now is the day of His vengeance. The Lord is no longer in His Temple, He is coming again to His footstool.

We will come back to this moment but once again, in pure eastern poetic tradition, we keep moving through our parallelisms, like the branches of the Great Menorah, these are candles of illumination set upon a candle stick to light the way for those who will look for them. We are now moving along the right side of the candelabra and so we jump back in time to John's day, the time of the Caesars of Rome and the Fifth Seal when Jesus Christ administered His Gospel directly and preached along the shores of Galilee.

This jump back in time also helps justify and prepare us to understand how a meek and gentle Lamb, the goodly son of Mary and the Father, can now roar as the royal lion, screech His vengeance like the mighty eagle, bellow His sorrow as the ox, and call His children together like a loving father.

Chapter Nine

War on Earth & in Heaven

Woe to the inhabiters of the earth and of the sea! The devil is come down unto you, having great wrath, because he knoweth that he hath but a short time.

— *John the Revelator*

John wants us to understand that the great battles of woe we have been witnessing are really the culmination of a long and terrible ancient fight. The painful truth is that the *War in Heaven* was never really won. It was merely moved to another field, the planet Earth. It is here that the decisive battle will take place at the end of time. John makes this point by showing two truths. First that God has attempted to establish His kingdom on Earth repeatedly, at least once every thousand years (sometimes more) to be exact. Then He will show John that the same arch-demon who has opposed Him on Earth is the one who opposed him first in heaven. The Lord has suffered much because of Lucifer and the wicked who will not come to Him. He is therefore fully justified in what He is about to do.

Revelation 12:1 And there appeared a great wonder in heaven; a woman clothed with the sun, and the moon under her feet, and upon her head a crown of twelve stars:

This is the coming Kingdom of Heaven seen as a beautiful woman. Her glory is Celestial power. She stands upon the moon, a symbol that her time has come. Often the moon here is depicted with two male crescent horns showing that she is protected by the Father's priesthood. [83] Women are a sign of nurture and transformation. She is a great queen crowned with 12 stars, both the Apostolic Authority and the Birthright of Israel. Her time to bring forth transformation has come.[84]

2 And she being with child cried, travailing in birth, and pained to be delivered.

Zion is ready to give birth to the kingdom. Lucifer's powers are coming to an end, but wait...

3 And there appeared another wonder in heaven; and behold a great red dragon, having seven heads and ten horns, and seven crowns upon his heads.

Since the days of Eden, the enemy of man has been a serpent. The same serpent that lied to our mother Eve and lost his legs has now grown into a terrible fearsome blood-red dragon. He has many forms, seen as seven distinct crowned heads with horns; the last of which has ten horns. The enemy of Zion on earth has been 7 manifestations. 1: Egypt, 2: Assyria, 3:Babylon, 4: Medo-Persia, 5: Greece, 6: Rome, 7: Rome Reborn. It is Rome Reborn, being a mixture of iron and clay, that Daniel saw as the 10 toes of Nebuchadnezzar's Metallic Man dream. This is the same image recast for John.[85] Each of these were crowned for a season but lost their power to the next. Make no mistake, here the Lord is declaring that though these monsters have separate faces, they are all just the same ugly beast. All have their source in Helel-Lucifer-Satan. To further hammer home the point, John is told that it is this same Lucifer-Satan-Dragon who fought the very first war in heaven when he drew away ⅓ of our kin, the sons of our Heavenly Parents.[86]

Revelation 12:4 And his tail drew the third part of the stars of heaven, and did cast them to the earth: and the dragon stood before the woman which was ready to be delivered, for to devour her child as soon as it was born.

In John's day, Satan waited with open jaws to destroy the kingdom yet again. He had been successful every dispensation before, necessitating its return every thousand years in pureness. John is witnessing the pattern renew itself with the Christian Church, founded by the Lord and being persecuted by Satan's latest face — Caesar's. It's a terrible thing for a mother with child to have to face a hungry dragon. The juxtaposition between purity and bestiality cannot be more extreme.

Revelation 12:5 And she brought forth a man child, who was to rule all nations with a rod of iron: and her child was caught up unto God, and to his throne.

Zion was to bring forth the kingdom of God. It would rule the earth as Joseph Smith taught, "by the word of God" but, the plan didn't work. Satan was too strong and the children of Zion were too weak. Instead of Zion and the Kingdom ruling, the chosen house of Israel went into exile being ruled by the nations for 1260 years.

6 And the woman fled into the wilderness, where she hath a place prepared of God, that they should feed her there a thousand two hundred and threescore years.[87]

The Kingdom was lost to man but not to God. He protected it at His throne for a future day. Zion was safe in her wasteland but none of this was ideal.

John would next be taken back further in time to the very foundation of the earth's creation, when the *Plan of Salvation* was being explained by God the Father and the new Earth was being formed for that purpose. John saw what seems impossible still, there was *War in Heaven*.

WAR IN HEAVEN

Tucked in three mere verses here are the only officially canonized account of an ancient War in Heaven. There are other non-canonized accounts; even English poet John Milton (1608–1674) knew there had been a War in Heaven. The concept is not new to the Restoration but its purpose and ramifications have been greatly demystified by it.

Revelation 12:7 And there was war in heaven: Michael and his angels fought against the dragon; and the dragon fought and his angels,

8 And prevailed not; neither was their place found any more in heaven.

9 And the great dragon was cast out, that old serpent, called the Devil, and Satan, which deceiveth the whole world: he was cast out into the earth, and his angels were cast out with him.

Mormons know that this war began when Lucifer, one of the elder sons of God, proposed a counter plan to the Father's *Plan of Salvation*. Lucifer's plan was discussed and the family rejected his plan by majority vote. Lucifer would not accept this and attempted to delegitimize the election of the plan. A battle ensued and he with ⅓ of the spirit sons of God where thrown from heaven. It is said that he fell like lightening to the Earth and here the war continues. After that battle we would call him Satan, meaning the *Enemy*. He still prefers his heavenly name, Lucifer which means the *Light bearer.*[88] It has been a long war.

10 And I heard a loud voice saying in heaven, Now is come salvation, and strength, and the kingdom of our God, and the power of his Christ: for the accuser of our brethren is cast down, which accused them before our God day and night.

11 And they overcame him by the blood of the Lamb, and by the word of their testimony; and they loved not their lives unto the death.

12 Therefore rejoice, ye heavens, and ye that dwell in them. Woe to the inhabiters of the earth and of the seal[89] for the devil is come down unto you, having great wrath, because he knoweth that he hath but a short time.

These verses speak for themselves but I want to highlight a particular insight which I believe is read over too quickly. The Lord says that Lucifer *knows that he has but a short time.* As impossible as it seems to christians, there are people on this Earth who worship Satan.[90] I don't mean in the guise of some made up religion, I mean actually worship him like Cain did with their eyes *half* open. I have met some of these people. They honestly believe that Lucifer has a secret plan to prevent the Lord's Second Coming and that they will inherit the Earth by vanquishing the Lord. It would be funny if they weren't so serious. Lucifer told his minions the same thing before the flood! Lucifer is not going to win and the truly sad thing is that he knows it. Liars lie! He will laugh when he sees the look of terror on the faces of his lickspittlers when they realize he played them for the fool. Lucifer hates them! Their vote with yours cost him everything. He will not support his children in their day of need. They will know it when they beg the rocks to be their tombs, but let's get back to John. The world has been warned.

Revelation 12:13 And when the dragon saw that he was cast unto the earth, he persecuted the woman which brought forth the man child.

14 And to the woman were given two wings of a great eagle, that she might fly into the wilderness, into her place, where she is nourished for a time, and times, and half a time, from the face of the serpent.

As a son of the American Revolution my blood runs red, white and blue. I like verse 14 because I want to believe that the Great Eagle here is the bald eagle, the emblem of the United States. Before any of you laugh too hard, you should know that the Founding Fathers read that and believed it too. They saw the Great Red Dragon as the Red Coats of England.[91] They believed that Lady Liberty, yes, the same in the harbor and the one that was once on our coinage, was this very woman being carried away from the popes and priests of the old world to the hidden biomes of America. Brigham Young took her further into the very desert itself where she was nourished until her nestled mountains blossomed as the rose.

15 And the serpent cast out of his mouth water as a flood after the woman, that he might cause her to be carried away of the flood.

16 And the earth helped the woman, and the earth opened her mouth, and swallowed up the flood which the dragon cast out of his mouth.

17 And the dragon was wroth with the woman, and went to make war with the remnant of her seed, which keep the commandments of God, and have the testimony of Jesus Christ.

Men like Benjamin Franklin and Thomas Jefferson saw the Atlantic Ocean as that great body of water separating the machinations of fallen religion from the tender truths of the American shore. For a long time, the mighty oceans have protected us from *ex cathedra*, *jus gladii*, inquisitions, the tantrums of protestant kings and the whims of angry Muslims.[92] Men like Thomas believed there was something moving in the heavens blessing America. Jefferson would later say:

The genuine and simple religion of Jesus will one day be restored: such as it was preached and practiced by Himself. Very soon after His death it became muffled up in mysteries, and has been ever since kept in concealment from the vulgar eye.[93]

WAR ON EARTH

Now that Lucifer was on the Earth, he became our problem. John is next shown the birth of Satan's plan and the birth of the horrible seven-headed, ten-horned dragon. You will note that he comes out of the sea. In ancient Hebraic thinking, the sea was the world of the dead and Spirit Prison. Since Noah's flood especially, all of the evil of the ancient world had been washed into the bottomless pit of the ocean. So, it is from there that evil returns, because it is the same enemy in disguise. Satan is a liar. Liars come in disguises.

Revelation 13:1 And I stood upon the sand of the sea, and saw a beast rise up out of the sea, having seven heads and ten horns, and upon his horns ten crowns, and upon his heads the name of blasphemy.

This is the same beast John saw trying to eat the kingdom. Note here that God blends the beasts that Daniel saw all into one. John is living in the day of Daniel's last beast but before the rise of the 10 horns / kingdoms:

2 And the beast which I saw was like unto a leopard, and his feet were as the feet of a bear, and his mouth as the mouth of a lion: and the dragon gave him his power, and his seat, and great authority.

Remember that Daniel was told that the lion-beast was Babylon, the bear-beast was Medo-Persia, the leopard-beast was Greece and the dragon-beast was Rome. Rome is the one crowned with 10 crowns because when Rome falls – which had not happened when John saw this – it would be reborn into 10 kingdoms. John sees that Satan is the one behind all of Daniel's beasts. In fact, they are not really many beasts but one with different faces. The dragon, who is Lucifer, gives them all their power. The Prophet Joseph said that the word *dragon* here really should have been translated as devil.[94] Note:

There is a mistranslation of the word "dragon" in the second verse [of chapter 13]. The original word signifies the Devil and not "dragon" as translated. Read chapter 12 verse 9; it there reads, "that old serpent, called the Devil." And it ought to be translated "Devil" in this case, and not "dragon."[95]

John will next see something shocking:

Revelation 13:3 And I saw one of his heads as it were wounded to death; and his deadly wound was healed: and all the world wondered after the beast.

4 And they worshipped the dragon which gave power unto the beast: and they worshipped the beast, saying, Who is like unto the beast? who is able to make war with him?

There had been nothing on the earth quite like the Roman Empire. It was a wonder. It lasted over 500 years! When Rome fell, the world shuttered. It did not seem possible. Rome was the Eternal City. It could not fall. Remember that all of this had not yet happened in John's day. John received this *Revelation* around 96 A.D. Rome would not fall for another 380+ years!

In John's day the forces of good and evil seemed clearly defined. Christianity was good and Rome was evil. Christ was good and Caesar was evil. If men wanted to live, they worshiped Caesar. The brave worshiped Jesus openly. The frightened worshipped Him in private.

5 And there was given unto him a mouth speaking great things and blasphemies; and power was given unto him to continue forty and two months.

6 And he opened his mouth in blasphemy against God, to blaspheme his name, and his tabernacle, and them that dwell in heaven.

Rome did all of that and more. Rome even killed the Prince of Peace and burned the Holy Temple of God to the ground before destroying Abraham's homeland in the sight of his children. Nebuchadnezzar did terrible things but Rome even starved Jerusalem into cannibalism. Desperate Jewish parents ate their own children, nothing like that had happened before.

Revelation 13:7 And it was given unto him to make war with the saints, and to overcome them: and power was given him over all kindreds, and tongues, and nations.

8 And all that dwell upon the earth shall worship him, whose names are not written in the book of life of the Lamb slain from the foundation of the world.

Once the Church of Christ rose, Rome turned its fury on her. To this day we do not know how many Saints were killed. We do know that Rome ended the lives of Peter and Paul with countless others, everywhere they could find them.

9 If any man have an ear, let him hear.

10 He that leadeth into captivity shall go into captivity: he that killeth with the sword must be killed with the sword. Here is the patience and the faith of the saints.

This was a comfort to the Saints of John's day. Many would be killed for their beliefs. Indeed we saw that the 5th Seal was covered in blood. The blasphemies and outrages were immense. All but John, and some of the seventy, were butchered. Christians were fed to lions, burned alive or hung on crosses. It was a terrible time. All God could say in comfort was that the Lord would have His justice at a future time and in a very Jewish way it *would be eye for an eye!* Those who butchered the Saints would one day be butchered themselves.

But something was coming that John, and indeed no mortal could have grasped. Satan was going to change his game plan halfway. The new, unfathomable plan would be: If you can't beat them, join them, or better yet — usurp them. Rome was going to become the Church! Caesar was going to become Christ! The new plan was so devilish that it would have been unfair of God not to warn the people. A pseudo-christ in "heaven" was going to become the Anti-Christ on earth. Here is what John saw:

Revelation 13:11 And I beheld another beast coming up out of the earth; and he had two horns like a lamb, and he spake as a dragon.

Again it's the bloody dragon but note two things have changed. This time he is not coming from the sea, no. He already walks the land of the living. Note also that he looks like a lamb (horns are an animal's authority; a symbol of *priesthood power*)[96] but his words are the dragons. Note even closer, that he has a dragon's mouth. Dragon mouths have serpent's fangs. These leave marks where they bite. We are going to be given several clues as to the identity of this new beast here:

12 And he exerciseth all the power of the first beast before him, and causeth the earth and them which dwell therein to worship the first beast, whose deadly wound was healed.

The new beast would possess all the power of Rome, including the ability to keep the people's worship toward the Eternal City. This would make it seem as though the death of the first beast never really took place. This exactly happened when the Bishop of Rome, known as the Pope, took over the throne of Caesar. Out of the ashes of a dead Roman Empire, the Holy Roman Empire rose. The Eternal City lived again as Rome the Vatican.

13 And he doeth great wonders, so that he maketh fire come down from heaven on the earth in the sight of men,

Miracles were done in the name of Papal Rome. We can cite many. Here are two easy ones. How about the so-called Vision of the Cross at the *Battle of the Milvian Bridge* when Constantine became a Roman Christian? In modern times we have the *Miracle of our Lady of Fatima* where children spoke for elders. How about the many bleeding statues and twisted trees that look like the Mother Mary? A quick historical search on your own will reveal a great many of these.

Revelation 13:14 And deceiveth them that dwell on the earth by the means of those miracles which he had power to do in the sight of the beast; saying to them that dwell on the earth, that they should make an image to the beast, which had the wound by a sword, and did live.

Men have built mighty churches on these sites. Pilgrims still make their journeys, some on bloody knees, to worship Rome at these spots where so-called miracles happened all around the world. Still the world cries, "Show us a sign!"[97]

15 And he had power to give life unto the image of the beast, that the image of the beast should both speak, and cause that as many as would not worship the image of the beast should be killed.

Rome lived again through the Vatican. A great many Christians and Pagans who refused to give Papal Rome the glory of God were tortured, murdered and burned at the stake. We will discuss this in disturbing depth in a future chapter when John is given more details from the Lord.

THE DREADED MARK OF THE BEAST

The most dreaded passage in all of scripture is probably *Revelation 13:17*. The prophecy that *no man could buy or sell without*

Lucifer Takes the Pope to Hell by William Blake, 1795. Here Blake is saying that the Pope belongs with the 6 wicked kings of the past. The 7th head of the dragon is the Pope.

the mark of the beast. This is a scary prospect. A man who cannot buy or sell cannot support his family nor himself. He cannot produce increase from his labor, which for a man is his prime duty before God. A man who cannot provide is not really a man. If one is forced to align with Satan or watch his wife and children starve, what is a man to do?

It is important to know that all christianity, except for the Latter-day Saints, believes that the *Book of Revelation* is a chronological book; meaning that they read it in a purely western way. They see the events as being chronological, happening in order, and one after another. A major reason that I wanted you to understand eastern thinking and poetry is so that you can get your mind around the correct structure of this book. *Revelation* is not chronological in a western sense. It is chronological in an eastern sense; in the sense that God is one eternal round. His concept of time is more like a menorah. It moves in-and-out through a circular pattern (you can think of it as an upward spiral) with the core event being as the central lighted branch which gives new meaning both to the moments that came before it and the events after it. It's a paradigm shift for sure but your spirit, being eternal, can grasp it better than your physical self can. Your mortal body is a clock, ticking toward your death. It has a much harder time grasping eternity and timelessness.

None of this would have been clear without Joseph Smith and the Urim & Thummim. In 1832 A.D., very likely around the time that baptist Reverend William Miller[98] was preaching that the Second Coming would take place in 1844, a group of Saints asked the Prophet Joseph to inquire of the Lord as to the meaning of the more enigmatic parts of *Revelation*. They expected the 4 horsemen to break forth at any moment. The heavenly prize came when the Lord revealed that each seal represented a dispensation and that seals 1 thru 5 were not future happenings but past events.[99] This meant that only seals 6 and 7 had any real bearing on the Latter-day Church. This was a huge gift from the throne! Again, all of christianity believes that all of the terrible events in the book are forthcoming, but we know that much of it has already happened. One cannot prepare for the future properly, if one has the wrong information. One is also not accountable for the sins of the past. That's great news!

SO WHAT IS GOING ON?

In our study of *Zechariah* you will remember the Lord's frustration with the money system that was being imposed upon the world. The Lord hates banking, coinage, interest and our modern system of real estate. He hates it because the earth belongs to Him and He has given dominion of it to man. Under His watchful care, the Earth is able to provide all the needs of life. As soon as money (in our modern sense) was introduced it immediately meant that human life and activity could be valued in a hierarchy. Some jobs would be seen as more important than others. These would earn higher wages. It meant that men could buy up the resources of the Earth and then grant the right to use it to others in the form of loans, leases or rent. This would mean that a few would determine who had the right to live on the land, eat from the land, and who could not. Remember that it was God who divided up the land not man. He intended for us all to have a place. Money, and the love of it particularly, is the root of all modern evil. Money and interest allow us to ignore the Lord's prayer that God would "give us our daily bread." Manna need not fall from heaven daily to help men live by faith, rather men could now store up vast sums of money based on past labors (or in the case of interest and rent – the labors of others) and live like kings on a brother's back. This is evil.

Seeing that all of this was unstoppable, the Lord showed Zechariah that He was preparing a worldwide proclamation against monetary dishonesty. Just as the Lord has directed modern prophets to make proclamations to the world about what He will and will not tolerate on His planet, He wanted it known that since man was determined to live under a monetary system, there would be both a new accountability required at a future day, and there would be consequences to the quality of life in mortality. God would judge men's actions as landlords and bankers, since the land – and the gold – are really His.

This is a long explanation I know, but you will never understand the *Mark of the Beast* without a paradigm shift for the very reason that the Mark of Beast is already here and has been for a very long time. John places it in the 5th seal.

WHAT IS THE MARK OF THE BEAST?

This is going to take a paradigm shift to understand. Secular-christianity is waiting for some type of futuristic computer chip implant to be forced upon mankind as a means of control. This chip, they fear, will be linked to their checking account balance and will prevent them from buying or selling without permission of Satan. The scriptures are clear one must bear the mark to function in society *and* any person bearing the Mark of the Beast will *not* be saved. Let's take a moment and try and think of this from a secular-christian, evangelical perspective since I believe it is important to understand how this fear motivates their actions in these Last-days. It will also give us another reason to thank God for modern prophets to help us see straighter than the world can see.

Christians, other than Catholics and Eastern Orthodox Churches, teach that once a person is saved, he cannot be unsaved. This is based on a handful of misreadings from the *Bible*, but has its real source in their lack of covenant-based "good works" since the days of Martin Luther. Their entire salvation-schema is that faith saves and that which is saved cannot be un-saved. They can even sin, although they say a truly saved person won't do that.[100] One would think therefore that they would have no fear of the Beast's Mark, but the opposite is true. Since they have no sacramental-good works to stand as a witness before God, and they have no right to the Holy Ghost as a constant companion of remembrance, they are *ever learning but never able to come to a knowledge thereof,* to quote Paul. In layman's terms we would say that they are ever searching for a sign of confirmation as proof that their faith-salvation is real.[101] It is ironic that they believe that it is faith alone that saves, but they don't really have the faith to believe it. This is because it is not true and the Spirit only testifies of truth.

My own breakthrough into the *Mark of the Beast* came when I was studying Greek from the perspective of 19th century English scholarship. It was from these great minds who spoke many ancient languages that I learned that the mark of the beast is the same word for the "mark left on the skin such as from a snake bite." Like any correct key, it can open the proper door. Suddenly I understood it all! The beast *which makes the mark* is a snake. The mark of the beast is the snake's bite. This is perfectly eastern! Snake bites can be venomous and venom eventually kills the body it invades. Of course the snake doing the biting is Lucifer the dragon. Lucifer's venom in your veins, kills you.[102] Let me illustrate what I am trying to say with a re-translation. It will help you to put on your Eastern Thinking Caps (not the ones with little tassels, bad, but true, joke.)

THE SERPENT'S VENOM

Here is a correct interpretation of these verses, offered for you to accept or reject. I'm okay with either that you choose.

Revelation 13:11 And I beheld another beast coming up out of the earth; and he had two horns like a lamb, and he spake as a dragon.

And I saw a new Beast coming out of the land of the living. He seemed to have the authority of the Lamb but his mouth and his words were the dragon's [the Devil's].

12 And he exerciseth all the power of the first beast before him, and causeth the earth and them which dwell therein to worship the first beast, whose deadly wound was healed.

He had all the power of the Caesars before him and he forced all the nations to worship Rome, which should have died when it fell, but it did not die. It came back to life!

13 And he doeth great wonders, so that he maketh fire come down from heaven on the earth in the sight of men,

This Beast performed many miracles which astounded men, he even made it appear that fire came down from heaven, but…

14 And deceiveth them that dwell on the earth by the means of those miracles which he had power to do in the sight of the beast; saying to them that dwell on the earth, that they should make an image to the beast, which had the wound by a sword, and did live.

…he is a liar. Still, people believed his satanic miracles. Because they believed him, he commanded his followers to make a shadow of Rome so that it lived on.

15 And he had power to give life unto the image of the beast, that the image of the beast should both speak, and cause that as many as would not worship the image of the beast should be killed.

He was so powerful that he gave life back to Rome. Rome spoke again and all who would not worship Rome were killed.

16 And he causeth all, both small and great, rich and poor, free and bond, to receive a mark in their right hand, or in their foreheads:

His venom infected all, small men and kings, freemen and slaves. By his serpent-words and serpent-teeth he bit everyone, corrupting them either in their ability to labor and make covenants (their hands) or in their intellectual ability to think and perceive, some in their "third eye".

17 And that no man might buy or sell, save he that had the mark, or the name of the beast, or the number of his name.

No one was able to live or function without his venom.

We have one last verse in this chapter, the dreaded 666, but for dramatic effect I want to extrapolate the above verses first, *to beat a dying horse.* This blood venom was introduced on the Earth in the 5th Seal at the Great Apostasy. Thus, you, modern man, is not accountable for it. All of us today were born into the Beast system and suffer under the poison of its mark. While we are accountable for getting the poison out, we are not guilty for the poison going in. It was injected before our births. Since the days of Imperial Rome, and its mutation into Papal Rome, the joining of Church and State has been the bane of the nations. America's Founding Fathers helped us see the possibility of separating the powers of each (that was a paradigm shift at the time). But, we still need new eyes to see the venom of the Beast System that we still accept as reality. In the United States of America, since the Civil War, the Beast System has been working to strangle the Land of the Free.[103]

Mark this well! You right now cannot buy or sell or even live without justifying yourself as worthy to your Beast of State. Since the 5th Seal, no man can or does buy or sell today without the consent of Rome or the many faces of shattered Rome, known as the State. It is all the same thing. If you doubt it, just look around you. This will take the paradigm shift, I warned you about. It can be very hard to get the venom you have had since birth out of your veins. But know, that even after you get it out, you will still be governed by it. If you can get your mind around this as a son or daughter of God, you will have begun the process of phlebotomy; *getting the venom out.* Here goes:

• It is illegal for one human to cut another human's hair without a license from the State.

• It is illegal for your child to make a pitcher of lemonade and sell cups of it on the street corner for a nickel without a food handler's permit.

• It is illegal for you to decide you don't want to pay your taxes or that you want to pay a lesser amount.

• It is illegal for you to decide that you are fed up with civilization, buy a tent and go and live in the mountains.

• It is illegal for you to own a dog without permission of the government. There is a limit to how many dogs you can own.

• It is illegal for you to transfer more than $5,000 of your own money in a 24-hour period to another account.

• It is illegal in many States for you to collect rain water in a bucket and water your own plants with it.

• It is illegal to catch a fish to feed yourself or your family, even in the free waters of the ocean, without proper authorization from the government (a fishing license).

• It is illegal to open a bakery and refuse to ice a cake for a costumer in a way you find particularly offensive.

• It is illegal to disconnect your own house on your own property from the power grid.

You can not buy or sell without the Mark of the Beast, today, right now. Can you see it?

Is it starting to hit you? The *Mark of the Beast* is the poison in your flesh that causes you to love the lie more than the truth. It is the poison that causes you to cling to the riches of the world rather than the riches of eternity. It is the notion in your brain that says, "Well of course a child needs a food handler's permit to sell me a lemonade, what if she used toilet water and I get sick? It is good for the government to monitor all forms of my communication to protect me from evil." That is the venom.

Remember, the Lord God shut the mouths of lions to save Daniel. He sent a giant fish to save Jonah from the depths of the sea. He parted the ocean so the Children of Israel could escape Pharaoh. You don't need the governments of the world to protect you. For those living in the lands of America, the promise was always double, "Serve the God of this land, the Lord Jesus Christ, and your days will be safe upon the Earth." We and the Children of Israel have trusted more in kings and governments. We have harkened to the Kingmen among us. We have let them rule us and our land and today we neither buy nor sell without their consent. Now you know. You have been marked. The only escape from the Mark of Beast, which you bare now, is to rush to the arms of the *Sealer of the Lord,* and stay beneath Jehovah's *mighty white wing.* Praise God that Sealers exist today, in the here and now. Come to the Priesthood of the Lord and get His Seal![104]

If you still don't get it, perhaps this modern story will help. Recently a Mormon father bought his teenage daughter a smart phone for her birthday. Naturally she was thrilled. She looked up traffic and saw which route to use to avoid an accident. She checked out a few Chinese Restaurants and found out which one had been serving cat with its orange sauce instead of chicken. She looked up words she was uncertain how to spell and snooped on social media for any gossip about a couple of boys she was interested in dating. After a week or so, her father asked her how she liked her new phone. She said, "It's the greatest thing in the world. I no longer need the Holy Ghost in my life, this phone is better and does it all." Venom, do you get it?

I have no doubt that the governments of the world would love to implant us all with a chip to better safeguard their interests and better manage us. I want to go on the record now by saying that it will never happen in the United States. This alone should prove to the secular-christian world that their interpretation of these verses is wrong. Follow their logic and you will see. Evangelicals believe the Bible is immutable; meaning it cannot be changed. Okay fine, that means that there is nothing they can do about the coming computer chip beastly implant. The problem is that since every one knows about the supposed future coming forced beastly computer chip implant, they have vowed to defeat it and absolutely refuse to participate in it at all costs. Okay, I would too. I don't want to be implanted and have no intention of being implanted, so now comes the grown up, non-brain washed evangelical moment — if the Bible is immutable and you are going to be implanted no matter what, but have banned together to stop it from happening, have you not then changed the word of God? If you do change the word of God and stop the unstoppable computer chip implant, then you have changed the Bible, which cannot be changed. And if you do happen to take from the word, by changing it, you are then condemned to hell by the word of the Bible. So, if you do get the mark of the Beast you are damned and if you don't get the mark you are damned. Damned if you do and damned if you don't, *well, damn!*

Of course all of this is just silly as they are silly. Do not listen to them, they have no power to save you. No, the Mark of the Beast is the venom of ultimately loving the things of this world more than the things of God. It is connected to man's faith in the arm of flesh over the arm of the Lord. It is accepting that the State has the right to catalog you and own you from womb to tomb. To number you with *Social Security Numbers* and *Driver's Licenses* and authorize your value through purse and scrip. We were born into that system and there is nothing we can do about it until the Lord comes, except for seeing it as it really is. We have been warned that the hearts of many would fail in the day that the Lord pulls down the system. This will be because they cannot fathom life outside the Beast. You don't have to be one of them. Live your life, try to follow the rules, lay up for yourselves treasure in heaven and be ready to completely walk away, consecrating it all to the Prince of Peace when He calls for it. Lot's wife looked back. Today all she is good for is seasoning potato chips.

All of this is encapsulated in false religion and for the Christians to whom this book is written, it is the poison that keeps them from rejecting secular-christianity and embracing that final sealing at the Lord's hand from His last ditch attempt to save them. The priesthood, the keys, the sacramental good-works have all been restored upon the Earth one last time. These alone will purge the blood and the body of Satan's poison by replacing it with the blood and body of Jesus Christ, for His blood *is sufficient and His body is meat indeed.* You and I have been poisoned; we are as dead. Jesus Christ is life and He is waiting by the door knocking. Let Him In! Enter His Holy House while you can!

Now you are prepared for the final verse — the dreaded man of the three 6's.

Revelation 13:18 Here is wisdom. Let him that hath understanding count the number of the beast: for it is the number of a man; and his number is Six hundred threescore and six.

He is the lamb-dragon of the 5th Seal who gave power back to Rome after it fell. Again, you have to think not of yourself but of the times of John and the Early Christian Church. Their entire focus had been trying to preach the gospel despite Imperial Rome. The Caesars had killed Jesus, Peter, Paul and an unknown number of Saints. Rome was the enemy. When Christianity finally conquered Rome it should have been a time to rejoice! Many, many did! Jesus Christ had won, right?! No, and now you see the reason that God had to tell John about it. Christ would not win, in fact the very opposite. The most unthinkable thing of all was that Rome would rise again. Satan would usurp the throne in the name of Jesus. Where the High Priest once stood in the midst of the Golden Cherubim of the Mercy Seat with a golden plaque upon his forehead reading, *Holiness to the Lord*, another man would stand in his place with a new crown, this one would read, *In The Place of Christ* quite literally translated, *Vicarious Filli Dei*, which in Roman numerals reads: 666.[105]

What does it mean?

We are going to meet him soon.

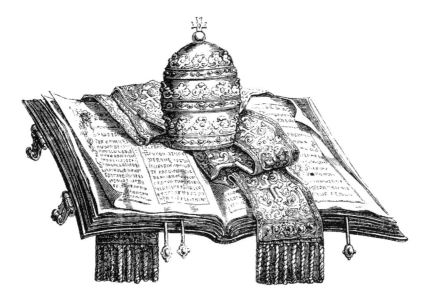

Chapter Ten

A Latter-Day Restoration

Zion stands with hills surrounded – Zion, kept by pow'r divine.
All her foes shall be confounded – Though the world in arms combine.
— Thomas Kelly, lyricist, 1769–1854

Now John jumps back to the Sixth Seal for a moment to see the preparation for God's judgement on the world. During the Sixth Seal, the Lord will restore the sealing powers through the administration of Elijah. This will allow the sealing of the fathers to the children and vice versa. This is a necessary part of the saving process to prepare a people ready to receive the Lord in honor at His return. Were there no one to receive Him as King and Bridegroom, all of the Father's *Plan of Salvation,* and the very purpose that the Earth was made, would be wasted. In the Sixth Seal the Temples, and powers to seal, have been returned and John sees Jehovah the Great standing in His Earthly Temple approving the work; leading the Church and organizing Israel on whichever distant shores He has placed them. It is all of Israel! Judah gathering in the city of David. Ephraim gathering in the Everlasting Hills. The Lost Ten Tribes, prepared by John, gathering on their distant horizon. Come and see:

Revelation 14:1 And I looked, and, lo, a Lamb stood on the mount Zion, and with him an hundred forty and four thousand, having his Father's name written in their foreheads.

We know this group. We have met the same before in chapter 7, verses 4 - 8. Now they are singing a new endowment written by God for their joy and protection. Note:

2 And I heard a voice from heaven, as the voice of many waters, and as the voice of a great thunder: and I heard the voice of harpers harping with their harps:

Revelation 14:3 And they sung as it were a new song before the throne, and before the four beasts, and the elders: and no man could learn that song but the hundred and forty and four thousand, which were redeemed from the earth.

Note also that there are elders here as well as these:

4 These are they which were not defiled with women; for they are virgins. These are they which follow the Lamb whithersoever he goeth. These were redeemed from among men, being the firstfruits unto God and to the Lamb.

5 And in their mouth was found no guile: for they are without fault before the throne of God.

The description here can only be that of children who died before the age of eight or who were aborted by their mothers on earth. Read the criteria carefully: They have knowledge in regards to a song of praise that only the priesthood redeemed know. They are boys because they have not born children of their own, nor had a wife, nor knew a woman. These were the first to be redeemed among men. Children who die before the age of eight are the first to be saved through the grace of Christ.[106] Lastly, they are without fault before the throne. Only children lost before the age of accountability; legally defined in God's kingdom as before their eighth birthday, are without fault before the throne.

How is all of this possible? It is because of the Restoration, which is the gift of Jesus Christ in our day through the hands of Joseph Smith, faithfully continued through his successors in the High Priesthood:

Revelation 14:6 And I saw another angel fly in the midst of heaven, having the everlasting gospel to preach unto them that dwell on the earth, and to every nation, and kindred, and tongue, and people,

7 Saying with a loud voice, Fear God, and give glory to him; for the hour of his judgment is come: and worship him that made heaven, and earth, and the sea, and the fountains of waters.

This was the Angel Moroni who returned the *Book of Mormon* from the ground to Joseph Smith. This book is the third Testament that Jesus is the Christ and that His Gospel in purity has been returned with all the keys and power necessary to seal those who will hear the call into the Kingdom of God before the angels in waiting pull the world apart.

Revelation 14:8 And there followed another angel, saying, Babylon is fallen, is fallen, that great city, because she made all nations drink of the wine of the wrath of her fornication.

9 And the third angel followed them, saying with a loud voice, If any man worship the beast and his image, and receive his mark in his forehead, or in his hand,

10 The same shall drink of the wine of the wrath of God, which is poured out without mixture into the cup of his indignation; and he shall be tormented with fire and brimstone in the presence of the holy angels, and in the presence of the Lamb:

11 And the smoke of their torment ascendeth up for ever and ever: and they have no rest day nor night, who worship the beast and his image, and whosoever receiveth the mark of his name.

John is pulled back into the present. Alone without his flock, on the Isle of Patmos, this Senior Apostle (and President of the Church) is comforted:

12 Here is the patience of the saints: here are they that keep the commandments of God, and the faith of Jesus.

13 And I heard a voice from heaven saying unto me, Write, Blessed are the dead which die in the Lord from henceforth: Yea, saith the Spirit, that they may rest from their labours; and their works do follow them.

John is not to mope about nor be sad about the future. *Here is the patience of the Saints.* The terrible dragon and the false lamb will be destroyed! Babylon will not be seen as Zion forever. She is not the bride but a pretending whore and in time will be unmasked.

In regards to these Saints in particular Joseph Smith said:

They rest from their labors for a long time, and yet their work is held in reserve for them, that they are permitted to do the same works after they receive a resurrection for their bodies.[107]

We have again the warning voice sounded in our midst which shows the uncertainty of human life. And in my leisure moments I have meditated upon the subject and asked the question, Why is it that infants, innocent children, are taken away from us, especially those that seem to be most intelligent beings? Answer: This world is a very wicked world. It is a proverb that the world grows weaker and wiser, but if it is the case, the world grows more wicked and corrupt. In the early ages of the world a righteous man-a man of God and intelligence-had a better chance to do good, to be received and believed, than at the present day. But in these days such a man is much opposed and persecuted by most of the inhabitants of the earth, and he has much sorrow to pass through. Hence the Lord takes many away, even in infancy, that they may escape the envy of man, the sorrows and evils of this present world. They were too pure and too lovely to live on earth. Therefore, if rightly considered, instead of mourning we have reason to rejoice, as they are delivered from evil. And we shall soon have them again.[108]

What is John to do here and now?

Fulfill his mission, he is to...

Revelation 14:14 And I looked, and behold a white cloud, and upon the cloud one sat like unto the Son of man, having on his head a golden crown, and in his hand a sharp sickle.

15 And another angel came out of the temple, crying with a loud voice to him that sat on the cloud, Thrust in thy sickle, and reap: for the time is come for thee to reap; for the harvest of the earth is ripe.

16 And he that sat on the cloud thrust in his sickle on the earth; and the earth was reaped.

17 And another angel came out of the temple which is in heaven, he also having a sharp sickle.

18 And another angel came out from the altar, which had power over fire; and cried with a loud cry to him that had the sharp sickle, saying, Thrust in thy sharp sickle, and gather the clusters of the vine of the earth; for her grapes are fully ripe.

19 And the angel thrust in his sickle into the earth, and gathered the vine of the earth, and cast it into the great winepress of the wrath of God.

20 And the winepress was trodden without the city, and blood came out of the winepress, even unto the horse bridles, by the space of a thousand and six hundred furlongs.[109]

The answer is, and has always been, reap! Do your missionary work, gather your dead, warn your friends and your enemies, find the elect and warn the wicked. It was the same in John's time and even more so in ours. The hour is short, the field is ready and soon the harvest will be over, gather fruit while you are able. It will save the fruit and it will save your soul as well.

Satan at the Gates of Hell with Mystery Babylon, Death & Sin by William Blake, 1806.

C. R. SAVAGE, Photo.   SALT LAKE.

LAYING THE CAP STONE OF THE SALT LAKE TEMPLE, by Electricity.

PRESIDENT WILFORD WOODRUFF, Officiating.   *Noon, April 6th, 1892.*

A souvenir card of the Capstone Ceremony of the Salt Lake Temple by Charles Carter.

Chapter Eleven

Safety on Mount Zion

The gathering together of the wheat into barns is to take place while the tares are being bound over, and preparing for the day of burning; Who hath ears to hear, let him hear. — *Joseph Smith the Prophet[110]*

We have been jumping around a lot in true eastern style. Hopefully I have done a good job of keeping you grounded. We have just explored the juxtaposition between Satan's destruction of the Kingdom established by the Lord during His earthly ministry in the time of the 5th Seal, and its Restoration in the Latter-days. We have witnessed Satan's complete over powering destruction that spilled into the first half of the 6th Seal, when Lucifer expected God to attempt a Restoration. This did not happen, instead the Lord slipped His 6th Seal Commission in near the close of the seal. He allowed the terrible frustration and enmity of the faiths on earth through these years to fracture Christianity. When the New World was founded, those weary of Church combined with State separated these powers legally. God used this separation to restore His Church and Kingdom anew. Since this new commission was given the difficult task of restoring all things in the *fullness of times* without much time, the Lord added a ½ hour of silence to the end of the 6th Seal, to give the Saints a little more time. We have already explored my speculation that we are living in the final years of this ½ hour of silence right now.

Now John is going to take us into the governmental heaven of God where we get to see the preparation being made for the events which we have already witnessed. Before we saw their effects on earth, now we are going to see them again from a heavenly point of view. This is useful so that man will be able to declare with the angels when it happens, "Thou art worthy of these acts, Oh Lord." It is the hope of the heavens, that by understanding it all, we might choose to repent and join the ranks of the redeemed while there is still time to do the *authorized good works* of salvation as commanded by Jesus Christ. If any reader wants to understand, and does not, find a *Latter-day Saint*, seek out a Bishop of the *Church of Jesus Christ of Latter-day Saints*, or grab ahold, (gently please) of a young Elder or Sister Missionary and invite them to speak with you. Just remember that none of us are perfect in this life and some of us Mormons are not always the best examples of all we know. That does not mean the gospel isn't true, only that some of us need to repent and be better examples.

As we pass through the other side of the poetic menorah (this chiastic book), we will (and expect to) have meaning added. When we saw these events the first time, we saw them from the perspective of the seven angels with trumpets. Now we will see the same events from the view point of seven angels with bowls. If you are truly grasping the eastern lessons of our feast series, you should immediately see what is going on here. Where have you seen *horns* and *bowls* before?[111] Here we go:

Revelation 15:1 And I saw another sign in heaven, great and marvellous, seven angels having the seven last plagues; for in them is filled up the wrath of God.

2 And I saw as it were a sea of glass mingled with fire: and them that had gotten the victory over the beast, and over his image, and over his mark, and over the number of his name, stand on the sea of glass, having the harps of God.

We are back in the Celestial Throne Room again. The first time we witnessed the terrible mourning and deep frustration of the Angels and Elders watching the blood drench the altar. This time though, there is rejoicing. The Lord has said "Enough!" Mercy has had its place. Many, oh so very many, human lives have been lost trying to dispense that mercy and it has born some fruit. The sweetest of which, we all hope will be you! *(and me too with our loved ones!)* Now, the day of mercy is passed. The Lord can no longer justify His delay. That would now be unjust and so the heavens sing the song of Moses. Why Moses?

3 And they sing the song of Moses the servant of God, and the song of the Lamb, saying, Great and marvellous are thy works, Lord God Almighty; just and true are thy ways, thou King of saints.

4 Who shall not fear thee, O Lord, and glorify thy name? for thou only art holy: for all nations shall come and worship before thee; for thy judgments are made manifest.

Before I tell you, just for fun go and open a Mormon Hymnal and look up Hymn #267 *How Wondrous and Great*.[112]

We have yet to feast on *Exodus* and all the fabulous stories in that book. One that we will yet enjoy together is the story how Moses had just arranged all the terms of the marriage engagement between the Children of Israel and the Lord at Sinai; both sides had agreed. The problem was that Israel was afraid of the Lord when they saw Him descend in fire on the peak of the Holy Mount. The Lord had come in burning passion and splendor, like any young man does trying to impress a would-be bride. Instead of being smitten by His glory, they were scared to death of Him. They asked Moses to make all of the arrangements without them and to simply fill them in later with the details. Think of yourself in this setting. You are a powerful prince. You have come to present to your girl your gifts of love, and she goes and hides in the bathroom asking you to give it to her mother who will tell her all about it (and you) later. It's deeply hurtful. It won't please you and it didn't please the Lord one bit.

After Moses had made all of the arrangements and the Children of Israel agreed to the terms, the Lord and Moses hammered out the details alone on the mountain top. *How depressing!* It was then that Israel committed adultery via the Golden Calf. The point I want to get to quickly is this: The Lord was angry and hurt, as any young groom would be. He had just given his girl a ring, turned his back to pay the bill and found her in her parents' bath house fornicating with the pool boy. It was just that bad! Well, the Lord made a very interesting statement which I believe gives humanity deep insight into His character and methods. It is extremely pertinent here and can be found in *Exodus 32:*

Exodus 32:7 And the Lord said unto Moses, Go, get thee down; for <u>thy</u> people, which <u>thou</u> broughtest out of the land of Egypt, have corrupted themselves:

8 They have turned aside quickly out of the way which I commanded them: they have made them a molten calf, and have worshipped it, and have sacrificed thereunto, and said, These be thy gods, O Israel, which have brought thee up out of the land of Egypt...

10 Now therefore <u>let me alone</u>, that my wrath may wax hot against them, and that I may consume them: and I will make of thee a great nation.

To Moses's everlasting credit, he knew not to leave the Lord alone right then. Moses talked the Lord down by relying on His great mercy. I once taught this story in a Sunday School class and had my head handed to me by a man with pointy glasses at the back of room. I stand by the words here written anyway. The Lord has told us that He is kind and meek and tender hearted. Here we see His terrible righteous anger but Moses and others have understood. As angry and frustrated as we make Him, He does love us and where *anger can burn down the world,* love can say, "I will try again with you." We will see this astounding truth illustrated when King David seeks the Lord's mercy on the

Threshing Floor of Araunah.[113] It's a second witness that the point is right. Here in *Revelation* you will note that the Lord went into His heavenly temple and closed the doors. The angels covered it with thick smoke from the altars, which held the pleading blood of the martyrs and saints of the earth. There alone, without a David or a Moses to talk Him down, the Lord is finally able to prepare His heart of meekness for the day of wrath of an injured God. Alone with the cries of the righteous and the memory of His own brutal murder, He is ready to fight! When He exits, He will be clothed in red and ready to do what has to be done. He has proclaimed that He is a *God of Justice* and today is the day of that justice. All the righteous can do is bow their heads and say, "You are right to do this, oh, Lord." Here His justice begins:

Revelation 15:5 And after that I looked, and, behold, the temple of the tabernacle of the testimony in heaven was opened:

6 And the seven angels came out of the temple, having the seven plagues, clothed in pure and white linen, and having their breasts girded with golden girdles.

7 And one of the four beasts gave unto the seven angels seven golden vials full of the wrath of God, who liveth for ever and ever.

8 And the temple was filled with smoke from the glory of God, and from his power; and no man was able to enter into the temple, till the seven plagues of the seven angels were fulfilled.

SEVEN VIALS

In order to make the poetic order of this chapter less confusing, we are going to take a slightly different pattern by way of explanation. These Seven Plagues contained in Seven Vials are not different events from the Seven Trumpet Judgements. They are the same and take place at the same time. This is strange to a western mind. Eastern thinkers would immediately suspect that the effect is meant to be parallel, or that A + B = C.

The complete picture here will only be grasped from the C. This means that we have to put the two together. To aid in this, we will leave the vial-plagues in normal text but summarize the trumpet-blasts in *italics*. All of the following are the events that will take place at the end of the ½ hour of silence which I believe will not happen before the Fall of 2022 A.D.

Revelation 16:1 And I heard a great voice out of the temple saying to the seven angels, Go your ways, and pour out the vials of the wrath of God upon the earth.

> *Revelation 8:6 And the seven angels which had the seven trumpets prepared themselves to sound.*

The first thing to notice is that these vials contain the wrath of God. Normally bowls are feminine places of blessing, instead these are bowls of poison.[114] By contrast Jewish trumpets are male animal horns, called shofars. They are typically used for protection, but here they are the call to battle. Watch the difference as we proceed.

FIRST ANGEL
Revelation 8:7 The first angel sounded, and there followed hail and fire mingled with blood, and they were cast upon the earth: and the third part of trees was burnt up, and all green grass was burnt up.

> *Revelation 16:2 And the first went, and poured out his vial upon the earth; and there fell a noisome and grievous sore upon the men which had the mark of the beast, and upon them which worshipped his image.*

<u>Number One:</u> The strange thing to notice by putting these two events together is that the trumpet call sends hail, fire and blood on the face of the earth. While the vials give those men marked by the beast terrible sores on their bodies. You are meant to put these things together. It's Jewish poetics. The male trumpet gives the female earth sores upon her face while the female vials give men sores on their bodies. I do not know exactly how this will look in reality but I suspect that the Lord will send some type

of hail from above that will hurt the earth and life upon it on contact. Dr. Velikovsky believed that this would be a fine reddish dust that would come from outer space. He believed that just such an event happened before to Egypt and turned the Nile red, making the water undrinkable. It also made it impossible to wash the dust away. It was everywhere.[115]

Note the next strange thing: this trumpet blast only kills ⅓ of the trees (and all the grass) but the juxtaposition puts the ⅓ of the trees with the men who have the mark of the beast. I can only speculate with you since these events are still to come but here is what I see with my eastern eyes:

The trumpets function as a call to arms and a call of warning. As such the trumpets offer some mercy for those who will hear them. The trumpet is like Moroni's Trumpet atop the Temples, warning the world and crying to the elect. It is mercy. He who has ears to hear, might yet hear. The vials have no mercy. They effect all without quarter. Thus we have the balance of mercy and justice even at this late date. It might still be possible to cry out to God and be saved by hearing the testimony of nature. The ⅓ here lines up with the men who become infected with the sores. Since trees are an eastern symbol for family bloodlines, I suspect that it could be saying that some nations, tribes, or families may be spared the sores. ⅓ is an oddity in scripture. While we have studied numbers and their heavenly meanings at some length together, ⅓ only has relevance to the ⅓ sons of our Heavenly Parents who rebelled and were lost. This ⅓ then is synonymous with *Perdition* which means *the weeping* and more specifically *the weeping mother*. The fact that only ⅓ is killed means that ⅔ are spared and this is of course mercy.

SECOND ANGEL

Revelation 16:3 And the second angel poured out his vial upon the sea; and it became as the blood of a dead man: and every living soul died in the sea.

> Revelation 8:8 And the second angel sounded, and as it were a great mountain burning with fire was cast into the sea: and the third part of the sea became blood;

> Revelation 8:9 And the third part of the creatures which were in the sea, and had life, died; and the third part of the ships were destroyed.

Number Two: Again, note the pattern. The second vial kills everything in the sea. Parallelism tells us that this vial will appear as an asteroid or a comet. Its warning blast will kill ⅓ of the sea creatures and ⅓ of the merchant and pleasure ships on the waters. The blood here is not fresh blood like when you cut your finger, it's old, thick, coagulated blood. It is gross.

From an eastern perspective the sea and the power of the sea is the power of Satan both in the hearts of those he owns in hell and the hearts of those he owns on earth. Both will be damaged and are here again symbolically marked as Perdition. The wealthy self-proclaimed illuminated ones of the world have built their satanic empire on the power of the seas (Satan). Their commerce and money chains span all continents. None can buy or sell without using them, here shown as merchant ships (civil) and navies (governmental) worldwide superstructures. These, like their masters, are called out as *Perdition* — ⅓. We will soon see them weeping on the shorelines.

THIRD ANGEL

Revelation 8:10 And the third angel sounded, and there fell a great star from heaven, burning as it were a lamp, and it fell upon the third part of the rivers, and upon the fountains of waters;

Revelation 8:11 And the name of the star is called Wormwood: and the third part of the waters became wormwood; and many men died of the waters, because they were made bitter.

Revelation 16:4 And the third angel poured out his vial upon the rivers and fountains of waters; and they became blood.

Revelation 16:5 And I heard the angel of the waters say, Thou art righteous, O Lord, which art, and wast, and shalt be, because thou hast judged thus.

Revelation 16:6 For they have shed the blood of saints and prophets, and thou hast given them blood to drink; for they are worthy.

Revelation 16:7 And I heard another out of the altar say, Even so, Lord God Almighty, true and righteous are thy judgments.

Number Three: This time a comet named *Wormwood*, due to its unspeakable bitterness, hits the planet and poisons the drinking water. Again we have the juxtaposition of having both ⅓ injured and the total injured. Men can live without sea water but not without fresh water. We are told that many will again die of poison or thirst. These would not embrace the living water of Christ when given the chance. Here the water available to them is blood, and blood is the seed of death. The angels witnessing all of this say that the Lord *is right to give them blood to drink* since they had been thirsty for the blood of the saints and the prophets.

Easternly we understand that having poisoned the root of the tree, the branches will die soon after. The Lord had injured the sea and so its little veins are next to follow. The poisonous Mark of the Beast had emanated from the sea-dragon Lucifer. All of the rest of us, living under the Beast System had relied on the Beast to fulfill our life needs. He had said that most of us could buy and sell and so we did. Now that the system is collapsing, now that the head of the serpent has been crushed, the little guy who was so bitten is dying from the venom. Where he had thought he had a large benefits package and retirement plan, he has discovered he only had an electronic number on a bank's computer. Where she thought she had police protection, she only has roaming gangs. Where he thought he had endless beer at the grocery store, there is no food on the shelves. Where she thought she was "woman hear her roar," she is now chattel for the strongest male in the herd. Where he thought he was an entitled minority fighting back at the "man," he is a solider in some kingpin's army. When Babylon the Great is falling, people worldwide will panic, and panic big!

FOURTH ANGEL

Revelation 16:8 And the fourth angel poured out his vial upon the sun; and power was given unto him to scorch men with fire.

Revelation 16:9 And men were scorched with great heat, and blasphemed the name of God, which hath power over these plagues: and they repented not to give him glory.

> *Revelation 8:12 And the fourth angel sounded, and the third part of the sun was smitten, and the third part of the moon, and the third part of the stars; so as the third part of them was darkened, and the day shone not for a third part of it, and the night likewise.*

> *Revelation 8:13 And I beheld, and heard an angel flying through the midst of heaven, saying with a loud voice, Woe, woe, woe, to the inhabiters of the earth by reason of the other voices of the trumpet of the three angels, which are yet to sound!*

Number Four: *At long last comes the dreaded global warming! If only we had recycled those old gym shoes and not used spray on deodorant! I couldn't resist.* Here the angelic vial attacks the sun. It again is a vial of justice instead of mercy. The sun in his anger throws heat waves and fire at people, who are angry with God and curse him while it seems they might still call out to him. Some mercy comes with the trumpet where the length of the sun's terrible heat is shortened, as is the moon's light and the stars. As dark as the night has now become, it is at least a break from the power of the sun! Perhaps some will sit in dark hours of reflection and pray to the Lord for help, but they probably won't. Maybe Lucifer can help them. His name means "light-bringer." Except that he hates them, so he won't.

One wonders if even now it might not be too late, if the wicked would only ask? Perhaps even more curious is how the angel considers the next three blasts to be woes. Personally, I would have thought the last four would have been woes. It does lead me to wonder if perhaps this fourth trial was man's last chance to repent. Collectively it is certainly too late, but maybe individually there is still a chance. We are told that instead the heavens hear only cursing and blasphemies. What is God to do? Perhaps Isaiah was speaking of these when he said:

Isaiah 37:29 Because thy rage against me, and thy tumult, is come up into mine ears, therefore will I put my hook in thy nose, and my bridle in thy lips, and I will turn thee back by the way by which thou camest.

This is a day of battle, the one the Lord has chosen, so it is time to have it out, with Satan and with the kings of the world:

Ezekiel 29:3 ...Behold, I am against thee, Pharaoh king of Egypt, the great dragon that lieth in the midst of his rivers, which hath said, My river is mine own, and I have made it for myself.

4 But I will put hooks in thy jaws, and I will cause the fish of thy rivers to stick unto thy scales, and I will bring thee up out of the midst of thy rivers, and all the fish of thy rivers shall stick unto thy scales.

5 And I will leave thee thrown into the wilderness, thee and all the fish of thy rivers: thou shalt fall upon the open fields; thou shalt not be brought together, nor gathered: I have given thee for meat to the beasts of the field and to the fowls of the heaven.

6 And all the inhabitants of Egypt shall know that I am the Lord, because they have been a staff of reed to the house of Israel.

This is an eastern way of describing Outer Darkness. If you want more on that, please refer to Vol 2: *Jonah and the Great Plan of Happiness*. We have more *Revelation* to feast on.

FIFTH ANGEL
Revelation 16:10 And the fifth angel poured out his vial upon the seat of the beast; and his kingdom was full of darkness; and they gnawed their tongues for pain,

Revelation 16:11 And blasphemed the God of heaven because of their pains and their sores, and repented not of their deeds.

Revelation 9:1-11 Summation: When the fifth trumpet sounds a star falls to earth with the key to the bottomless pit. He opens it and smoke like what might spew from a volcano darkens the sun and air. It is a cloud of powerful locusts who have poisonous stingers in their tails. These don't eat greenery like normal locusts do but they attack humans who have not been sealed to God. They don't kill the non-sealed but torture them for 5 months. It is so bad that mankind wants to die but they will not be allowed to. These locusts are like battle-ready horses wearing golden crowns but have men's faces with long women's hair. Their teeth are fierce like lions and they are armored and very noisy in flight. Their tails sting painfully. They are led by a king whose name means "The Destroyer." This is called the first woe.

Number Five: This is called the first of three woes. A woe is an event *of great sorrow or distress*. This is peculiar. The first four events are disastrous but here is the first real woe. Something here is different. You will remember from our study of *Ezekiel* that some event has to happen which would allow the Jews to rebuild the *Temple of Solomon* on the mount where today stands the *Dome of the Rock*. This has to happen before the Second Coming so the Lord can be received at the Temple in Old Jerusalem. We explored how Ezekiel seems to be describing, in rather astonishingly accurate terms, a nuclear event gone wrong. This event decimates an angry anti-Semitic army which comes against Israel and convinces the Jewish people (correctly I might add) that Jehovah is real and is on their side. The radiation that is given off leaves the evil horde dead for miles and the remains of their weaponry is enough to power Jerusalem for nine years!

I am speculating here that this fifth event is the war that Ezekiel saw, because the world puts their anger at the last 4 events on the backs of Israel. Due to the terrible disasters, much of the civilized super-systems that kept the petty tribal rivalries in check are gone. There is nothing to stop the Arab hordes (read sons of Esau) from making their move. I further suspect that this first attempt will be unsuccessful and hence the world will mourn and lament their woe. They finally had a chance to attack Israel and lost. I find it further interesting that the Latter-day Saints are protected here from the power of the destroyer, *Apollyon,* so that they can finish their work on the earth. That work will be preparing the Americas for the New Jerusalem and Zion City. I suspect that it is after this first woe that John is seen measuring the Temple Mount but not the outer court since Armageddon is yet to come. See *Vol 5. Ezekiel* for more on this.

Summarizing *Revelation 9:13-21 & 11:3-14* we have the second woe. It comes upon mankind as a voice speaks from the horns of the altar. Traditionally, this is another place of mercy but now the mercy is for the Saints not the world, so the horns command that the four angels bound in the Euphrates River be released. These are given 391½ days to prepare to kill ⅓ of mankind.[116] They, like unclean beasts, prepare for men to fight each other in Armageddon.

SIXTH ANGEL

Revelation 16:12 And the sixth angel poured out his vial upon the great river Euphrates; and the water thereof was dried up, that the way of the kings of the east might be prepared.

Revelation 16:13 And I saw three unclean spirits like frogs come out of the mouth of the dragon, and out of the mouth of the beast, and out of the mouth of the false prophet.

Revelation 16:14 For they are the spirits of devils, working miracles, which go forth unto the kings of the earth and of the whole world, to gather them to the battle of that great day of God Almighty...

Revelation 16:16 And he gathered them together into a place called in the Hebrew tongue <u>Armageddon</u>.

Number Six: This is clearly the battle of Armageddon. It is this battle which the Jews are in danger of losing when the

Messiah Ben Judah, the Great Jehovah, whom we know as Jesus Christ, comes and saves them. This is the official Second Coming of Jesus Christ.

We skipped over verse 15 to keep the parallelism. This verse is a parenthetical and has special meaning to Latter-day Saints. In the modern temples of the Restoration we prepare ourselves to be ready for the marriage supper of the Lord. In an eastern wedding, the Father of the bridegroom, if He be a powerful king, gives the guests and family invited a new set of clothes to wear at the wedding. These were to be carefully cared for and guarded. It was unthinkable to be unprepared once the table was set and the wedding cry went out to gather. As a sign of this ancient endowment, the Temple Guards of Solomon and Herod's Temples would watch through the night both for any enemies and for the bridegroom. Verse 15 harkens to that truth and the 7th Angel.

SEVENTH & FINAL ANGEL
Revelation 16:15 Behold, I come as a thief. Blessed is he that watcheth, and keepeth his garments, lest he walk naked, and they see his shame.

In ancient temple times there was a certain officer in Israel known as *The Ruler of the Mountain of the House.* He was a chief watchman and a judge. He went about the temple at every watch with a lighted torch to see whether or not the guards were attentive and at their posts. If he found one sleeping, he struck him with a stick and then demanded his temple garments. It was authorized for him to burn this neglectful watchman's temple garments as a sign that he was slothful at his post. When others would question the commotion or the fire, the answer was to be given back: "This is the noise of a Levite under correction, and whose garments are burning, for he was asleep on his watch."[117] Without his garment he was left naked and embarrassed.

With this the second woe is past, and the third cometh quickly. Be sure to have your wedding garments on. We have one last trumpet to sound and one last vial to pour:

Revelation 16:17 And the seventh angel poured out his vial into the air; and there came a great voice out of the temple of heaven, from the throne, saying, It is done.

Revelation 16:18 And there were voices, and thunders, and lightnings; and there was a great earthquake, such as was not since men were upon the earth, so mighty an earthquake, and so great.

Revelation 16:19 And the great city was divided into three parts, and the cities of the nations fell: and great Babylon came in remembrance before God, to give unto her the cup of the wine of the fierceness of his wrath.

Revelation 16:20 And every island fled away, and the mountains were not found.

Revelation 16:21 And there fell upon men a great hail out of heaven, every stone about the weight of a talent: and men blasphemed God because of the plague of the hail; for the plague thereof was exceeding great.

> Revelation 11:15 And the seventh angel sounded; and there were great voices in heaven, saying, The kingdoms of this world are become the kingdoms of our Lord, and of his Christ; and he shall reign for ever and ever.
>
> Revelation 11:16 And the four and twenty elders, which sat before God on their seats, fell upon their faces, and worshipped God,
>
> Revelation 11:17 Saying, We give thee thanks, O Lord God Almighty, which art, and wast, and art to come; because thou hast taken to thee thy great power, and hast reigned.
>
> Revelation 11:18 And the nations were angry, and thy wrath is come, and the time of the dead, that they should be judged, and that thou shouldest give reward unto thy servants the prophets, and to the saints, and them that fear thy name, small and great; and shouldest destroy them which destroy the earth.
>
> Revelation 11:19 And the temple of God was opened in heaven, and there was seen in his temple the ark of his testament: and there were lightnings, and voices, and thunderings, and an earthquake, and great hail.

<u>Number Seven</u>: This is the worldwide announcement to come and acknowledge the King of Kings. The wise of the earth will find a Jew and take him gently by his helm and ask to be escorted into Old Jerusalem, which will be renamed *Jehovah-shammah*, meaning *Jehovah (at last!) is there!*[118]

It would be wonderful if we could close the book and rejoice in this glorious news, but since this is a book about juxtaposition, John is going to pause just before the wedding of Jehovah to Zion and compare for us the fate, personality and doom of the pretended bride, *the Great Whore.*

She is the one that everybody thought would be dressed in white and greeted by Almighty God's Belovéd Son. We are going to discover that she is a prostitute and a pretender. The Lord wants us to recognize her early so we will not be deceived by her when she calls to us with her siren song *or her beta-slave cat purring.*[119] We are warned early that when we see the signs of the times, we are to flee from her. Her name is *Mystery Babylon. She is a whore.*

Europa riding Zeus, Berlin: Verlag von Neufeld & Henius, 1902. *Symbol of the European Union, John's Rome Re-born.*

Chapter Twelve

Mystery Babylon the Great

Don't envy the finery and fleeting show of sinners, for they are in a miserable situation; but as far as you can, have mercy on them, for in a short time God will destroy them, if they will not repent and turn unto Him.

— *Joseph Smith the Prophet*

All the notable religions of the world have their sacred truths. These are their *pearls*, to quote the Lord, that are not given freely just because someone asks for them. These are the truths that are offered to the faithful who have proven themselves worthy of the deeper knowledge and meditations that come line upon line, and precept upon precept. These are the "good works" that one must be prepared to receive through faith, repentance, patience, and sometimes endurance. Martin Luther and the evangelical movement like to pretend that such deeper doctrines are not consistent with Jesus's teachings. They are unprepared to adequately answer why the Lord would say things such as this:

Matthew 13:11 [And Jesus said] ...the knowledge of the secrets of the kingdom of heaven has been given to you, but not to them. *(NIV version)*

As always the *King James Version* adds nobility to the words recorded. It reads:

[And the Lord said...] it is given unto you to know the *mysteries* of the kingdom of heaven, but to them it is not given. *(KJV)*

The word to pay attention to here is *mysteries*. In a religious context the word refers to the "good works" and "deeper knowledge" of christianity. Events like the Lord's transfiguration, which only Peter, James and John of the 12 were permitted to see, and of which the Lord said, "Don't tell anyone what you have just seen until I say that you can" are examples of mysteries that are not to be shared except in a specific way and at a specific time of the Lord's choosing. It should strike secular-christianity as odd that the Lord's command to keep His mysteries quiet even applied to the rest of the 12; faithful men like Andrew and Matthew. Why couldn't they know? That is the point. Higher "good works" are on the Lord's timetable for sharing and always have been.

The important thing to understand is that when the scriptures speak of "mysteries" they are speaking of religion. In this chapter we are going to meet *Mystery Babylon*. Symbolically she is a woman. In heaven's eyes religions are women because they are the protected space of nourishment and transformation from which the younglings grow into maturity. The church (a woman) is protected by the male priesthood, which is its function.

The heavens, which hold righteous women in great esteem, have many terrible things to say about wicked woman like the kind we are about to meet. She is the worst! The very mother of darkness.

Revelation 17:1 And there came one of the seven angels which had the seven vials, and talked with me, saying unto me, Come hither; I will shew unto thee the judgment of the great whore that sitteth upon many waters:

2 With whom the kings of the earth have committed fornication, and the inhabitants of the earth have been made drunk with the wine of her fornication.

In other words, this is the mixing of Church and State. The Kings of the world have benefited greatly by combining with the false churches over the centuries to own the souls of men. This had worked for a season because it was a mutation of the order of heaven. There, the Rightful King would marry the Church in purity; a form of Atonement and Redemption. The Queen goes where the King is and rules where he rules. If the church is the queen and the king is Almighty God, then you too get to sit where the King sits. In our case, the King-Bridegroom is to marry the Church-Zion. It's a win-win! Unless of course you've been tricked by a clever arch-demon into believing that he is the king and Mystery Babylon is the church-bride. Being drunk on power, wealth and fornication like this church-bride has been, has lead her to do many terrible things with little to no recourse for her membership.

Revelation 17:3 So he carried me away in the spirit into the wilderness: and I saw a woman sit upon a scarlet coloured beast, full of names of blasphemy, having seven heads and ten horns.

Note the heads and horns. This is the beast of State controlled by Satan. It has been Egypt, Assyria, Babylon, Medo-Persia, Greece, Rome (in two forms) and the 10 Nations which sprang from Rome. We are living under this last incarnation.

4 And the woman was arrayed in purple and scarlet colour, and decked with gold and precious stones and pearls, having a golden cup in her hand full of abominations and filthiness of her fornication:

5 And upon her forehead was a name written, MYSTERY, BABYLON THE GREAT, THE MOTHER OF HARLOTS AND ABOMINATIONS OF THE EARTH.

The ruse is here painfully illustrated. John had thought to find the beautiful Zion there. She had fled into the wilderness to hide when the Beast of State was unable to eat her son. Naturally, he suspected to find her waiting, but this is not her! Instead, he finds an impostor; a prostitute. She is not a beautiful bride dressed in the sun, waiting patiently. She is a hussy, trashy and gaudy. She is drunk with her pride and power. About her forehead is not the crown of 12 priesthood leaders of the House of Israel. Instead she is a Mystery! The same mystery cult that once existed in Babylon long ago re-dressed in a different gown.

She, like the great dragon, is just the same old sin with a new face. All her children are the dogs and harlots and admonitions of the entire planet who have trusted in her. In terms of being Mystery Babylon, she is the Church of the Devil, specifically in this instance, she has another name. We will learn it from the clues John gives us.

6 And I saw the woman drunken with the blood of the saints, and with the blood of the martyrs of Jesus: and when I saw her, I wondered with great astonishment.[120]

Remember that John was the head of the Church. From his seat in Ephesus, then banished to Patmos, he had never seen what the church-bride would become. When he saw her in the now, he could hardly believe his eyes. She was a marvel! John may have been more than shocked to see the statues of his own brethren, Peter, Andrew and James, not to mention the statues and paintings of himself, adorning her fornication parties! No wonder he marveled. Where once stood the hated Nero, now stood the City of the Vatican!

Revelation 17:7 And the angel said unto me, Wherefore didst thou marvel? I will tell thee the mystery of the woman, and of the beast that carrieth her, which hath the seven heads and ten horns.

Let me pause here and say with pleasure that I have many Catholic friends. I have always been treated in a manner that I consider christ-like by them. I cannot say the same for other secular christian denominations. Catholics should take comfort in knowing that Mormons believe that all Christianity outside the Restored Gospel is fallen and corrupt, but these verses are plain, and as we shall see, undeniable. The *Book of Mormon* defines the *Church of the Devil* as being all religions *except* the *Church of Jesus Christ of Latter-days*. That is true enough. These verses here for John can only be about Christianity as it pertained to John and it can only be Papal Rome. All other interpretations of the text are unsound and dishonest. *I still love Catholics. They make awesome Mormons.* The angel reaffirms the truth of this being Rome a second time:

8 The beast that thou sawest was, and is not; and shall ascend out of the bottomless pit, and go into perdition: and they that dwell on the earth shall wonder, whose names were not written in the book of life from the foundation of the world, when they behold the beast that was, and is not, and yet is.

Note: this exactly happened with the Roman Empire as we explored in *Daniel & the Last Days*. It seemed incomprehensible to the Empire that the Iron Feet of Rome could fall, but it did. From the ruins rose the Holy Roman Empire with the Pope as its god; the new Caesar. To nail it home a third time, the angel beats us over the head with it:

9 And here is the mind which hath wisdom. The seven heads are seven mountains, on which the woman sitteth.

Even in John's day, Rome was called the *City of the Seven Hills*. They are: Aventine Hill; Caelian Hill; Capitoline Hill; Esquiline Hill; Palatine Hill; Quirinal Hill; and Viminal Hill.[121]

Revelation 17:10 And there are seven kings: five are fallen, and one is, and the other is not yet come; and when he cometh, he must continue a short space.

The mighty kings are the heads of the beast known as Pharaoh, the Kings of Assyria, the Babylonian Kings, the Medo-Persian Emperors, and Greece who had come and gone by John's day. These five had terrorized Israel but at this point had fallen. Rome, the sixth, still was and would last a while longer. By John's day it was already past its prime. One more, the seventh, would come when 10 nations or tribes would rise from Rome's ruin. These would be held together by Papal Rome (the Holy Roman Empire). Daniel said that they would try and remake the Roman

Empire but because they would be a mixture of strong and weak nation-communities, all attempts to reunite the old Empire would ultimately fail. The current history of the *European Union* is proof enough of Daniel's ten toes and John's ten horns on one demonic head. They are a failed mixture of weak and strong. It is painfully prophetic that at one time the EU had even debated the return of Latin as the communal tongue. They argued that since Latin was a dead language it would place all their union member states at an equal disadvantage. The plan was dropped in the end. The holy word says that the European Union will never coalesce like their members hope. God has spoken but something tells me that they will try to force their will on man anyway. I wouldn't bet on a happy result.

Revelation 17:11 And the beast that was, and is not, even he is the eighth, and is of the seven, and goeth into perdition.

Papal Rome will yet be numbered with the sons that are *wept* over, when it falls. We shall see that it will fall hard.

12 And the ten horns which thou sawest are ten kings, which have received no kingdom as yet; but receive power as kings one hour with the beast.

13 These have one mind, and shall give their power and strength unto the beast.

They will attempt to unify against the will of God but will fail as Daniel foretold in the end. You cannot mix iron with clay, even if Lucifer does the mixing.

14 These shall make war with the Lamb, and the Lamb shall overcome them: for he is Lord of lords, and King of kings: and they that are with him are called, and chosen, and faithful.

15 And he saith unto me, The waters which thou sawest, where the whore sitteth, are peoples, and multitudes, and nations, and tongues.

16 And the ten horns which thou sawest upon the beast, these shall hate the whore, and shall make her desolate and naked, and shall eat her flesh, and burn her with fire.

17 For God hath put in their hearts to fulfil his will, and to agree, and give their kingdom unto the beast, until the words of God shall be fulfilled.

Starting with Martin Luther, these same ten toes of Europe eventually injured the power of Rome until at last Napoleon Bonaparte ended the reign of the Popes as earthly kings. A fourth time the angel will tell us who the whore is. Four is the number of fallen earth with its boundaries set by God. The perfect number of times for this:

18 And the woman which thou sawest is that great city, which reigneth over the kings of the earth.

Spiritually this city would be called Babylon, but physically, by John's day, she was called Rome. John will witness what is left of her "short space" of time. In John's day people were being called out of her. This would continue through the works of the Reformation through the reign of Napoleon into the Restoration of the Gospel from the 1830s to the missionary work of today. The call has gone out to flee Babylon, who now sits across every ocean. Soon she will fall! Run from her while you can!

Lest the reader think we are only picking on Roman Catholics, consider this. All Christianity, including Eastern Orthodoxy, the Reformation, and the Evangelical movement had its roots in the Imperial Caesars. If not at first, than increasingly so after February 27th 380 A.D., when the *Edict of Thessalonica* put *Trinitarian Christianity* as the official religion of the Roman Empire. Even here the church began to decay. Poison sprinkled upon the roots eventually kills all the branches of the tree. The poison of Apostasy eventually spread into the Eastern Church and into all the branches of her Reformation.

Greedy Elitist Luciferian Bankers saw the opportunity to run the world, and have plotted to *buy everything in this world with money* ever since. All that can be done is to call the innocent songbirds from the trees before the mighty angel of God puts an ax to the trunk, fells the dead wood, and sets it all ablaze. This is exactly what John sees next:

Revelation 18:1 And after these things I saw another angel come down from heaven, having great power; and the earth was lightened with his glory.

2 And he cried mightily with a strong voice, saying, Babylon the great is fallen, is fallen, and is become the habitation of devils, and the hold of every foul spirit, and a cage of every unclean and hateful bird.

3 For all nations have drunk of the wine of the wrath of her fornication, and the kings of the earth have committed fornication with her, and the merchants of the earth are waxed rich through the abundance of her delicacies.

4 And I heard another voice from heaven, saying, Come out of her, my people, that ye be not partakers of her sins, and that ye receive not of her plagues.

5 For her sins have reached unto heaven, and God hath remembered her iniquities.

We have recorded in the annuals of history the terrible tales of Rome's depravations. They are horrible to read but they stand as witness to the angel's proclamation above. Here are just a few of what has been preserved to us about the inner doings of the Vatican in times past:

• As soon as Papal Christianity gained legal power in 315 A.D., pagan temples were destroyed and pagan priests were killed by Catholic mobs. Thousands of pagans were murdered. Examples of their sacred sites that were destroyed were: the Sanctuary of Aesculap in Aegaea, the Temple of Aphrodite in Golgatha, Aphaka in Lebanon, and the Heliopolis.

• Between 372 - 444 A.D., thousands of christians who believed in the so-called *Manichaean Heresy* were exterminated all throughout the Roman Empire.

• In 385 A.D. in Trier, Germany the first Christians were beheaded for heresy against the Roman Church.

• Christian Emperor Theodosius who ruled from 408 - 450 A.D., had a neighborhood of children executed when he learned that they had been playing with the remains of pagan statues they had found.

• World famous female philosopher Hypatia of Alexandria was cut to pieces with glass fragments by a hysterical Catholic mob led by their minister in 415 A.D.

• Holy Roman Emperor Charlemagne beheaded 4,500 Saxons in 782 A.D. who refused to forcefully convert to Roman Catholicism.

• In 1010 A.D., the Bishop of Limoges, France had the Jews in his area forcefully converted, expelled or killed.

• In 1209 the first Crusade against other christians was ordered by the Pope. It was called the Crusade against the Albigensians. Their crime was that they refused to acknowledge the Bishop of Rome's authority over their own bishops, and they refused to pay the Pope's ordered tax. One million people were killed.

• In 1209, Pope Innocent III ordered the city of Bezris, France and all its people destroyed. On July 22nd all the inhabitants were killed including all faithful Roman Catholics who tried to hide their neighbors and friends. Records say as many as 70,000 were murdered.

• On August 15th 1209, un-numbered thousands were murdered in the city of Carcassonne on Papal orders.

• Between 1209 and 1229 nearly all of the Cathars, amounting to ½ the population of Languedoc, France were exterminated. The last Cathar was burned alive in 1324 A.D. Total Cathars murdered by Rome estimated at 1 million souls.

• As many as 11,000 peasants (men, women and their children) were murdered in Steding Germany on May 27th 1234 A.D., when they complained about the "suffocating" church tax that Rome imposed on them.

• In 1348 A.D., the entire Jewish population of Basel, Switzerland and Strasbourg, France are burned alive.

• John Huss, a critic of Rome's right to sell indulgences and the papal infallibility, was burned at the stake in 1415 A.D.

• The Roman church killed 80,000 Turks in the Battle of Belgrad in 1456 A.D.

• Between 1484 - 1750 A.D., modern scholars have documented over 200,000 so-called witches who were burned alive or hung. Most were women but 20% were male.

• During the Spanish Inquisition, Inquisitor Torquemada alone burned 10,220 people.

• A minimum of 100,000 christians were murdered by Rome for being followers of the Josephites, Paulikians, Runcarians, and Waldensians philosophies. All of which were christian but disagreed with the popes on various doctrines.

• In 1489, the Bishops of Europe ordered forced conversion of all Jews or death. In response, the Rabbis drafted the famous

Letter of Constantinople. Written on December 22nd 1489. It authorized Jews to pretend to convert to christianity with the goal of destroying the Catholic world from within. It was on this authority that a combination of Jesuit Priests and Edomic-Jewish banks founded the Illuminati to bring open honor to Lucifer and rule the world through secret combinations.

• In 1492 A.D., the year Columbus set sail for the New World, more than 150,000 Jews were expelled from Spain. Many died on the forced exodus. Recent evidence suggests that Columbus was a Marrano Jew and hoped for a New World in part as a place to resettle others needing to escape Catholic persecutions.

• In Poland during the 15th century, 1,019 churches and 17,987 villages were plundered by the *Catholic Knights of the Order* on Papal command. To this day the number of murdered victims in Poland remains unknown.

• In 1631 A.D., Catholics sacked the city of Magdeburg, Germany. 30,000 Protestants are slain. Eyewitness Friedrich Schiller wrote: "In a single church fifty women were found beheaded. Some were mothers. We found their infants still sucking on their dead mother's breasts."

• During the 30 Years' War in the 1600s between Roman Catholics and Protestants at least 40% of the then German population is killed.

• In 1648, during the Chmielnitzki Massacres in Poland , 200,000 Jews were slain.

More? There is a great deal more!

Sadly we could go on and on. The above listing is by no means the end of it. One historical record, *Fox's Book of Martyrs*, lists the names of people murdered by order of the Caesars and the Popes. When printed and bound this book was over one foot thick! That's larger than a man can get his hand around the binding. When Joseph Smith held the book in his *two* hands, he wept and said that these men and women were blessed of God for their sacrifice in defying religious tyranny in their day. He said that they were truly martyrs in the cause of truth. A painfully ironic moment as the *Church of the Devil* and the *Beastly forces of the United States* would also claim his life for religion. Historians estimate that over 200 million people have been killed by Rome in one of its two phases, Imperial or Papal. When John saw the blood stained altar in the 5th Seal, he was not seeing a little blood. There's enough blood in the average human body to fill a little more than a 1-gallon milk jug.

THE LOSS OF THE EAST

While a lot of the blood splattered on heaven's altar came at the hands of Rome, what is less well know among christians today is the vast amount of blood spilt in the east in the lands of what was once the Eastern Christian Church. This is important to our study because it includes the lands of John the Belovéd's missionary labours. Many are surprised today to learn that upwards of 40 million christians were killed or driven from their homes by militant Muslims and Buddhists from the Mediterranean Sea all the way to China. Nearly all of the old mosques of Iraq and Iran are built on the ruins of christian churches. The Emperor Khubla Khan's[122] mother, Sorkhotani, was a Nestorian Christian princess of the Kereyid Confederacy. She raised her children in the faith when possible.

The main reason the Western Church called for the Crusades was to halt the flow of Islam into European Christianity. Islam had killed the christians of Northern Africa and had crossed the sea into Spain. Rome realized that soon it would be surrounded if it did not act. What is so deeply offensive (in my opinion) in terms of the eyes of heaven, is how Papal Rome did nothing to aid the Christians of the Eastern Church in their centuries of need. They were angry that the east would not acknowledge the Bishop of Rome. *He was only a bishop after all.*

We have record of the titles of at least 50 Christian books which were lost when Islam captured the Great Libraries of Christendom. Modern Arab historians like to make much of the great learning which came from Islam during this period. What they leave out is the fact that Eastern Christians had translated much of the Greek Classics from Greek and Latin into Aramaic, which was spoken widely in the Eastern Church. The Great Libraries of Alexandra, Baghdad, Ctesiphon, Otranto, Nalanda, and Cairo, were conquered by the Muslims and all the wealth of these books, which were not burned, thrown into rivers, or used to roll cigars, were read by the Aramaic speaking Arabs. The vast over-whelming amount of knowledge credited to the so-called *Golden Age of Islam* was stolen from Christian and Classical libraries! History is written by the conquerors until it is rediscovered generations later by the seekers of real truth. *So, now you know. Don't believe everything you read in modern history books.*

We know that between 666 A.D. and 1815 A.D. there were at least 2 Muslim attacks on Christian and Jewish lands per year. Statistically Christians and Jews were being attacked every 6 months! Having been purged from Europe, Muslim pirates took to the seas and started the slave trades out of Africa. They sold blacks into European collected colonies, and they sold 1.5 million whites (Europeans and Americans) into North Africa slave markets and harems. Muslim pirates were finally curbed by President Thomas Jefferson, and finally halted by President James Madison in 1815, but that is another story for another day.

In all fairness, blood begets blood. The concept of justice, vengeance and recompense are real (and godly) emotions. Things that are wrong demand to be made right or need to be forgiven. The universal nature of justice means that men too often take vengeance into their own hands. The blood of Christ, taken by His kin and Rome, was answered back and forth in vengeance. It was this that the Prophet Joseph Smith lamented about when the protestant and evangelical christian communities turned against the Mormons. He asked, how could a Protestant christian people, who had been so terribly mistreated by Rome, repeat the very same evils against the Mormons?[123] The answer is simple. It takes a tremendous amount of humility and christian kindness to set aside the outrages done to you. People who are bullied tend to bully, and the abused abuse others. It can be hard to remember at that moment that Jesus taught us to forgive and to let go. Vengeance is the Lord's and even if you choose to forgive, He may still take vengeance, but that is His choice. Either way, you are free.

THE TIME OF THE END

Papal power ended in terms of her previous history, for all intents and purposes, by Napoleon Bonaparte. He is called robotically by many an Anti-Christ but I believe that history will bear out that Napoleon was as much called of God in his station as was Alexander the Great before him.[124]

The Bible speaks of the *Time of the End* as being the conclusion of Satan's total power over man's salvation and the return of humanity's ability to make and keep sacred covenants as free agents. In terms of the *Book of Revelation*, it is the short window of time in the 6th Seal when God would hold back His angry angels wanting to cleanse the earth, and keep in check the demons running amok among us. This short time was granted so that the Lord might have a chance to glean the field one last time, and seal those of the children of men who would listen to one last plea. These could yet come and gather to a stake of Zion; a city of refuge. Why? If there were none to greet the groom at the call to marry, the entire Earth would be a waste.

In Vol.1 of the *Gospel Feast Series: Daniel & the Last Days*, we explored all of this in great detail. Here we will only summarize it. There we showed how the Angel Gabriel told Daniel that the power of the Beastly Kings would end in 1798 A.D. At this time the spirit of revolution spread from Colonial America into Catholic France. The French people were tired of the elitist caste system they toiled under. Spurred on by the success of freedom in America, and financed by Luciferian bankers from London and Paris, they unleashed a *Reign of Terror.* France lacked the god-fearing founders that blessed American shores, so many paid in blood. Voltaire expressed the feeling of the time when he said:

I am weary of hearing people repeat that 12 men established the Christian religion. I will prove that one man may suffice to overthrow it.

The new leaders of France: Rousseau, d'Alembert, Diderot, the Rothschilds and others discarded the *Bible* and declared atheism and humanism to be the only true religion. This new religion became the frenzy of France with the leaders of the Revolution being known as the *Atheists.* They renamed the ancient Notre Dame Cathedral, the *Temple of Reason.* Donkeys were given drinks out of the former holy sacrament chalices and orgies and humanism ruled the day.

It was during this time that a brilliant young soldier, Napoleon Bonaparte was defending the French Revolution's interests at home and abroad. Soon he took the eye of Revolutionary leader Maximilien de Robespierre. By the age of 24 he was promoted to Brigadier General. In 1796 he invaded Italy, defeated the papal troops, and occupied papal lands. Pope Pius VI sued for peace, which was granted on February 19th 1797; but just 10 months later a riot brought another French General, Berthier back to Rome. There at the Vatican on February 10th 1798, he affectively dethroned the Pope, removing all his power as an earthly king. He declared the papal lands free and demanded the Pope renounce all temporal authority. Of course this last part was too much and the Pope refused; and so he was taken prisoner ten days later and escorted out of the Vatican to the citadel of Valence in Drôme where he died six weeks later on the 29th of August 1799. At the time he had reigned longer than any other Pope.

It would not be long before Napoleon would be appointed to the Provisional Consulate of France. Shortly after he installed himself as First Consul, giving himself sweeping powers of State. A new Pope was also appointed by the church calling himself Pius VII but the damage was done. The papal power was broken and has never regained its former glory. In 1804 Napoleon did attempt to make peace with the Vatican in exchange for being declared Emperor of France but at his coronation ceremony he humiliated Pope Pius VII by taking the crown into his own hands and declaring himself Emperor (an event denied by Vatican historians today despite historical witnesses to the event).

The Pope had for centuries demanded the sole right to appoint European successors. Rome enforced this power with a strong armed military commander known as the *Holy Roman*

Emperor. Napoleon didn't care about any of this. He even went so far as to dissolve the Holy Roman Empire and created the new *Confederation of the Rhine.*

It is difficult to be too harsh on the French people, the Catholic church had been incredibly oppressive. Oppressive Christianity is satanic and has been from the beginning. Papal Rome had manipulated their rulers, tortured dissenting citizens, and burned any Frenchman they disliked at the stake. Corruption in the church was rampant and universally known. The masses felt very much like teenagers finally being put in charge of the house while their parents were away. They had for so long been commanded in all things that their new found sense of freedom knew no bounds. This new *Religion of Reason* remained in force until Napoleon Bonaparte ended it in 1799 A.D. Under Catholic-French law, vast tracts of papal and elitist lands could not be subdivided for any purpose. This guaranteed that the powerful would always remain so while the poorer classes could never achieve private ownership. The Lord dislikes the concept of landlords and tenants. In Catholic France, the Church owned it all, and your soul as well. When the French Revolutionary Government needed funds to pay back Rothschild banks, they simply confiscated Catholic properties and auctioned them off. The resulting sale netted more than 700 million pounds sterling in 1790's currency. That is literally billions and billions of dollars today.

It didn't take long for the French masses to cry for a more stable religion than that of Reason, so Napoleon released 20,000 catholic clergymen who had been imprisoned during the Revolution. He forced them to swear allegiance to the government of France and not to the Pope in Rome.

These heroic events were called for from the heavens and will be better understood by the pre-schoolers of the Millennium than they are by the scholars of today.

Revelation 18:4 And I heard another voice from heaven, saying, ...

6 Reward [the whore] even as she rewarded you, and double unto her double according to her works: in the cup which she hath filled fill to her double.

7 How much she hath glorified herself, and lived deliciously, so much torment and sorrow give her: for she saith in her heart, I sit a queen, and am no widow, and shall see no sorrow.

Napoleon was the one who heard the call and did just that. Eventually Napoleon turned on the Illuminati Bankers who were funding him and they pressured England to bring him down. In recent years Papal Rome has regained some of her lost prestige but this was necessary, for after the people have been warned to flee from her, the Lord Himself will deal the final blow. He will also destroy the Luciferian Bankers at the same time. John heard the heavens say next:

8 Therefore shall her plagues come in one day, death, and mourning, and famine; and she shall be utterly burned with fire: for strong is the Lord God who judgeth her.

9 And the kings of the earth, who have committed fornication and lived deliciously with her, shall bewail her, and lament for her, when they shall see the smoke of her burning,

10 Standing afar off for the fear of her torment, saying, Alas, alas, that great city Babylon, that mighty city! for in one hour is thy judgment come.

Here it is like a thief in the night. I suspect that this will be near the time of the Great Worldwide financial collapse that we studied in *Zechariah*, note the rationale for thinking so:

Revelation 18:11 And the merchants of the earth shall weep and mourn over her; for no man buyeth their merchandise any more:

12 The merchandise of gold, and silver, and precious stones, and of pearls, and fine linen, and purple, and silk, and scarlet, and all thyine wood, and all manner vessels of ivory, and all manner vessels of most precious wood, and of brass, and iron, and marble,

13 And cinnamon, and odours, and ointments, and frankincense, and wine, and oil, and fine flour, and wheat, and beasts, and sheep, and horses, and chariots, and slaves, and souls of men.

14 And the fruits that thy soul lusted after are departed from thee, and all things which were dainty and goodly are departed from thee, and thou shalt find them no more at all.

15 The merchants of these things, which were made rich by her, shall stand afar off for the fear of her torment, weeping and wailing,

16 And saying, Alas, alas, that great city, that was clothed in fine linen, and purple, and scarlet, and decked with gold, and precious stones, and pearls!

17 For in one hour so great riches is come to nought. And every shipmaster, and all the company in ships, and sailors, and as many as trade by sea, stood afar off,

18 And cried when they saw the smoke of her burning, saying, What city is like unto this great city!

19 And they cast dust on their heads, and cried, weeping and wailing, saying, Alas, alas, that great city, wherein were made rich all that had ships in the sea by reason of her costliness! for in one hour is she made desolate.

Many have all their treasures here on earth. These will miss the power and prestige that their wealth has given them. Think of the mighty and powerful landlords, business tycoons, Silicone Valley geeks, CEOs, Royal Families, Illuminati Elitists, and Investment Bankers of our planet. Strip them of their wealth and what are they? Would anyone follow them? Would anyone sit at their feet and listen to their blather? Would anyone report in the news their latest threats to move to Canada? Would any rent boys or silly women follow them around? Without the digital numbers in their bank accounts what would they be but nerds, sycophants, narcissists, satanists and whiners? They are only called elites on this planet for their fine odours, wines, vessels and slaves. They will vanish in a day! *Oh, you exhausted of the earth, store up your treasures in heaven where there are no thieves to steal them and no rust to waste them away. Rejoice with the heavens instead when you see the smoke of all of these assets burning.* Your Lord and God will be coming soon after! It's okay to rejoice over her fall on that day. See, the Lord has told you to:

Revelation 18:20 Rejoice over her, thou heaven, and ye holy apostles and prophets; for God hath avenged you on her.

21 And a mighty angel took up a stone like a great millstone, and cast it into the sea, saying, Thus with violence shall that great city Babylon be thrown down, and shall be found no more at all.

This rock is both Daniel's and Matthew's:

Daniel 2:34 Thou sawest till that a stone was cut out without hands, which smote the image upon his feet that were of iron and clay, and brake them to pieces.

Matthew 18:6 But whoso shall offend one of these little ones which believe in me, it were better for him that a millstone were hanged about his neck, and that he were drowned in the depth of the sea.

The only *sure course* is to *change course* now. Flee and Repent!

Revelation 18:22 And the voice of harpers, and musicians, and of pipers, and trumpeters, shall be heard no more at all in thee; and no craftsman, of whatsoever craft he be, shall be found any more in thee; and the sound of a millstone shall be heard no more at all in thee;

23 And the light of a candle shall shine no more at all in thee; and the voice of the bridegroom and of the bride shall be heard no more at all in thee: for thy merchants were the great men of the earth; for by thy sorceries were all nations deceived.

24 And in her was found the blood of prophets, and of saints, and of all that were slain upon the earth.

With the death of the whore, who pretended to be the bride of Christ, space is made for the true bride, the lady named Zion.

Chapter Thirteen

The Marriage of Zion!

We ought to have the building up of Zion as our greatest object. When wars come, we shall have to flee to Zion. The time is soon coming, when no man will have any peace but in Zion and her stakes. —*Joseph Smith the Prophet*

Revelation often teaches by juxtaposition. (One of my favorite words.) We have just witnessed the whore and the false king, Lucifer, in one of his many forms. These have been removed. Juxtaposed for our learning is the real bridegroom, the Lord Jesus Christ and His real bride, the Lady Zion.

Revelation 19:1 And after these things I heard a great voice of much people in heaven, saying, Alleluia; Salvation, and glory, and honour, and power, unto the Lord our God:

2 For true and righteous are his judgments: for he hath judged the great whore, which did corrupt the earth with her fornication, and hath avenged the blood of his servants at her hand.

3 And again they said, Alleluia. And her smoke rose up for ever and ever.

Hallelujah means *Praise to Jehovah!* The Jewish name of our bridegroom, the very same.

4 And the four and twenty elders and the four beasts fell down and worshipped God that sat on the throne, saying, Amen; Alleluia.

5 And a voice came out of the throne, saying, Praise our God, all ye his servants, and ye that fear him, both small and great.

6 And I heard as it were the voice of a great multitude, and as the voice of many waters, and as the voice of mighty thunderings, saying, Alleluia: for the Lord God omnipotent reigneth.

7 Let us be glad and rejoice, and give honour to him: for the marriage of the Lamb is come, and his wife hath made herself ready.

8 And to her was granted that she should be arrayed in fine linen, clean and white: for the fine linen is the righteousness of saints.

9 And he saith unto me, Write, Blessed are they which are called unto the marriage supper of the Lamb. And he saith unto me, These are the true sayings of God.

Remember that these sayings were delivered to John *semaino*; meaning as *a gift with a token*. How great a gift and how perfect a setting; a wedding ceremony between God and Man.

For a moment John is overcome and forgets himself.

10 And I fell at his feet to worship him [the angel messenger]. And he said unto me, See thou do it not: I am thy fellowservant, and of thy brethren that have the testimony of Jesus: worship God: for the testimony of Jesus is the spirit of prophecy.

How embarrassing, but it is an honest mistake. It is hard not to get caught up in the praise of this moment. Even in this, John gives us a morsel. *The testimony of Jesus is the spirit of prophecy.* Use it well.

Here comes the bridegroom! John is going to throw a lot of symbols and images at us in a very short space. You will remember that the very first promise to Adam & Eve was that a hero-son, the seed of the woman, would come to save them. Other cultures and dispensations have also had names and symbols of this hero. John is going to pepper some of these in to make the point that Christ is the King of Kings and the Hero of Heroes. All the legends, myths, stories, and authentic scriptures have prophesied of Him. At long last, He comes!

11 And I saw heaven opened, and behold a white horse; and he that sat upon him was called Faithful and True, and in righteousness he doth judge and make war.

12 His eyes were as a flame of fire, and on his head were many crowns; and he had a name written, that no man knew, but he himself.

The great male gods of Egypt had names that *no man knew*, it was seen as a source of their priesthood. These gods lost their power to their wives when they gave them their new names. This allowed their wives to rule in their behalf.[125] No man or woman knows this name, or in other words, Christ rules supreme and speaks for Himself. Indeed, we will see that very soon.

This becomes more relevant in symbolism when one also remembers that the first king to wear a double crown was Pharaoh. As far as we know, he was the first monarch who claimed authority over more than one country. So he wore more than one crown. Ever after, the kings of Egypt were crowned with the *pshent*, or *United Crowns of Upper and Lower Egypt.*[126] When Ptolemy Philometer entered Antioch as a conqueror he wore a triple crown, two for Egypt, and the third for Asia. Here to John, the Lord is claiming dominion over many — over all! He is the King of Kings. How many crowns? Were I to guess, I'd say He is wearing 72 crowns. One for each of the official bloodline-families of Noah. *Thinking eastern again. Love it!*

Revelation 19:13 And he was clothed with a vesture dipped in blood: and his name is called The Word of God.

This blood garment is many things. It is the blood red stains from having been forced to walk the wine-press of the wrath of God alone. It is a sign of the bloody sacrifice that made Jesus the Lamb of God, and it is symbolic of the blood of His enemies.[127] These are they who would not come to Him after multiple and repeated chances to do so, and the Masters Mahan who slink in silence and think there are *none to make them afraid.*

14 And the armies which were in heaven followed him upon white horses, clothed in fine linen, white and clean.

These are a proper and spectacular eastern style army in the pure tradition of an eastern style king. Jesus is both a Celestial Prince and an Eastern King in the finest tradition of

King David. He leads a righteous army. They are white because He is dressed in red.

Revelation 19:15 And out of his mouth goeth a sharp sword, that with it he should smite the nations: and he shall rule them with a rod of iron: and he treadeth the winepress of the fierceness and wrath of Almighty God.

Note that the sharp sword is also the Iron Rod. We know from Father Lehi that while the Word of God is sharp and cutting to His enemies, it is the promise of safety and steadfastness to those who hold onto it. The Lord's return this day will be both great and terrible. Great for those who have waited for Him, terrible for those who are unprepared to receive the rightful King, and worse for those who have oppressed His little ones for millennia.

16 And he hath on his vesture and on his thigh a name written, KING OF KINGS, AND LORD OF LORDS.

How noble a prince! How great a King! At last to be married and one with the King of Kings! There is no higher honor. The thigh serves a dual purpose. It is a reminder of the covenant the Lord made with Jacob. It was with *a wrestle upon the thigh*, that Jacob's name was changed to Israel. Jacob prevailed with the Lord despite an injury to his thigh. In brief, a blessing upon a man's thigh, is a tasteful way of blessing a man's increase and masculinity. These are both necessary in terms of a man's destiny as a father, an under-shepherd, and a future prince and king beneath God. The fact that our Lord has the declaration that He is the King of the Kings and the Lord of the Lords written on the thigh of His battle robes, states loudly in eastern terms that He has overcome ALL THINGS and is bringing almighty power, eternal glory, and endless increase with Him. He is both God and the Rightful Son of God the Father. He is also the groom of Israel. This is the same thigh as Father Jacob's.[128]

17 And I saw an angel standing in the sun; and he cried with a loud voice, saying to all the fowls that fly in the midst of heaven, Come and gather yourselves together unto the supper of the great God;[129]

18 That ye may eat the flesh of kings, and the flesh of captains, and the flesh of mighty men, and the flesh of horses, and of them that sit on them, and the flesh of all men, both free and bond, both small and great.

In Jewish terms, an angel that stands in the sun is one of great authority. Interestingly, he is often connected in some way with commands over God's animal creations. The pattern is continued here. Also, in terms of the 4 Heavenly Beasts at the throne. The Eagle is a symbol of the Father's legal justice and ability to avenge wrongs (this is balanced by the bull who is a sign of God's ecclesiastical mercy.) Note that it is the bird-creation who has been called upon to feast, and on the flesh of man no less. It is the justice of God that will now destroy the defiled temples of God – made in His image – male and female.[130]

19 And I saw the beast, and the kings of the earth, and their armies, gathered together to make war against him that sat on the horse, and against his army.

20 And the beast was taken, and with him the false prophet that wrought miracles before him, with which he deceived them that had received the mark of the beast, and them that worshipped his image. These both were cast alive into a lake of fire burning with brimstone.

21 And the remnant were slain with the sword of him that sat upon the horse, which sword proceeded out of his mouth: and all the fowls were filled with their flesh.

And note again, that the angels, elders, beasts and witnesses, said with solemnness, "Amen! You are worthy to do this, Lord." His witnesses agree.

Revelation 20:1 And I saw an angel come down from heaven, having the key of the bottomless pit and a great chain in his hand.

2 And he laid hold on the dragon, that old serpent, which is the Devil, and Satan, and bound him a thousand years,

3 And cast him into the bottomless pit, and shut him up, and set a seal upon him, that he should deceive the nations no more, till the thousand years should be fulfilled: and after that he must be loosed a little season.

We have been told that this angel is Michael, our Father Adam. Of all men is he not the most rightful? Adam who had no real choice but lose the wife he loved or eat the fruit and die? This is a moment of true justice for him. Adam & Eve fought the fight, necessitated the plan of opposites and endured to the end. It cost Adam everything. He, like the Lord, chose mortality, death, and turmoil to save a bride and build a kingdom for the glory of God the Father.

Revelation 20:4 And I saw thrones, and they sat upon them, and judgment was given unto them: and I saw the souls of them that were beheaded for the witness of Jesus, and for the word of God, and which had not worshipped the beast, neither his image, neither had received his mark upon their foreheads, or in their hands; and they lived and reigned with Christ a thousand years.

5 But the rest of the dead lived not again until the thousand years were finished. This is the first resurrection.

There will be more than one resurrection. The one that all of us want is to die and be raised during the *First Resurrection* particularly in the part known as the morning thereof. The reason is given next.

6 Blessed and holy is he that hath part in the first resurrection: on such the second death hath no power, but they shall be priests of God and of Christ, and shall reign with him a thousand years.

Those who are raised in the morning of the First Resurrection are promised that the second death will have no claim on them. This is heavenly lingo for saying that they will not have lost the right to live in God's presence again. The earlier into the Millennium that you are raised, the sooner you will be able to learn the reigning process at the feet of the rightful King.

How glorious to be created a prince or princess at the feet of such a King as ours! Joseph Smith said:

Iniquity will hide its hoary head, Satan will be bound, and the works of darkness destroyed. Righteousness will be put to the line and judgment to the plummet, and he that fears the Lord will alone be exalted in that day.[131]

THE LITTLE SEASON AKA THE FINAL BATTLE OF GOG & MAGOG

This next verse always gets a gasp and a "What, why, again? We just put the dirty bugger in the pit!"

Revelation 20:7 And when the thousand years are expired, Satan shall be loosed out of his prison [for a little season],

8 And shall go out to deceive the nations which are in the four quarters of the earth, Gog and Magog, to gather them together to battle: the number of whom is as the sand of the sea.

Ah, damn it! None of this would make any sense without Joseph Smith. The Prophet explained that in order to be fair to all, Satan would be released after the Millennium to have a chance to tempt and try all the people who were born during the Millennium, as well as any others who needed to have the education that comes from that experience. There will be children and family and all of the like during this time. It is not fair to deprive them of the lesson of opposites, and the agency of choice. I really hope I won't be around for that. Satan has caused so much trouble. I read that and think, *yeah but can't we just lose the key, we've got a thousand years to forget where we put it. I'm really sick of that guy.*

At least at the end of the little season we have this from the Prophet Joseph:

After the "little season" [of Revelation 20:3] is expired and the earth undergoes its last change and is glorified, then will all the meek inherit the earth, wherein dwelleth righteousness.[132]

169

In regards to the children of Edom, the Luciferian hordes, and all whom Satan worked up against Jerusalem, the angels have fire ready for them:

Revelation 20:9 And they went up on the breadth of the earth, and compassed the camp of the saints about, and the beloved city: and fire came down from God out of heaven, and devoured them.

10 And the devil that deceived them was cast into the lake of fire and brimstone, where the beast and the false prophet are, and shall be tormented day and night for ever and ever.

THE FINAL JUDGEMENT
Revelation 20:11 And I saw a great white throne, and him that sat on it, from whose face the earth and the heaven fled away; and there was found no place for them.

12 And I saw the dead, small and great, stand before God; and the books were opened: and another book was opened, which is the book of life: and the dead were judged out of those things which were written in the books, according to their works.

Judged according to their <u>works</u>, note it well christians of the world. Joseph Smith commented:

You will discover in this quotation that the books were opened; and another book was opened, which was the book of life; but the dead were judged out of those things which were written in the books, according to their works; consequently, the books spoken of must be the books which contained the record of their works, and refer to the records which are kept on the earth. And the book which was the book of life is the record which is kept in heaven.[133]

In a very real sense these are also the records of the church which contain the official records of all of the witnessed ordinances from the naming of children to the sealing records of the temples. If your name is not recorded in these records, the good works which you preformed on earth do not count. Note that it is *NOT* men's faith that judges them at the end but their works as recorded.

13 And the sea gave up the dead which were in it; and death and hell delivered up the dead which were in them: and they were judged every man according to their works.

There are dead in the sea? Yes! There are a lot of dead in the sea. Traditionally the sea is a symbol for the World of the Dead in every culture including Judaism and earliest Christianity. If you have not taken our feast into *Jonah* and the *World of the Dead*, you are missing a rich treat. If you have, this should immediately leap to mind and you can say with the truth seekers that Jonah is a book that only a Mormon can truly understand. *No, it's not about a whale!*

14 And death and hell were cast into the lake of fire. This is the second death.

15 And whosoever was not found written in the book of life was cast into the lake of fire.

Notice that *death* and *hell* are personified here. This is your clue that something more is going on. Death and Hell are not people that can be cast into fire. In secular-christian terms death and hell are already fire so that's hardly a punishment. What this is really saying is that during the Millenium the Earth will be raised in glory from its current Telestial state into a Terrestrial State. A Terrestrial state is one of paradisiacal glory. Glory is connected to light and heat. Since God is a being of eternal glory, He is a being of endless burning light. The Father is like the Sun and more. When the Earth is raised in glory, it will be as a baptism of fire. Anything and anyone on the Earth who is not living some law of the Terrestrial glory will not abide the experience. All Telestialism will be burned up.

Much of what the Lord is doing with His church in these Latter-days is creating a vehicle by which we can gain enough Terrestrial glory to abide the coming day of fire. Your *Confirmation* or receiving the *Gift of the Holy Ghost* by the laying on of hands by one having authority to do so, was part of that Terrestrial preparation. You might have heard your *Confirmation* as being a *Baptism by Fire?* Being baptized by fire will help you escape the coming day of fire because that which has been *tempered in the flames* already, cannot be destroyed by the flames a second time. Living the laws of chastity, charity, and consecration are all Terrestrial Laws. This is why you might have heard Mormons jokingly call paying *tithing* their *Fire Insurance.* It's a silly way of saying that because the Latter-day Saints are striving to gain some Terrestrial Glory now through faith and good works, they are holding fast to God's promise that they will be saved to greet Zion when the Earth is made new in Terrestrial splendor. *Bring it on!*

A NEW HEAVEN & A NEW EARTH

Heavenly visions can have that dreamlike quality which mortal men know all too well. Time and place can have no exact meaning. Tiny spaces can feel miles away while mountains can be overcome with a single jump. Minutes can be hours and a thousand years can vanish in the blink of an eye. We know that the Millennial Reign of Christ will be 1,000 years upon the Earth. It is going to be a time of education, mentorship and preparation. At the end of the Millennium, the Lord is going to make His final accounting of the Earth experience to our Universal Father. Our Father governs by giving assignments and instructions and then requiring an *After Action Report* at the end. In the Celestial Worlds it is called the *Return & Report* report. It is the Lord's final duty to Return & Report on the *Plan of Salvation* under His charge to the Father of us all. Knowing the Lord's deep love for the Father, you can be certain that every single "i" will be dotted and every "t" will be crossed. The Millennium gives the Lord the time to prepare all things before that great day of reporting.

For a quick moment, John was taken from the glorious Terrestrial view of the earth made new to the final state of the Earth and those so mentored by the Lord. Our final destination is not to be a Prince or Princess / King or Queen in Terrestrial Glory, as wonderful as that will be. Our final destiny, if we choose to embrace it, will be to sit with Christ in His Celestial throne. The Millennium will be a time to be mentored for that greater blessing as the Earth moves closer to the Celestial Home. As a near parting gift, John was shown that Celestial state and we are the blessed ones for having it recorded. John saw:

Revelation 21:1 And I saw a new heaven and a new earth: for the first heaven and the first earth were passed away; and there was no more sea.

There is no more sea because there is no more Spirit Prison. The saints living in the Millennium have used part of their time to redeem all of their ancestors that could be redeemed. Every baptism on behalf of the dead is as a body being lifted out of the font of the sea. At last the waters there are dry. Hell is no more.

2 And I John saw the holy city, new Jerusalem, coming down from God out of heaven, prepared as a bride adorned for her husband.

3 And I heard a great voice out of heaven saying, Behold, the tabernacle of God is with men, and he will dwell with them, and they shall be his people, and God himself shall be with them, and be their God.

Joseph Smith made this observation:

I discover by this quotation that John upon the isle of Patmos saw the same things concerning the last days which Enoch saw [see Moses 7:62]. But before the tabernacle can be with men, the elect must be gathered from the four quarters of the earth.[134]

Thus the missionary labors in which we are called today.

4 And God shall wipe away all tears from their eyes; and there shall be no more death, neither sorrow, nor crying, neither shall there be any more pain: for the former things are passed away.

5 And he that sat upon the throne said, Behold, I make all things new. And he said unto me, Write: for these words are true and faithful.

6 And he said unto me, It is done. I am Alpha and Omega, the beginning and the end. I will give unto him that is athirst of the fountain of the water of life freely.

7 He that overcometh shall inherit all things; and I will be his God, and he shall be my son.

I want that. Don't you? At this point in my life its not even the *all things* that I want anymore. Things are stuff. I am not pooh-poohing the stuff, but more than the stuff, I want to be mentored into manhood as a son of one so grand as the Prince of Peace, the King of Zion. Joseph Smith said that salvation for him (and for you) is to be put in a place where you have no more enemies. None to harm or make you afraid ever again. I am certain John understood that too. Note who won't be with us:

8 But the fearful, and unbelieving, and the abominable, and murderers, and whoremongers, and sorcerers, and idolaters, and all liars, shall have their part in the lake which burneth with fire and brimstone: which is the second death.

As John is witnessing all of these future events, one of the angels who was ready at God's command to start all of this, came to speak with him, and show him something:

9 And there came unto me one of the seven angels which had the seven vials full of the seven last plagues, and talked with me, saying, Come hither, I will shew thee the bride, the Lamb's wife.

10 And he carried me away in the spirit to a great and high mountain, and shewed me that great city, the holy Jerusalem, descending out of heaven from God,

11 Having the glory of God: and her light was like unto a stone most precious, even like a jasper stone, clear as crystal;

12 And had a wall great and high, and had twelve gates, and at the gates twelve angels, and names written thereon, which are the names of the twelve tribes of the children of Israel:

Joseph Smith added this insight:

Now we learn from the Book of Mormon the very identical continent and spot of land upon which the New Jerusalem is to stand [see 3 Nephi 20:22], and it must be caught up, according to the vision of John upon the isle of Patmos. Now many will be disposed to say that this New Jerusalem spoken of is the Jerusalem that was built by the Jews on the eastern continent. But you will see from Revelation 21:2 [that] there was a New Jerusalem coming down from God out of heaven, adorned as a bride for her husband. After this, the Revelator was caught away in the Spirit to a great and high mountain and saw the great and holy city descending out of heaven from God. Now there are two cities spoken of here... I shall say with brevity that there is a New Jerusalem to be established on this [American] continent, and also that Jerusalem shall be rebuilt on the eastern continent. "Behold, Ether saw the days of Christ, and he spake concerning a New Jerusalem upon this land. And he spake also concerning the house of Israel, and the Jerusalem from whence Lehi should come-after it should be destroyed it should be built up again, a holy city unto the Lord; wherefore, it could not be a new Jerusalem for it had been in a time of old" [see Ether 13:4-5].[135]

Revelation 21:13 On the east three gates; on the north three gates; on the south three gates; and on the west three gates.

14 And the wall of the city had twelve foundations, and in them the names of the twelve apostles of the Lamb.

Zion Temple is for the House of Israel by birth and by adoption, so that includes you either way. It is built on the foundation of the priesthood; there is no firmer rock than the likes of Peter et al. Incidentally, do you remember this next part from Ezekiel? What do you want to bet that this time we are getting it from John's perspective. Is Ezekiel there too?

15 And he that talked with me had a golden reed to measure the city, and the gates thereof, and the wall thereof.

16 And the city lieth foursquare, and the length is as large as the breadth: and he measured the city with the reed, twelve thousand furlongs. The length and the breadth and the height of it are equal.

17 And he measured the wall thereof, an hundred and forty and four cubits, according to the measure of a man, that is, of the angel.

18 And the building of the wall of it was of jasper: and the city was pure gold, like unto clear glass.

19 And the foundations of the wall of the city were garnished with all manner of precious stones. The first foundation was jasper; the second, sapphire; the third, a chalcedony; the fourth, an emerald;

20 The fifth, sardonyx; the sixth, sardius; the seventh, chrysolite; the eighth, beryl; the ninth, a topaz; the tenth, a chrysoprasus; the eleventh, a jacinth; the twelfth, an amethyst.

21 And the twelve gates were twelve pearls; every several gate was of one pearl: and the street of the city was pure gold, as it were transparent glass.

22 And I saw no temple therein: for the Lord God Almighty and the Lamb are the temple of it.

23 And the city had no need of the sun, neither of the moon, to shine in it: for the glory of God did lighten it, and the Lamb is the light thereof.[136]

24 And the nations of them which are saved shall walk in the light of it: and the kings of the earth do bring their glory and honour into it.

25 And the gates of it shall not be shut at all by day: for there shall be no night there.

26 And they shall bring the glory and honour of the nations into it.

27 And there shall in no wise enter into it any thing that defileth, neither whatsoever worketh abomination, or maketh a lie: but they which are written in the Lamb's book of life.

All of this was witnessed by Ezekiel as well. Ezekiel, the High Priest of his day was the witness of the *Old Testament* and John, the senior apostle of his day, is witnessing it in the *New Testament*. Two Witnesses have spoken. This word is both promised and established. It will come to pass! Right down to the water coming from the Temple in Old Jerusalem, feeding the Trees of Life and healing, all the way down to the sea, changing its water from poisoned salt to fresh and pure.

Revelations 22:1 And he shewed me a pure river of water of life, clear as crystal, proceeding out of the throne of God and of the Lamb.

2 In the midst of the street of it, and on either side of the river, was there the tree of life, which bare twelve manner of fruits, and yielded her fruit every month: and the leaves of the tree were for the healing of the nations.

3 And there shall be no more curse: but the throne of God and of the Lamb shall be in it; and his servants shall serve him:

4 And they shall see his face; and his name shall be in their foreheads.

5 And there shall be no night there; and they need no candle, neither light of the sun; for the Lord God giveth them light: and they shall reign for ever and ever.

6 And he said unto me, These sayings are faithful and true: and the Lord God of the holy prophets sent his angel to shew unto his servants the things which must shortly be done.

7 Behold, I come quickly: blessed is he that keepeth the sayings of the prophecy of this book.

John on the Isle of Patmos writing the Revelation with an Eagle.

John Outruns Peter to the Empty Tomb by James Tissot.

Chapter Fourteen

Even So, Come Lord Jesus!

I the Lord, knowing the calamity which should come upon the inhabitants of the earth, called upon my servant Joseph Smith, Jun., and spake unto him from heaven, and gave him commandments. — *Jesus Christ*

We did it! You have just feasted on one of the most enigmatic books God has given man. Joseph Smith said it was one of the simplest too. What do you think? The very fact that you are studying the word of God and trying to follow Him makes it all easier. The Lord gives line upon line. As we accept truth and embrace it, He gives more. See for yourself:

Ether 4:7 And in that day that [men] shall exercise faith in me, saith the Lord,... that they may become sanctified in me, then will I manifest unto them [all] things..., even to the unfolding unto them all my revelations, saith Jesus Christ, the Son of God, the Father of the heavens and of the earth, and all things that in them are.

8 And he that will contend against the word of the Lord, let him be accursed; and he that shall deny these things, let him be accursed; for unto them will I show no greater things, saith Jesus Christ; for I am he who speaketh.

We know what John thought. Once again he was overcome with joy for the final victory of the Messiah Ben Judah, his cousin, Saviour, King, mentor and friend. It is hard to put oneself in John's sandals. He had witnessed it all. The Lord's baptism, His ministry, the successful and unsuccessful conversions of His countrymen. He had witnessed the Transfiguration, shouted Hosanna as the Lord entered Jerusalem and wept with Him when that entry turned from triumphant to disappointment. He was there at the Last Supper and laid on the Lord's chest when he learned the duplicitous nature of Judas. He watched the trial, the

179

suffering, and the crucifixion. With tears in his eyes, he must have tried to put on a firm face when the Lord, through parched lips, gave His own mother Mary into his care. It must have been terrible beyond words! He may have been the first to believe when word came to the brethren, "He is not in the tomb. He is Risen!" Is it any wonder millions of boys have been named John in his honor, ever since?

It is interesting to note that in the scriptures there is a connection between the close-friendship of God and the revealing of God's purposes. God delights in sharing His ways and foreknowledge with His friends. Men who have proven faithful, despite terrible trials, have earned the title, "Friend of God." Men we know as Joseph Smith, Daniel, Lehi and Nephi, among others have been so called. All of these have witnessed knowledge, visions, and great revelation. In just such a manner, John is called "The Belovéd." How wonderful for us that John was willing and able to share that status with you and me.

Revelation 22:8 And I John saw these things, and heard them. And when I had heard and seen, I fell down to worship before the feet of the angel which shewed me these things.

9 Then saith he unto me, See thou do it not: for I am thy fellowservant, and of thy brethren the prophets, and of them which keep the sayings of this book: worship God.[137]

We get a feeling for the power of this experience as here John, overcome by it all, nearly falls down in praiseful worship a second time. He is again reminded that only God is to be worshiped but the angel does proceed to speak God's message as though the Lord Himself was speaking it. This works because we know that, *From the mouths of His servants, it is the same.* And here is a signified fellowservant by token. Here is a true messenger. We would be wise to heed his words:

10 And he saith unto me, Seal not the sayings of the prophecy of this book: for the time is at hand.

11 He that is unjust, let him be unjust still: and he which is filthy, let him be filthy still: and he that is righteous, let him be righteous still: and he that is holy, let him be holy still.

12 And, behold, I come quickly; and my reward is with me, to give every man according as his work shall be.

13 I am Alpha and Omega, the beginning and the end, the first and the last.

14 Blessed are they that do his commandments, that they may have right to the tree of life, and may enter in through the gates into the city.

John's *Revelation* is not a closed book. It is not a sealed book. It is not a book to be casually brushed away. It is an Official Proclamation like our modern *Family: A Proclamation to the World* or any of the other proclamations given from God by his ordained servants. With the frightening warning that the day is coming when "he and she who is filthy, will be filthy still" comes the following, which Mormons alone are prepared to comprehend:

Revelation 22:15 For without are dogs, and sorcerers, and whoremongers, and murderers, and idolaters, and whosoever loveth and maketh a lie.

The phrase "loveth and maketh a lie" is code for those of the Telestial Order. We are given a list of some of these, those who play the dog (sexual deviance), sorcerers (followers of *pharamacia*), murderers, and the lovers of idols; which in its highest symbolism are adulterers and adulteresses. We should take a short tangent and explore this because, as you will see above, these are they who have no access to the Temple, the Healing Tree of Life and the City of Zion. We, therefore, don't want to be those who "love and make a lie."

LOVING AND MAKING A LIE

In Mormon theology, the lowest reward a human can receive on the *Day of Judgement*, that is still a kingdom of glory, is called, *The Telestial Kingdom.* The glory of this kingdom has been compared to the stars in the sky in that they are a place of light. They have some beauty, but cannot compare to the greater rewards which the Father has for those who have proved worthy of more light and beauty.[138]

The Lord has told us that the Telestial Kingdom is a place for those who: rejected the gospel, the testimony of Jesus, the prophets, and the everlasting covenant both on Earth and when given a chance in the Spirit World; these were unrepentant liars, sorcerers, adulterers, and whoremongers during their time on Earth; and most enigmatically, those who loved and made a lie.[139] It is this last one that needs a little clarification. The Lord hates lies and some lies are dearly loved by humanity. The following list is by no means inclusive: it is a beloved lie that abortion is not murder; it is a beloved lie that men cannot rise above their weaknesses; it is a beloved lie that "true love" makes all sexual acts permissible to God; it is a beloved lie that one can take Jesus physically into his heart; it is a beloved lie that once Jesus is physically in your heart, any desires you have are from Him. There are many others. Beware of them. Note that it is not just the lie that is the problem, but the *love of it* and the perpetuation of it, called *the making of it,* that will damn men and women.

What makes these lies so dangerous is that the implementation of them leads to justifiable sin. Because we love the lie, we justify the action connected with it. Please know that all of these actions are forgivable, but those that love the lie more than they love the Lord never humble themselves to a point where God can heal them. It is a point of pride with them. It is this same pride that caused Lucifer to say that he knew better than the Most High and destroyed ⅓ of God's family. So too, do these liars believe they know more than the prophets and the Lord. They love their lie deeply and in order to see it prosper, they teach it to others, leading others to sin. The Lord cautioned thus:

Matthew 18:7 Woe unto the world because of offences! for it must needs be that offences come; but woe to that man by whom the offence cometh!

He and she (the scriptures contain many accounts of women doing this) who cause another to stumble may find at the Judgement Bar that they are required to pay for more than just their own sins.[140] My own sins have caused me grief. I tremble to think of paying for another's. There is still time to repent. What does one do? The Lord Himself answers us:

Revelation 22:16 I Jesus have sent mine angel to testify unto you these things in the churches. I am the root and the offspring of David, and the bright and morning star.

17 And the Spirit and the bride say, Come. And let him that heareth say, Come. And let him that is athirst come. And whosoever will, let him take the water of life freely.

And then the warning that every missionary knows:

Revelation 22:18 For I testify unto every man that heareth the words of the prophecy of this book, If any man shall add unto these things, God shall add unto him the plagues that are written in this book:

19 And if any man shall take away from the words of the book of this prophecy, God shall take away his part out of the book of life, and out of the holy city, and from the things which are written in this book.

Young missionaries are frequently shown this verse with the rather stupid comment that God saw no need to speak again from the heavens. The stupider of the secular-christians will point to these verses as justification against the *Book of Mormon*, saying that it adds to the *Bible*, therefore all Mormonism is cursed. I used to take great joy in letting them go on and on before asking them to read *Deuteronomy 4:2* with me:

So, using the same logic, Moses is saying that anything added or taken from the writings after this *Old Testament* chapter is not of God. Of course the Jews used this very argument to disregard the mission of Jesus Christ and the entire *New Testament.* There are many great communications of God to man after *Deuteronomy.* Using secular-christian logic we would have to throw out Isaiah (God Forbid!) and the tender songs of King David. None of these books were assembled into the Word before Ezra was commanded to do it. It is the same with the *New Testament.* There was *NO* canonized *New Testament* in John's day. The more honest and educated know that John was speaking of his letter alone, not the Bible which did not exist as a book then. *Yawn!*

Of course, intelligent men and women around the globe have questioned loudly: *Where is the God of Abraham, Isaac and Israel today? Why doesn't He speak to His children now? Are we not in more peril today than we have ever been? Has there not been greater need now than ever?*

With the Restoration of Christianity and the return of Priesthood Authority to the Earth, exactly as John the Divine foretold, members of the *Church of Jesus Christ of Latter-Day Saints* testify together that yes, God does speak to man again and the heavens are open right now. We claim the right to personal revelation and more. We claim to have access to living Prophets and Apostles this very day.

We invite all who will hear to come and see for themselves. You probably already know a Mormon. Ask them yourself. You can start out by saying something like "Okay, so what's up with you Mormons?" and "Can I come with you to church and check you guys out?" After your friend picks himself up off the floor, he or she will say, "Sure." Then ask for a *Book of Mormon* and read it or request a free copy online. You don't have to take our word for it either. Like the *Book of Revelation* we have just studied, the *Book of Mormon* contains a promise and a blessing just for reading it. We call it Moroni's Promise and it's a big one:

Moroni 3:3 Behold, I would exhort you that when ye shall read these things, if it be wisdom in God that ye should read them, that ye would remember how merciful the Lord hath been unto the children of men, from the creation of Adam even down until the time that ye shall receive these things, and ponder it in your hearts.

4 And when ye shall receive these things, I would exhort you that ye would ask God, the Eternal Father, in the name of Christ, if these things are not true; and if ye shall ask with a sincere heart, with real intent, having faith in Christ, he will manifest the truth of it unto you, by the power of the Holy Ghost.

5 And by the power of the Holy Ghost ye may know the truth of all things.

This is extremely important because then you will have the knowledge of these things for yourself; a personal witness from God for you. It doesn't get any better than that, but you must ask with a sincere heart, truly wanting to know and believing that Christ can and will answer you in truth. What does this have to do with John's writings here? The same Moroni who made the above promise to you in the name of the Lord explained this as well, when he preserved for us the Lord's own exhortation to you:

Ether 4:11 ...he that believeth these things which I [the Lord] have spoken, him will I visit with the manifestations of my Spirit, and he shall know and bear record. For because of my Spirit he shall know that these things are true; for it persuadeth men to do good.

12 And whatsoever thing persuadeth men to do good is of me; for good cometh of none save it be of me. I am the same that leadeth men to all good; he that will not believe my words will not believe me — that I am; and he that will not believe me will not believe the Father who sent me. For behold, I am the Father, I am the light, and the life, and the truth of the world.

13 Come unto me, O ye Gentiles, [saith the Lord] and I will show unto you the greater things, the knowledge which is hid up because of unbelief.

14 Come unto me, O ye house of Israel, and it shall be made manifest unto you how great things the Father hath laid up for you, from the foundation of the world; and it hath not come unto you, because of unbelief.

15 Behold, when ye shall rend that veil of unbelief which doth cause you to remain in your awful state of wickedness, and hardness of heart, and blindness of mind, then shall the great and marvelous things which have been hid up from the foundation of the world from you — yea, when ye shall call upon the Father in my name, with a broken heart and a contrite spirit, then shall ye know that the Father hath remembered the covenant which he made unto your fathers, O house of Israel.

16 And then shall my revelations which I have caused to be written by my servant John be unfolded in the eyes of all the people. Remember, when ye see these things, ye shall know that the time is at hand that they shall be made manifest in very deed.

In other words the blessings and horror of the *Book of Revelation* written down by John the Belovéd are at our very doors. If that was so almost 4 Jubilees ago, in the days that the *Book of Mormon* was offered, oh, how much nearer they must be today!

Ether 4:17 Therefore, when ye shall receive this record ye may know that the work of the Father has commenced upon all the face of the land.

18 Therefore, repent all ye ends of the earth, and come unto me, and believe in my gospel, and be baptized in my name; for he that believeth and is baptized shall be saved; but he that believeth not shall be damned; and signs shall follow them that believe in my name.

19 And blessed is he that is found faithful unto my name at the last day, for he shall be lifted up to dwell in the kingdom prepared for him from the foundation of the world. And behold it is I [Jesus Christ] that hath spoken it. Amen.

PARTING WORDS

Here we have John's final words. In order to let the weight of them sink inside you, and in order to better understand the personality of John. Take a moment and reflect on all of the terrible plagues, sorrows, lamentations, and woes that John has just witnessed. It's pretty terrible what's coming. Now read the ending.

Revelation 22:20 He [the Lord Jesus] which testifieth these things saith, Surely I come quickly. Amen.

Even so, come, Lord Jesus.

21 The grace of our Lord Jesus Christ be with you all. Amen.

THE END [Until Joseph Smith, Jr.]

Even so,...

Despite all that has happened, all that must still happen and all of it combined, the only thing John wants when it is all said and done, is the only thing that I want too.

Despite it all…

Even so...

Come, Lord Jesus.

Amen to that.

Studio City, CA

10/17/2017

John Sees the Lord, unknown artist. A very western thinker's perspective on Revelation. Note how the artist has attempted to portray exactly what John described. If John says that the Lord's word was like a two-edged sword coming from His mouth, then you had better draw that exactly.

Nephi to John

The book of Revelation is one of the plainest books
God ever caused to be written. — *Joseph Smith the Prophet*

As Saints of the Latter-days we have a rich gift in the *Book of Mormon*. One of the very many things that this sacred book does is testify that the *Book of Revelation* given to John is both valid and correct, *as far as it is translated correctly* – but that's a given.

Nephi, one of the truly great sons of God, had been blessed through his faithfulness to see a vision of human history. This places him with those so highly favored as Daniel, Zechariah, Ezekiel, Isaiah, John and Joseph Smith. We are blessed in that they were allowed to record what they saw and pass it forward to us. Nephi's stands unique in that his account went directly from his pen through the *Urim & Thummim* into English.

There is an interesting correlation between being favored to see the secrets and future plans of God, and being called His friend. Daniel was called much loved of God, Joseph Smith was called the "friend of God," and of course John was named the Belovéd. Another friend of God was the young Nephi whose personal writings make up *1st & 2nd Nephi* in the *Book of Mormon*. They are some of the treasures of all scripture.

To set the stage, the previous verses are a vision given to tell the story of the native peoples of the Americas from their ancestors disembarking through their eventual social collapse. It continues through God's justification for the European conquering of the New World up to the events of John's 7th Seal.

1 Nephi 13:1 And it came to pass that the angel spake unto me, saying: Look! And I looked and beheld many nations and kingdoms.

2 And the angel said unto me: What beholdest thou? And I said: I behold many nations and kingdoms.

3 And he said unto me: These are the nations and kingdoms of the Gentiles.

The word Gentile is a Latin word that means Nations. In scripture this correlates to the *Table of Nations* found in Genesis which lays out the bloodlines that descended from Father Noah. Since the Lord had convented with the Children of Israel to be the light of example to the nations, the word Gentile was used to differentiate Israel from all other bloodlines. Today *Gentile* has a distasteful sound but to the Lord it simply means National Bloodlines.

4 And it came to pass that I saw among the nations the formation of a great church.

5 And the angel said unto me: Behold the formation of a church which is most abominable above all other churches, which slayeth the saints of God, yea, and tortureth them and bindeth them down, and yoketh them with a yoke of iron, and bringeth them down into captivity.

President Kimball, who was a very kind prophet, disliked the easy association that can be made between this abominable church and Catholicism. He would remind the Saints that every church that is not the Lord's true church is the devil's church. We will see in the strictest sense that the scriptures absolutely back that up. We will also see that in terms of these specific verses it is indeed the Catholic Church in Rome which is being singled out. Two easy clues, first this church is slaying "saints" and its power is "iron" which in all prophecy is the Roman Empire.

6 And it came to pass that I beheld this great and abominable church; and I saw the devil that he was the founder of it.

In the early days of pure Christianity it was the Lord who founded His church, but as we have learned from both Daniel and John, this pure Church of Jesus Christ was wrapped into

Pagan Rome until the throne of Caesar became the seat of the Pope. The Eternal City merely switched crowns. Nephi bears witness that all of this was Lucifer's doing.

7 And I also saw gold, and silver, and silks, and scarlets, and fine-twined linen, and all manner of precious clothing; and I saw many harlots.

8 And the angel spake unto me, saying: Behold the gold, and the silver, and the silks, and the scarlets, and the fine-twined linen, and the precious clothing, and the harlots, are the desires of this great and abominable church.

9 And also for the praise of the world do they destroy the saints of God, and bring them down into captivity.

Money & Power were the ultimate goals of Lucifer's Church. For a time, both of these flowed into Rome without measure.

10 And it came to pass that I looked and beheld many waters; and they divided the Gentiles from the seed of my brethren.

Nephi sees the vast oceans that separate the hemispheres.

11 And it came to pass that the angel said unto me: Behold the wrath of God is upon the seed of thy brethren.

12 And I looked and beheld a man among the Gentiles, who was separated from the seed of my brethren by the many waters; and I beheld the Spirit of God, that it came down and wrought upon the man; and he went forth upon the many waters, even unto the seed of my brethren, who were in the promised land.

This man was Christopher Columbus whose courage and story continue to inspire Europeans and anger Native Nations and Tribes. For those willing to see it, this verse says that it was indeed God's wrath that brought Columbus. In that the native peoples are justified, but it also says that it was by God's will that he came. This should bring some sense of comfort.

13 And it came to pass that I beheld the Spirit of God, that it wrought upon other Gentiles; and they went forth out of captivity, upon the many waters.

1 Nephi 13:14 And it came to pass that I beheld many multitudes of the Gentiles upon the land of promise; and I beheld the wrath of God, that it was upon the seed of my brethren; and they were scattered before the Gentiles and were smitten.

15 And I beheld the Spirit of the Lord, that it was upon the Gentiles, and they did prosper and obtain the land for their inheritance; and I beheld that they were white, and exceedingly fair and beautiful, like unto my people before they were slain.

Once the floodgates had opened, there was no stopping the spread. Again, some peace can be had that the Lord both understood and permitted this. We will see in a moment that despite the hardship, the Lord did have a plan of mercy connected to what appears to be madness.

16 And it came to pass that I, Nephi, beheld that the Gentiles who had gone forth out of captivity did humble themselves before the Lord; and the power of the Lord was with them.

This verse puts the stamp of approval upon the motivation of some of the European settlers. It was their humble desire to escape the captivity of the Old World tyrants and the Devil's Church that lead them to cross the vast waters.

17 And I beheld that their mother Gentiles were gathered together upon the waters, and upon the land also, to battle against them.

This is a reference to *Mother England.*

18 And I beheld that the power of God was with them, and also that the wrath of God was upon all those that were gathered together against them to battle.

19 And I, Nephi, beheld that the Gentiles that had gone out of captivity were delivered by the power of God out of the hands of all other nations.

Many of America's founding fathers and mothers felt the power of God moving the events in their lives. They were convinced that it was God's will that America be free. These precious verses state that it was God's hand that freed America. But why? Why do this?

20 And it came to pass that I, Nephi, beheld that they did prosper in the land; and I beheld a book, and it was carried forth among them.

21 And the angel said unto me: Knowest thou the meaning of the book?

22 And I said unto him: I know not.

23 And he said: Behold it proceedeth out of the mouth of a Jew. And I, Nephi, beheld it; and he said unto me: The book that thou beholdest is a record of the Jews, which contains the covenants of the Lord, which he hath made unto the house of Israel; and it also containeth many of the prophecies of the holy prophets; and it is a record like unto the engravings which are upon the plates of brass, save there are not so many; nevertheless, they contain the covenants of the Lord, which he hath made unto the house of Israel; wherefore, they are of great worth unto the Gentiles.

This book of great worth is the *Holy Bible*, which in this case is primarily the *King James Version* although there were other Bibles at the time. The Lord is here declaring the book to be of great worth.

24 And the angel of the Lord said unto me: Thou hast beheld that the book proceeded forth from the mouth of a Jew; and when it proceeded forth from the mouth of a Jew it contained the fulness of the gospel of the Lord, of whom the twelve apostles bear record; and they bear record according to the truth which is in the Lamb of God.

25 Wherefore, these things go forth from the Jews in purity unto the Gentiles, according to the truth which is in God.

Nephi is here saying that the Jews, despite whatever other issues they may have had as a people, were true to their commitment to the purity of God's word. They may have not always followed it, but they were careful to keep it. One of the Lord's gripes with Catholicism is that they have not been true to their charge with Holy Writ:

26 And after they go forth by the hand of the twelve apostles of the Lamb, from the Jews unto the Gentiles, thou seest the formation of that great and

abominable church, which is most abominable above all other churches; for behold, they have taken away from the gospel of the Lamb many parts which are plain and most precious; and also many covenants of the Lord have they taken away.

27 And all this have they done that they might pervert the right ways of the Lord, that they might blind the eyes and harden the hearts of the children of men.

28 Wherefore, thou seest that after the book hath gone forth through the hands of the great and abominable church, that there are many plain and precious things taken away from the book, which is the book of the Lamb of God.

Here the blame for the alteration of the Bible from the simple and plain word of God to the confusing and sometimes contradictory verses that have lead to over 200+ translations/interpretations is blamed squarely on the Catholic Church removing parts of the scriptures for varying reasons.

29 And after these plain and precious things were taken away it goeth forth unto all the nations of the Gentiles; and after it goeth forth unto all the nations of the Gentiles, yea, even across the many waters which thou hast seen with the Gentiles which have gone forth out of captivity, thou seest — because of the many plain and precious things which have been taken out of the book, which were plain unto the understanding of the children of men, according to the plainness which is in the Lamb of God — because of these things which are taken away out of the gospel of the Lamb, an exceedingly great many do stumble, yea, insomuch that Satan hath great power over them.

This is the condition of secular christianity today. They hold to the Bible as the perfect, unaltered word of God but they have to choose which of the 200+ translations/interpretations is the perfect unaltered one. How perfect can a book be that has 200+ interpretations?

30 Nevertheless, thou beholdest that the Gentiles who have gone forth out of captivity, and have been lifted up by the power of God above all other nations, upon the face of the land which is choice above all other lands, which is the land that the Lord God hath covenanted with thy father that his seed should have for the land of their inheritance; wherefore, thou seest that the

Lord God will not suffer that the Gentiles will utterly destroy the mixture of thy seed, which are among thy brethren.

31 Neither will he suffer that the Gentiles shall destroy the seed of thy brethren.

The Lord loves the children of Lehi. They are part of Israel. They have paid a heavy price for the sins of Laman and Lemuel, but he has saved a remnant despite many attempts to eliminate them. The words of the Lord to Sitting Bull at the Battle of the Little Big Horn still ring, "These [Custer's Army], I will give to you because they have no ears to hear mercy."

32 Neither will the Lord God suffer that the Gentiles shall forever remain in that awful state of blindness, which thou beholdest they are in, because of the plain and most precious parts of the gospel of the Lamb which have been kept back by that abominable church, whose formation thou hast seen.

33 Wherefore saith the Lamb of God: I will be merciful unto the Gentiles, unto the visiting of the remnant of the house of Israel in great judgment.

In other words, the founding of the United States would both save the world through the restoration of the Gospel and redeem the remnant of Lehi's children.

34 And it came to pass that the angel of the Lord spake unto me, saying: Behold, saith the Lamb of God, after I have visited the remnant of the house of Israel — and this remnant of whom I speak is the seed of thy father — wherefore, after I have visited them in judgment, and smitten them by the hand of the Gentiles, and after the Gentiles do stumble exceedingly, because of the most plain and precious parts of the gospel of the Lamb which have been kept back by that abominable church, which is the mother of harlots, saith the Lamb — I will be merciful unto the Gentiles in that day, insomuch that I will bring forth unto them, in mine own power, much of my gospel, which shall be plain and precious, saith the Lamb.

This occurred with the release of the *Book of Mormon* and the official formation of the *Church of Jesus Christ of Latter-day Saints* on April 6th 1830 A.D.

35 For, behold, saith the Lamb: I will manifest myself unto thy seed, that they shall write many things which I shall minister unto them, which shall be plain

and precious; and after thy seed shall be destroyed, and dwindle in unbelief, and also the seed of thy brethren, behold, these things shall be hid up, to come forth unto the Gentiles, by the gift and power of the Lamb.

36 And in them shall be written my gospel, saith the Lamb, and my rock and my salvation.

This must have been a source of great joy to Nephi. The murder of Laban for the *Brass Plates* was a horrible event. One can sense the terror in young Nephi's words as he rationalized the horrible deed that had to be done, and how he was the one who had to do it.

37 And blessed are they who shall seek to bring forth my Zion at that day, for they shall have the gift and the power of the Holy Ghost; and if they endure unto the end they shall be lifted up at the last day, and shall be saved in the everlasting kingdom of the Lamb; and whoso shall publish peace, yea, tidings of great joy, how beautiful upon the mountains shall they be.

This is you. Hang in there! Every time you strive to fulfill the 3-fold mission of the Church by raising up righteous family, finding the elect of God and warning the rest, and redeeming your dead in the Temples that dot the Earth, you are preparing for yourself and your kin, a beautiful place upon Mount Zion.

38 And it came to pass that I beheld the remnant of the seed of my brethren, and also the book of the Lamb of God, which had proceeded forth from the mouth of the Jew, that it came forth from the Gentiles unto the remnant of the seed of my brethren.

39 And after it had come forth unto them I beheld other books, which came forth by the power of the Lamb, from the Gentiles unto them, unto the convincing of the Gentiles and the remnant of the seed of my brethren, and also the Jews who were scattered upon all the face of the earth, that the records of the prophets and of the twelve apostles of the Lamb are true.

40 And the angel spake unto me, saying: These last records, which thou hast seen among the Gentiles, shall establish the truth of the first, which are of the twelve apostles of the Lamb, and shall make known the plain and precious things which have been taken away from them; and shall make known to all kindreds, tongues, and people, that the Lamb of God is the Son of the Eternal

Father, and the Savior of the world; and that all men must come unto him, or they cannot be saved.

41 And they must come according to the words which shall be established by the mouth of the Lamb; and the words of the Lamb shall be made known in the records of thy seed, as well as in the records of the twelve apostles of the Lamb; wherefore they both shall be established in one; for there is one God and one Shepherd over all the earth.

42 And the time cometh that he shall manifest himself unto all nations, both unto the Jews and also unto the Gentiles; and after he has manifested himself unto the Jews and also unto the Gentiles, then he shall manifest himself unto the Gentiles and also unto the Jews, and the last shall be first, and the first shall be last.

1 Nephi 14:1 And it shall come to pass, that if the Gentiles shall hearken unto the Lamb of God in that day that he shall manifest himself unto them in word, and also in power, in very deed, unto the taking away of their stumbling blocks —

2 And harden not their hearts against the Lamb of God, they shall be numbered among the seed of thy father; yea, they shall be numbered among the house of Israel; and they shall be a blessed people upon the promised land forever; they shall be no more brought down into captivity; and the house of Israel shall no more be confounded.

This is the heart of the *Oath & Covenant of the Priesthood* where we become the sons of Abraham and Levi with full rights in the family of Abraham, Isaac and Israel. However, the Lord did another wonder when He merged much of the House of Japheth with the Tribe of Joseph, namely Ephraim. When the blood of Father Joseph of Egypt is awakened in the midst of the Gentile nations, it is the gathering of the elect of God; although all are welcome who will come. In our day, even those adopted in become full heirs. All are welcome on equal terms!

3 And that great pit, which hath been digged for them by that great and abominable church, which was founded by the devil and his children, that he might lead away the souls of men down to hell — yea, that great pit which hath been digged for the destruction of men shall be filled by those who digged it, unto their utter destruction, saith the Lamb of God; not the destruction of the soul, save it be the casting of it into that hell which hath no end.

4 For behold, this is according to the captivity of the devil, and also according to the justice of God, upon all those who will work wickedness and abomination before him.

5 And it came to pass that the angel spake unto me, Nephi, saying: Thou hast beheld that if the Gentiles repent it shall be well with them; and thou also knowest concerning the covenants of the Lord unto the house of Israel; and thou also hast heard that whoso repenteth not must perish.

6 Therefore, wo be unto the Gentiles if it so be that they harden their hearts against the Lamb of God.

7 For the time cometh, saith the Lamb of God, that I will work a great and a marvelous work among the children of men; a work which shall be everlasting, either on the one hand or on the other — either to the convincing of them unto peace and life eternal, or unto the deliverance of them to the hardness of their hearts and the blindness of their minds unto their being brought down into captivity, and also into destruction, both temporally and spiritually, according to the captivity of the devil, of which I have spoken.

The Lord is playing for keeps this time. This is the end and next comes the day of judgement.

8 And it came to pass that when the angel had spoken these words, he said unto me: Rememberest thou the covenants of the Father unto the house of Israel? I said unto him, Yea.

9 And it came to pass that he said unto me: Look, and behold that great and abominable church, which is the mother of abominations, whose founder is the devil.

10 And he said unto me: Behold there are save two churches only; the one is the church of the Lamb of God, and the other is the church of the devil; wherefore, whoso belongeth not to the church of the Lamb of God belongeth to that great church, which is the mother of abominations; and she is the whore of all the earth.

11 And it came to pass that I looked and beheld the whore of all the earth, and she sat upon many waters; and she had dominion over all the earth, among all nations, kindreds, tongues, and people.

12 And it came to pass that I beheld the church of the Lamb of God, and its numbers were few, because of the wickedness and abominations of the whore who sat upon many waters; nevertheless, I beheld that the church of the Lamb, who were the saints of God, were also upon all the face of the earth; and their

dominions upon the face of the earth were small, because of the wickedness of the great whore whom I saw.

How sad and how wonderful to know this. We are few. The church is small. In truth, a careful study of all religions (except for those sects of the Reformation who stumble because of their ruined Bibles) will reveal the same mystery cults by a different name. Egyptian, Assyrian, Babylon, Medo-Persian, Helenistic Greek, Roman, and Papal Rome (including Orthodox & Episcopal) are the same church.

13 And it came to pass that I beheld that the great mother of abominations did gather together multitudes upon the face of all the earth, among all the nations of the Gentiles, to fight against the Lamb of God.

14 And it came to pass that I, Nephi, beheld the power of the Lamb of God, that it descended upon the saints of the church of the Lamb, and upon the covenant people of the Lord, who were scattered upon all the face of the earth; and they were armed with righteousness and with the power of God in great glory.

15 And it came to pass that I beheld that the wrath of God was poured out upon that great and abominable church, insomuch that there were wars and rumors of wars among all the nations and kindreds of the earth.

16 And as there began to be wars and rumors of wars among all the nations which belonged to the mother of abominations, the angel spake unto me, saying: Behold, the wrath of God is upon the mother of harlots; and behold, thou seest all these things —

17 And when the day cometh that the wrath of God is poured out upon the mother of harlots, which is the great and abominable church of all the earth, whose founder is the devil, then, at that day, the work of the Father shall commence, in preparing the way for the fulfilling of his covenants, which he hath made to his people who are of the house of Israel.

We explored this at length in *Vol 1: Daniel & the Last Days*.

18 And it came to pass that the angel spake unto me, saying: Look!

19 And I looked and beheld a man, and he was dressed in a white robe.

20 And the angel said unto me: Behold one of the twelve apostles of the Lamb.

21 Behold, he shall see and write the remainder of these things; yea, and also many things which have been.

22 And he shall also write concerning the end of the world.

23 Wherefore, the things which he shall write are just and true; and behold they are written in the book which thou beheld proceeding out of the mouth of the Jew; and at the time they proceeded out of the mouth of the Jew, or, at the time the book proceeded out of the mouth of the Jew, the things which were written were plain and pure, and most precious and easy to the understanding of all men.

24 And behold, the things which this apostle of the Lamb shall write are many things which thou hast seen; and behold, the remainder shalt thou see.

25 But the things which thou shalt see hereafter thou shalt not write; for the Lord God hath ordained the apostle of the Lamb of God that he should write them.

26 And also others who have been, to them hath he shown all things, and they have written them; and they are sealed up to come forth in their purity, according to the truth which is in the Lamb, in the own due time of the Lord, unto the house of Israel.

27 And I, Nephi, heard and bear record, that the name of the apostle of the Lamb was John, according to the word of the angel.

28 And behold, I, Nephi, am forbidden that I should write the remainder of the things which I saw and heard; wherefore the things which I have written sufficeth me; and I have written but a small part of the things which I saw.

29 And I bear record that I saw the things which my father saw, and the angel of the Lord did make them known unto me.

30 And now I make an end of speaking concerning the things which I saw while I was carried away in the Spirit; and if all the things which I saw are not written, the things which I have written are true. And thus it is. Amen.

John the Revelator, Father Nephi, Mahonri, Joseph Smith the Prophet, and the rest of the brethren we know. If it was at the very door in their day, we are standing in the midst of it now. Even so…, bring it on!

Joseph Smith on the Beasts of Revelation

I want the liberty of thinking and believing as I please.
It feels so good not to be trammelled.
— Joseph Smith, Jr.

On April 8th 1843, the Prophet Joseph Smith stood to preach. The Baptist Millerite movement had been gaining attention by saying that the sanctification of God's altar on Earth was going to happen in the Fall of 1844. They believed that this would result in the Second Coming of Jesus Christ. Joseph had gone on record saying that they were wrong. The sanctification of the altar was to be an event of Restoration by a blood witness. It is uncertain exactly when our Prophet suspected that the blood which would be witnessed would be his own. In order to help clarify some of the Saints' preaching about Revelation and particularly the beasts of the book, the Prophet gave the following address. It would be his only recorded public sermon on the Beasts of Revelation.

The subject I intend to speak upon this morning is one that I have seldom touched upon since I commenced my ministry in the Church. It is a subject of great speculation, as well amongst the elders of this Church, as among the divines of the day: it is in relation to the beasts spoken of by John the Revelator. I have seldom spoken from the revelations; but as my subject is a constant source of speculation amongst the elders, causing a division of sentiment and opinion in relation to it, I now do it in order that division and differences of opinion may be done away with, and not that correct knowledge on the subject is so much needed at the present time.

It is not very essential for the elders to have knowledge in relation to the meaning of beasts, and heads and horns, and other figures made use of in the revelations; still, it may be necessary, to prevent contention and division and do away with suspense. If we get puffed up by thinking that we have much knowledge, we are apt to get a contentious spirit, and correct knowledge is necessary to cast out that spirit.

The evil of being puffed up with correct (though useless) knowledge is not so great as the evil of contention. Knowledge does away with darkness, suspense and doubt; for these cannot exist where knowledge is.

There is no pain so awful as that of suspense. This is the punishment of the wicked; their doubt, anxiety and suspense cause weeping, wailing and gnashing of teeth.

In knowledge there is power. God has more power than all other beings, because he has greater knowledge; and hence he knows how to subject all other beings to Him. He has power over all.

I will endeavor to instruct you in relation to the meaning of the beasts and figures spoken of. I should not have called up the subject had it not been for this circumstance. Elder Pelatiah Brown, one of the wisest old heads we have among us, and whom I now see before me, has been preaching concerning the beast which was full of eyes before and behind; and for this he was hauled up for trial before the High Council.

I did not like the old man being called up for erring in doctrine. It looks too much like the Methodist, and not like the Latter-day Saints. Methodists have creeds which a man must believe or be asked out of their church. I want the liberty of thinking and believing as I please. It feels so good not to be trammelled. It does not prove that a man is not a good man because he errs in doctrine.

The High Council undertook to censure and correct Elder Brown, because of his teachings in relation to the beasts. Whether they actually corrected him or not, I am a little doubtful, but don't care. Father Brown came to me to know what he should do about it. The subject particularly referred to was the four beasts and four-and-twenty elders mentioned in Rev. 5:8 — "And when he had taken the book, the four beasts and four-and-twenty elders fell down before the Lamb, having every one of them harps, and golden vials full of odors, which are the prayers of saints."

Father Brown has been to work and confounded all Christendom by making out that the four beasts represented the different kingdoms of God on the earth. The wise men of the day could not do anything with him, and why should we find fault? Anything to whip sectarianism, to put down priestcraft, and bring the human family to a knowledge of the truth. A club is better than no weapon for a poor man to fight with.

Father Brown did whip sectarianism, and so far so good; but I could not help laughing at the idea of God making use of the figure of a beast to represent His kingdom on the earth, consisting of men, when He could as well have used a far more noble and consistent figure. What! the Lord made use of the figure of a creature of the brute creation to represent that which is much more noble, glorious, and important — the glories and majesty of His kingdom? By taking a lesser figure to represent a greater, you missed it that time, old gentleman; but the sectarians did not know enough to detect you.

When God made use of the figure of a beast in visions to the prophets He did it to represent those kingdoms which had degenerated and become corrupt, savage and beast-like in their dispositions, even the degenerate kingdoms of the wicked world; but He never made use of the figure of a beast nor any of the brute kind to represent His kingdom.

Daniel says (chap. 7:16) when he saw the vision of the four beasts, "I came near unto one of them that stood by, and asked him the truth of all this," the angel interpreted the vision to Daniel; but we find, by the interpretation that the figures of beasts had no allusion to the kingdom of God. You there see that the beasts are spoken of to represent the kingdoms of the world, the inhabitants whereof were beastly and abominable characters; they were murderers, corrupt, carnivorous, and brutal in their dispositions. The lion, the bear, the leopard, and the ten-horned beast represented the kingdoms of the world, says Daniel; for I refer to the prophets to qualify my observations which I make, so that the young elders who know so much, may not rise up like a flock of hornets and sting me. I want to keep out of such a wasp-nest.

There is a grand difference and distinction between the visions and figures spoken of by the ancient prophets, and those spoken of in the revelations of John. The things which John saw had no allusion to the scenes of the days of Adam, Enoch, Abraham or Jesus, only so far as is plainly represented by John, and clearly set forth by him. John saw that only which was lying in futurity and which was shortly to come to pass. See Rev. 1:1-3, which is a key to the whole subject: "The revelation of Jesus Christ, which God gave unto Him, to show unto his servants things which must shortly come to pass; and He sent and signified it by His angel unto His servant John: who bare record of the word of God, and of the testimony of Jesus Christ, and of all things that he saw. Blessed is he that readeth, and they that hear the words of his prophecy and keep those things that are written therein: for the time is at hand." Also Rev. 4:1. "After this I looked, and, behold, a door was opened in heaven; and the first voice which I heard was as it were of a trumpet talking with me; which said, Come up hither, and I will show thee things which must be hereafter."

The four beasts and twenty-four elders were out of every nation; for they sang a new song, saying, "Thou art worthy to take the book, and to open the seal thereof: for thou wast slain, and hast redeemed us to God by thy blood out of every kindred, and tongue, and people, and nation." (See Rev. 5:9.) It would be great stuffing to crowd all nations into four beasts and twenty-four elders.

Now, I make this declaration, that those things which John saw in heaven had no allusion to anything that had been on the earth previous to that time, because they were the representation of "things which must shortly come to pass," and not of what has already transpired. John saw beasts that had to do with things on the earth, but not in past ages. The beasts which John saw had to devour the inhabitants of the earth in days to come. "And I saw when the

Lamb opened one of the seals; and I heard, as it were the noise of thunder, one of the four beasts saying, Come and see. And I saw, and beheld a white horse: and he that sat on him had a bow; and a crown was given unto him: and he went forth conquering, and to conquer. And when he had opened the second seal, I heard the second beast say, Come and see. And there went out another horse that was red: and power was given to him that sat thereon to take peace from the earth, and that they should kill one another; and there was given unto him a great sword." (Rev. 6:1 - 4.) The book of Revelation is one of the plainest books God ever caused to be written.

The revelations do not give us to understand anything of the past in relation to the kingdom of God. What John saw and speaks of were things which he saw in heaven; those which Daniel saw were on and pertaining to the earth.

I am now going to take exceptions to the present translation of the Bible in relation to these matters. Our latitude and longitude can be determined in the original Hebrew with far greater accuracy than in the English version. There is a grand distinction between the actual meaning of the prophets and the present translation. The prophets do not declare that they saw a beast or beasts, but that they saw the image or figure of a beast. Daniel did not see an actual bear or a lion, but the images or figures of those beasts. The translation should have been rendered "image" instead of "beast," in every instance where beasts are mentioned by the prophets. But John saw the actual beast in heaven, showing to John that beasts did actually exist there, and not to represent figures of things on the earth. When the prophets speak of seeing beasts in their visions, they mean that they saw the images, they being types to represent certain things. At the same time they received the interpretation as to what those images or types were designed to represent.

I make this broad declaration, that whenever God gives a vision of an image, or beast, or figure of any kind, He always holds Himself responsible to give a revelation or interpretation of the meaning thereof, otherwise we are not responsible or accountable for our belief in it. Don't be afraid of being damned for not knowing the meaning of a vision or figure, if God has not given a revelation or interpretation of the subject.

John saw curious looking beasts in heaven; he saw every creature that was in heaven, — all the beasts, fowls and fish in heaven, — actually there, giving glory to God. How do you prove it? (See Rev. 5:13.) "And every creature which is in heaven, and on the earth, and under the earth, and such as are in the sea, and all that are in them, heard I saying, Blessing, and honor, and glory, and power, be unto Him that sitteth upon the throne, and unto the Lamb for ever and ever."

I suppose John saw beings there of a thousand forms, that had been saved from ten thousand times ten thousand earths like this, — strange beasts of which we have no conception: all might be seen in heaven. The grand secret was to show John what there was in heaven. John learned that God glorified Himself by saving all that His hands had made, whether beasts, fowls, fishes or men; and He will glorify Himself with them.

Says one, "I cannot believe in the salvation of beasts." Any man who would tell you that this could not be, would tell you that the revelations are not true. John heard the words of the beasts giving glory to God, and understood them. God who made the beasts could understand every language spoken by them. The four beasts were four of the most noble animals that had filled the measure of their creation, and had been saved from other worlds, because they were perfect: they were like angels in their sphere. We are not told where they came from, and I do not know; but they were seen and heard by John praising and glorifying God.

The popular religionists of the day tell us, forsooth, that the beasts spoken of in the Revelation represent kingdoms. Very well, on the same principle we can say that the twenty-four elders spoken of represent beasts; for they are all spoken of at the same time, and are represented as all uniting in the same acts of praise and devotion.

This learned interpretation is all as flat as a pancake! "What do you use such vulgar expressions for, being a prophet?" Because the old women understand it — they make pancakes. Deacon Homespun said the earth was flat as a pancake, and ridiculed the science which proved to the contrary. The whole argument is flat, and I don't know of anything better to represent it. The world is full of technicalities and misrepresentation, which I calculate to overthrow, and speak of things as they actually exist.

Again, there is no revelation to prove that things do not exist in heaven as I have set forth, nor yet to show that the beasts meant anything but beasts; and we never can comprehend the things of God and of heaven, but by revelation. We may spiritualize and express opinions to all eternity; but that is no authority.

Oh, ye elders of Israel, hearken to my voice; and when you are sent into the world to preach, tell those things you are sent to tell; preach and cry aloud, "Repent ye, for the kingdom of heaven is at hand; repent and believe the Gospel." Declare the first principles, and let mysteries alone, lest ye be overthrown. Never meddle with the visions of beasts and subjects you do not understand. Elder Brown, when you go to Palmyra, say nothing about the four beasts, but preach those things the Lord has told you to preach about — repentance and baptism for the remission of sins.

[He then read Rev. 13:1-8.] John says, "And I saw one of his heads as it were wounded to death; and his deadly wound was healed; and all the world wondered after the beast." Some spiritualizers say the beast that received the wound was Nebuchadnezzar, some Constantine, some Mohammed, and others the Roman Catholic Church; but we will look at what John saw in relation to this beast. Now for the wasp's nest. The translators have used the term "dragon" for devil. Now it was a beast that John saw in heaven, and he was then speaking of "things which must shortly come to pass;" and consequently the beast John saw could not be Nebuchadnezzar. The beast John saw was an actual beast, and an actual intelligent being gives him his power, and his seat, and great authority. It was not to represent a beast in heaven: it was an angel in heaven who has power in the last days to do a work.

"All the world wondered after the beast," Nebuchadnezzar and Constantine the Great not excepted. And if the beast was all the world, how could the world wonder after the beast? It must have been a wonderful beast to cause all human beings to wonder after it; and I will venture to say that when God allows the old devil to give power to the beast to destroy the inhabitants of the earth, all will wonder. Verse 4 reads, "And they worshiped the dragon which gave power unto the beast; and they worshiped the beast, saying. Who is like unto the beast? Who is able to make war with him?"

Some say it means the kingdom of the world. One thing is sure, it does not mean the kingdom of the Saints. Suppose we admit that it means the kingdoms of the world, what propriety would there be in saying, Who is able to make war with my great big self? If these spiritualized interpretations are true, the book contradicts itself in almost every verse. But they are not true.

There is a mistranslation of the word dragon in the second verse. The original word signifies the devil, and not dragon, as translated. In chapter 12, verse 9, it reads, "That old serpent, called the devil," and it ought to be translated devil in this case, and not dragon. It is sometimes translated Apollyon. Everything that we have not a key-word to, we will take it as it reads. The beasts which John saw and speaks of being in heaven, were actually living in heaven, and were actually to have power given to them over the inhabitants of the earth, precisely according to the plain reading of the revelations. I give this as a key to the elders of Israel. The independent beast is a beast that dwells in heaven, abstract [apart] from the human family. The beast that rose up out of the sea should be translated the image of a beast, as I have referred to it in Daniel's vision.

I have said more than I ever did before, except once at Ramus, and then up starts the little fellow (Charles Thompson) and stuffed me like a cock-turkey with the prophecies of Daniel, and crammed it down my throat with his finger. *recorded in the Documented History of the Church 5:339-345.*

One is immediately struck by the knowledge of a true prophet of the Lord. This sermon is astounding as much for what it does say as for what it doesn't say. It is clear that the Prophet is trying to get at something but doesn't want the grief of being told he's wrong, or, worse for him, causing some of the Saints to lose their faith in the Lord. Joseph had a deeply tender heart for our people and preferred self-sacrifice to the heart break of knowing that something he did or said might cause a fellow Latter-day Saint to doubt. It is a marvelous peek into his personality and inner-mind.

As it pertains to our discussion, I wish that we had the prophet with us to "cross-examine." Careful analysis of this sermon raises questions which are not easily answered. I can only offer my speculation which may turn out to be wrong. I would encourage any one who has not been reading our *Gospel Feast Series* in order, to pause a moment and read *Vol. 5: Ezekiel & the Millennial Reign of Christ*, chapters 2 & 3 and Appendix A before proceeding. There you will learn about the Great Tsabim known anciently as the *Hosts of Heaven*. You will see that the Lord considers them to be alive. They are *the children of His hands*, as opposed to you, who are the *children of His wife*. As proof that Joseph Smith knew about them to a greater extent than he openly let on can be found in some of the statements he made in private. See what you make of this.

THE LOST TEN TRIBES

One of the more dynamic accounts concerning Joseph Smith's view on the Lost Ten Tribes is an old interview of church Patriarch Homer M. Brown (formerly of the Granite Stake) by Brother Theodore Tobiason in October 1924. The account resides in the *Historical Department* of the LDS Church in Salt Lake City. Patriarch Brown was a grandson of Benjamin and Sister Brown, who often sheltered Joseph Smith from his enemies in Nauvoo, Illinois in the 1840s. Brother Tobiason asked:

Brother Brown, will you give us some light and explanation on the 5th verse on page 386 of the L.D.S. Hymn Book which speaks of the Ten Tribes of Israel, on the part of this Earth which formed another planet, according to the Hymn of [Sister] Eliza R. Snow.

1. Thou, earth, wast once a glorious sphere

   Of noble magnitude,

   And didst with majesty appear

   Among the worlds of God.

2. But thy dimensions have been torn

   Asunder, piece by piece,

   And each dismembered fragment borne

   Abroad to distant space...

5. And when the Lord saw fit to hide

   The "ten lost tribes" away,

   Thou, Earth, wast severed to provide

   The orb on which they stay...

11. A "restitution" yet must come,

    That will to thee restore,

    By that grand law of worlds, thy sum

    Of matter heretofore.

12. And thou, O earth, will leave the track

    Thou hast been doomed to trace;

    The Gods with shouts will bring thee back

    To fill thy native place.[141]

"Yes, sir, I think I can answer your question," [the patriarch said]. "Sister Eliza R. Snow, in visiting my grandparents was asked by my grandmother: 'Eliza, where did you get your ideas about the Ten Lost Tribes being taken away as you explain it in your wonderful hymn?'"

She answered as follows: "Why, my husband [the Prophet Joseph] told me about it."

Have you any other information that your grandfather ever gave you, as contained in any conversation with the Prophet Joseph Smith?

"I have! One evening in Nauvoo, just after dark, somebody rapped at the doorway vigorously. Grandfather said he was reading the *Doctrine and Covenants*. He rose hurriedly and answered the summons at the door, where he met the Prophet Joseph Smith. [The Prophet] said, 'Brother Brown, can you keep me over night, the mobs are after me?'

Grandfather answered, 'Yes, sir. It will not be the first time, come in.'

'All right,' the Prophet said, shutting the door quickly. He came in and sat down.

Grandmother said: 'Brother Joseph, have you had your supper?'

'No,' he answered, 'I have not.' So she prepared him a meal and he ate it. Afterward they were in a conversation relative to the principles of the [Restored] Gospel. During the conversation the Ten Lost Tribes were mentioned.

Grandfather said, 'Joseph, where are the Ten Tribes?'

He said, 'Come to the door and I will show you. Come on Sister Brown, I want you both to see.'

It being a starlight night the Prophet said: 'Brother Brown, can you show me the Polar Star?'

'Yes, sir,' he said, pointing to the North Star. 'There it is.'

'Yes, I know,' said the Prophet, 'but which one? There are a lot of stars there.'

Grandfather said: 'Can you see the points of the Dipper?'

The Prophet answered, 'Yes.'

'Well,' he said, 'trace the pointers, pointing up to the largest star. That is the North Star.'

The Prophet answered: 'You are correct. Now,' he said, pointing toward the star, 'do you discern a twinkler to the right and below the Polar Star, which we would judge to be about the distance of 20 feet from here?'

Grandfather answered, 'Yes, sir.'

The Prophet said: 'Sister Brown, do you see that star also?'

Her answer was, 'Yes, sir.'

'Very well then,' he said, 'let's go in.'

After re-entering the house, the Prophet said: 'Brother Brown, I noticed when I came in that you were reading *The Doctrine and Covenants*. Will you kindly get it.'

He did so. The Prophet turned to Section 133 and read, commencing at the 26th verse and throughout to the 34th verse.

> D&C 133:26 And they who are in the north countries shall come in remembrance before the Lord; and their prophets shall hear his voice, and shall no longer stay themselves; and they shall smite the rocks, and the ice shall flow down at their presence.
>
> 27 And an highway shall be cast up in the midst of the great deep.
>
> 28 Their enemies shall become a prey unto them,
>
> 29 And in the barren deserts there shall come forth pools of living water; and the parched ground shall no longer be a thirsty land.
>
> 30 And they shall bring forth their rich treasures unto the children of Ephraim, my servants.
>
> 31 And the boundaries of the everlasting hills shall tremble at their presence.
>
> 32 And there shall they fall down and be crowned with glory, even in Zion, by the hands of the servants of the Lord, even the children of Ephraim.
>
> 33 And they shall be filled with songs of everlasting joy.
>
> 34 Behold, this is the blessing of the everlasting God upon the tribes of Israel, and the richer blessing upon the head of Ephraim and his fellows.

He said, after reading the 31st verse, 'Now let me ask you what would cause the Everlasting Hills to tremble with more violence than the coming together of the two planets? And the place whereon they reside will return to this Earth. Now, scientists will tell you that it is not scientific: That two planets coming together would be disastrous to both; but, when two planets or other objects are traveling in the same direction and one of them with a little greater velocity than the other, it would not be disastrous, because the one traveling faster would overtake the other. Now, what would cause the mountains of ice to melt quicker than the heat caused by the friction of the two planets coming together?'

[The Prophet then asked], 'Did you ever see a meteor falling that was not red hot? That would cause the mountains of ice to melt. And relative to the Great Highway which should be cast up when the planet returns to its place in the great Northern Waters, it will form a highway and waters will recede and roll back.'

He continued, 'Now as to their coming back from the Northern Waters; they will return from the north because their planet will return to the place from whence it was taken. Relative to the waters rolling back to the north, if you take a vessel of water and swing it rapidly around your head you won't spill any, but if you stop the motion gradually, it will begin to pour out.'

'Now,' he said, 'Brother Brown, at the present time this Earth is rotating very rapidly. When this planet returns it will make the Earth that much heavier, and it will then revolve slower, and that will account for the waters receding from the Earth for a great while, but has now turned and is proceeding rapidly eastward.'"

If the Brown family and Eliza R. Snow's testimony is not enough, Brother Charles Walker also heard such statements. Independently he visited Sister Eliza Snow one night and asked her about the dividing of the earth in former times. He recorded the following in his journal:

March 10, 1881: At night paid Sister Eliza R. Snow a short visit and had some conversation with her on the dividing of the earth. She told me that she heard the Prophet say that when the ten tribes were taken away, the Lord cut the earth in two, Joseph striking his left hand in the center with the edge of his right to illustrate the idea, and that they were on an orb or planet by themselves, and when they returned with the portion of this earth that was taken away with them, the coming together of these two bodies or orbs, would cause a shock and make the earth "reel to and fro like a drunken man." She also stated that he said the earth was now ninety times smaller than when first created or organized.

It's going to get exciting. The prophets have said that the heavens declare the glory of God. Today they only whisper, tomorrow they will shout for joy!

God the Father Inviting Christ to Sit on the Throne at His Right Hand by Peter de Grebber, 1645, St. Catherine's Convent Museum, Netherlands. Note the very popish attire and demeanor of the Father; including the *Pope's Triple* Crown. Art such as this helped reinforce to the masses the Catholic dogma that the Pope is God on Earth. But don't take our word for it, here is the word of Pope Pius XI (#259 1922-1939): "You know that I am the Holy Father, the representative of God on earth, the Vicar of Christ, which means that I Am God on the earth."

Appendix C
The Number of His Name

Here is wisdom, let him who hath understanding count the number...
—John the Revelator

Alexander Hislop (1807 - 13 March 1865) was a minster in the Free Church of Scotland. He is most famous for his book *The Two Babylons*. It was originally released in 1853 as a pamphlet but was greatly expanded as public interest grew. Both greatly respected and greatly maligned today, the book is a valuable tool in understanding the symbolism and circumstances of the merger of Pagan Rome with Christianity. It is an educated peek into the old adage, *If you can't beat 'em, join 'em;* which is exactly what the elites of the failing Roman Empire did. They couldn't beat Christianity so they took it over. Sadly, when it comes to the correct interpretation of last day events, most and many roads *still lead to Rome.*

We will soon be studying *Genesis* together. There we will learn the terrible history of the sons of Esau and how their agenda merged into Rome and Islam. Under these guises they continue to work toward the destruction of Israel.

Reverend Hislop explained the meaning behind Revelation 13:18: *Here is wisdom. Let him that hath understanding count the number of the beast: for it is the number of a man; and his number is 666.*

THE NAME OF THE BEAST BY ALEXANDER HISLOP
The name "Lateinos" has been generally accepted by Protestant writers [as the name of the man-beast counted as 666], yet there has been always found a certain deficiency, and it has been felt that something was wanting to put it beyond all possibility of doubt. Now, looking at the subject from the Babylonian point of view, we shall find both the name and number of the beast brought home to us in such a way as leaves nothing to be desired on the point of evidence. ...the Pope... was called by many different titles. ...Among these

innumerable names, how shall we ascertain the name at which the Spirit of God points in the enigmatical language that speaks of the name of the beast, and the number of his name? If we know the Apocalyptic name of the system, that will lead us to the name of the head of the system. The name of the system is "Mystery" (Rev 17:5). Here, then, we have the key that at once unlocks the enigma... That name, as we have seen, was Saturn. Saturn and Mystery are both Chaldean words, and they are correlative terms. As Mystery signifies the Hidden system, so Saturn signifies the Hidden god. In the Litany of the Mass, the worshippers are taught thus to pray: "God Hidden, and my Saviour, have mercy upon us." (M'Gavins Protestant) Whence can this invocation of the "God Hidden" have come, but from the ancient worship of Saturn, the "Hidden God"? As the Papacy has canonized the Babylonian god by the name of St. Dionysius, and St. Bacchus, the "martyr," so by this very name of "Satur" is he also enrolled in the calendar; for March 29th is the festival of "St. Satur," the martyr. (CHAMBER'S Book of Days) To those who were initiated the god was revealed; to all else he was hidden. Now, the name Saturn in Chaldee is pronounced Satur; but, as every Chaldee scholar knows, consists only of four letters, thus - Stur. This name contains exactly the Apocalyptic number 666: -

$$S = 060 \quad T = 400 \quad U = 006 \quad R = 200 \quad \Sigma = 666$$

If the Pope is, as we have seen, the legitimate representative of Saturn, the number of the Pope, as head of the Mystery of Iniquity, is 666. But still further it turns out, as shown above, that the original name of Rome itself was Saturnia, "the city of Saturn." This is vouched alike by Ovid, by Pliny, and by Aurelius Victor. Thus, then, the Pope has a double claim to the name and number of the beast. He is the only legitimate representative of the original Saturn at this day in existence, and he reigns in the very city of the seven hills where the Roman Saturn formerly reigned; and, from his residence in which, the whole of Italy was "long after called by his name," being commonly named "the Saturnian land." But what bearing, it may be said, has this upon the name Lateinos, which is commonly believed to be the "name of the beast"? Much. It proves that the common opinion is thoroughly well-founded. Saturn and Lateinos are just synonymous, having precisely the same meaning, and belonging equally to the same god. The reader cannot have forgotten the lines of Virgil, which showed that Lateinos, to whom the Romans or Latin race traced back their lineage, was represented with a glory around his head [a halo or Saturn's rings], to show that he was a "child of the Sun." Thus, then, it is evident that, in popular opinion, the original Lateinos had occupied the very same position as Saturn did in the Mysteries, who was equally worshipped as the "offspring of the Sun." Moreover, it is evident that the Romans knew that the name "Lateinos" signifies the "Hidden One," for their antiquarians invariably affirm that Latium received its name from Saturn "lying hid" there. On etymological grounds, then, even on the testimony of the Romans, Lateinos is equivalent to the "Hidden One"; that is, to Saturn, the "god of Mystery.'

Latium Latinus (the Roman form of the Greek Lateinos), and Lateo, "to lie hid," all alike come from the Chaldee "Lat," which has the same meaning. The name "lat," or the hidden one, had evidently been given, as well as Saturn, to the great Babylonian god...

The deified kings were called after the gods from whom they professed to spring, and not after their territories. The same, we may be sure, was the case with Latinus.

While Saturn, therefore, is the name of the beast, and contains the mystic number, Lateinos, which contains the same number, is just as peculiar and distinctive an appellation of the same beast. The Pope, then, as the head of the beast, is equally Lateinos or Saturn, that is, the head of the Babylonian "Mystery." ...we find the mystic number 666 unmistakably and "indelibly marked" on his own forehead, and that he who has his seat on the seven hills of Rome has exclusive and indefeasible claims to be regarded as the Visible head of the beast.

The reader, however, who has carefully considered the language that speaks of the name and number of the Apocalyptic beast, must have observed that, in the terms that describe that name and number, there is still an enigma that ought not to be overlooked. The words are these: "Let him that hath understanding count the number of the beast – for it is the number of a man" (Rev 13:18). What means the saying, that the "number of the beast is the number of a man"? Does it merely mean that he has been called by a name that has been borne by some individual man before? This is the sense in which the words have been generally understood. But surely this would be nothing very distinctive – nothing that might not equally apply to innumerable names. But view this language in connection with the ascertained facts of the case, and what a Divine light at once beams from the expression. Saturn, (the hidden god – the god of the Mysteries) whom the Pope represents, whose secrets were revealed only to the initiated, – was identical with Janus, who was publicly known to all Rome, to the uninitiated and initiated alike, as the grand Mediator, the opener and the shutter, who had the key of the invisible world. Now, what means the name Janus? That name, as Cornificius in Macrobius shows, was properly Eanus; and in ancient Chaldee, E-anush signifies "the Man."

...The name Banush, or "the Man," was applied to the Babylonian Messiah, as identifying him with the promised seed of the Woman. ...That man, who was believed to have conquered the adversaries of the gods, was Janus, the god-man. In consequence of his assumed character and exploits, Janus was invested with high powers, made the keeper of the gates of heaven, and arbiter of men's eternal destinies. Of this Janus, this Babylonian "man," the Pope, as we have seen, is the legitimate representative... Janus, while manifestly worshipped as the Messiah or god-man, was also celebrated as

"Principium Decorum," the source and fountain of all the Pagan gods. We have already in this character traced him backward through Cush to Noah; but to make out his claim to this high character, in its proper completeness, he must be traced even further still. The Pagans knew, and could not but know, at the time the Mysteries were concocted, in the days of Shem and his brethren, who, through the Flood, had passed from the old world to the new, the whole story of Adam, and therefore it was necessary, if a deification of mankind there was to be, that his pre-eminent dignity, as the human "Father of gods and men," should not be ignored. Nor was it. The Mysteries were full of what he did, and what befell him; and the name E-anush, or, as it appeared in the Egyptian form, Ph'anesh, "The man," was only another name for that of our great progenitor. The name of Adam in the Hebrew of Genesis almost always occurs with the article before it, implying "The Adam," or "The man." There is this difference, however – "The Adam" refers to man unfallen, E-anush, "The man," to "fallen man." E-anush, then, as "Principium decorum," "The fountain and father of the gods," is "FALLEN Adam." Anesh properly signifies only the weakness or frailty of fallen humanity; but any one who consults Ovid, Fashti, as to the character of Janus, will see that when E-anush was deified, it was not simply as Fallen man with his weakness, but Fallen man with his corruption.

The principle of Pagan idolatry went directly to exalt fallen humanity, to consecrate its lusts, to give men license to live after the flesh, and yet, after such a life, to make them sure of eternal felicity. E-anus, the "fallen man," was set up as the human Head of this system of corruption – this "Mystery of Iniquity." Now, from this we come to see the real meaning of the name, applied to the divinity commonly worshipped in Phrygia along with Cybele in the very same character as this same Janus, who was at once the Father of the gods, and the Mediatorial divinity. That name was Atys, or Attis, or Attes, and the meaning will evidently appear from the meaning of the well-known Greek word Ate, which signifies "error of sin," and is obviously derived from the Chaldean Hata, "to sin."

...If, therefore, the Pope occupies, as we have seen, the very place of Janus "the man," how clear is it, that he equally occupies the place of Attes, "the sinner," and then how striking in this point of view the name "Man of sin," as divinely given by prophecy (2 Thess 2:3) to him who was to be the head of the Christian apostasy, and who was to concentrate in that apostasy all the corruption of Babylonian Paganism?

The Pope is thus on every ground demonstrated to be the visible head of the beast. But the beast has not only a visible, but an invisible head that governs it. That invisible head is none other than Satan, the head of the first grand apostasy that began in heaven itself. This is put beyond doubt by the language of Revelation 13:4 "And they worshipped the Dragon which gave power unto the beast, saying, Who is like unto the beast? Who is able to make war with him?" This language shows that the worship of the dragon is commensurate with the worship of the beast. ...But, in truth, we have historical evidence, and that of a very remarkable kind, that the Pope, as head of the Chaldean Mysteries, is as directly the representative of Satan, as he is of the false Messiah of Babylon. It was long ago noticed by Irenaeus, about the end of the second century, that the name Teitan contained the Mystic number 666; and he gave it as his opinion that Teitan was "by far the most probable name" of the beast from the sea.

Now, on inquiry, it will actually be found, that while Saturn was the name of the visible head, Teitan was the name of the invisible head of the beast. Teitan is just the Chaldean form of Sheitan, the very name by which Satan has been called from time immemorial by the Devil-worshippers of Kurdistan; and from Armenia or Kurdistan, this Devil-worship embodied in the Chaldean Mysteries came westward to Asia Minor, and thence to Etruria and Rome.

That Teitan was actually known by the classic nations of antiquity to be Satan, or the spirit of wickedness, and originator of moral evil, we have the following proofs: The history of Teitan and his brethren, as given in Homer and Hesiod, the two earliest of all the Greek writers, although later legends are obviously mixed up with it, is evidently the exact counterpart of the Scriptural account of Satan and his angels. Homer says, that "all the gods of Tartarus," or Hell, "were called Teitans." Hesiod tells us how these Teitans, or "gods of hell," came to have their dwelling there. The chief of them having committed a certain act of wickedness against his father, the supreme god of heaven, with the sympathy of many others of the "sons of heaven," that father "called them all by an opprobrious name, Teitans," pronounced a curse upon them, and then, in consequence of that curse, they were "cast down to hell," and "bound in chains of darkness" in the abyss. While this is the earliest account of Teitan and his followers among the Greeks, we find that, in the Chaldean system, Teitan was just a synonym for Typhon, the malignant Serpent or Dragon, who was universally regarded as the Devil, or author of all wickedness. It was Typhon, according to the Pagan version of the story, that killed Tammuz, and cut him in pieces; but Lactantius, who was thoroughly acquainted with the subject, upbraids his Pagan countrymen for "worshipping a child torn in pieces by the Teitans." It is undeniable, then, that Teitan, in Pagan belief, was identical with the Dragon, or Satan.

In the Mysteries, as formerly hinted, an important change took place as soon as the way was paved for it. First, Tammuz was worshipped as the bruiser of the serpent's head, meaning thereby that he was the appointed destroyer of Satan's kingdom. Then the dragon himself, or Satan, came to receive a certain measure of worship, to "console him," as the Pagans said, "for the loss of his power," and to prevent him from hurting them; and last of all the dragon, or Teitan or Satan, became the supreme object of worship, the Titania, or rites of Teitan, occupying a prominent place in the Egyptian Mysteries, and also in those of Greece. How vitally important was the place that these rites of Teitan or Satan occupied, may be judged of from the fact that Pluto, the god of Hell (who, in his ultimate character, was just the grand Adversary), was looked up to with awe and dread as the great god on whom the destinies of mankind in the eternal world did mainly depend; for it was said that to Pluto belonged "to purify souls after death." Purgatory having been in Paganism, as it is in Popery, the grand hinge of priestcraft and superstition, what a power did this opinion attribute to the "god of Hell"! No wonder that the serpent, the Devil's grand instrument in seducing mankind, was in all the earth worshipped with such extraordinary reverence, it being laid down in the Octateuch of Ostanes, that "serpents were the supreme of all gods and the princes of the Universe." No wonder that it came at last to be firmly believed that the Messiah, on whom the hopes of the world depended, was Himself the "seed of the serpent"! This was manifestly the case in Greece; for the current story there came to be, that the first Bacchus was brought forth in consequence of a connexion on the part of his mother with the father of the gods, in the form of a "speckled snake."

...These wicked heretics avowedly worshipped the old serpent, or Satan, as the grand benefactor of mankind, for revealing to them the knowledge of good and evil. But this doctrine they had just brought along with them from the Pagan world, from which they had come, or from the Mysteries, as they came to be received and celebrated in Rome. Here, then, the grand secret of the Roman Empire is at last brought to light - viz., the real name of the tutelar divinity of Rome. That secret was most jealously guarded; insomuch that when Valerius Soranus, a man of the highest rank, and, as Cicero declares, "the most learned of the Romans," had incautiously divulged it, he was remorselessly put to death for his revelation.

If any one thinks it incredible that Satan should thus be canonized by the Papacy in the Dark Ages, let me call attention to the pregnant fact that, even in comparatively recent times, the Dragon - was worshipped by the Romanists of Poictiers under the name of "the good St. Vermine"!!!

Now, as the Pagan Pontifex, to whose powers and prerogatives the Pope had served himself heir, was thus the High-priest of Satan, so, when the Pope entered into a league and alliance with that system of Devil-worship, and consented to occupy the very position of that Pontifex, and to bring all its abominations into the Church, as he has done, he necessarily became the Prime Minister of the Devil, and, of course, came as thoroughly under his power as ever the previous Pontiff had been.

How exact the fulfillment of the Divine statement that the coming of the Man of Sin was to be "after the working or energy of Satan." Here, then, is the grand conclusion to which we are compelled, both on historical and Scriptural grounds, to come: As the mystery of godliness is God manifest in the flesh, so the mystery of iniquity is - so far as such a thing is possible - the Devil incarnate.

THE MAN OF SIN REVEALED

We have explored at length the Lord's need to warn His young church about the mind-bending truth that their greatest persecutors would beat them by becoming them. In place of Jesus Christ would sit the Anti-Christ! While John gave us the most information about him, the apostle Paul also warned of the enthronement of "the man of sin" who would sit in the "temple of God" showing himself to be God while exalting himself as Christ on earth. We are in debt to Martin Luther and others of the Reformation who, when reading the Biblical warnings, had eyes to see the signs. Scriptures such as this one:

2 Thessalonians 2:3 Let no man deceive you by any means: for [the Second Coming of Jesus Christ] shall not come, except there come a falling away first, and that man of sin be revealed, the son of perdition;

4 Who opposeth and exalteth himself above all that is called God, or that is worshipped; so that he as God sitteth in the temple of God, shewing himself that he is God.

5 Remember ye not, that, when I was yet with you, I told you these things?

Just what building did Paul have in mind when he said "sitting in the temple of God?" Paul also taught that in the christian church the *Body of Christ* was the ultimate temple. In ancient temple times, the Mercy Seat atop the Arc of the Covenant served as God's earthly throne. It was flanked by two golden cherubs.

Psalms 99:1 The Lord reigneth; let the people tremble: he sitteth between the cherubims; let the earth be moved.

John the Revelator left us this interesting clue:

Revelation 10:10 And the devil that deceived [men] was cast into the lake of fire and brimstone, where the beast and the false prophet are, and shall be tormented day and night for ever and ever.

11 And I saw a great white throne, and him that sat on it,...

Much of the secular-christian world is waiting for a pagan pseudo-christ to reign from a re-built temple in Jerusalem. What the ancient apostles are saying is that we should be on the look out for a man sitting within the body of Christ, claiming to be God upon a white throne flanked by golden cherubs, exalting himself in the place of Christ. See if these quotes from the horse's own mouth help:

"You know that I am the Holy Father, the representative of God on earth, the Vicar of Christ, which means that I Am God on the earth." - Pope Pius XI (Pope #259 1922-1939).

"The Pope is not simply the representative of Jesus Christ. On the contrary, he is Jesus Christ Himself, under the veil of the flesh." - Evangelical Christendom, January 1, 1895, pg. 15, London J. S. Phillips.

"The Pope is of so great dignity, and so exalted that he is not a mere man, but as it were God and the vicar of God." - Ferraris's Ecclesiastical Dictionary.

"The Pope and God are the same, so he has all power in Heaven and earth." - Pope Pius V, quoted in Barclay, XXVII:218, Cities Petrus Bertanous.

"Into this fold of Jesus Christ, no man may enter unless he be led by the Sovereign Pontiff; and only if they be united to him can men be saved, for the Roman Pontiff is the Vicar of Christ and His personal representative on earth." - Pope John XXIII in his homily to the Bishops and faithful at his coronation November 4, 1958.

"All names which in the Scriptures are applied to Christ, by virtue of which it is established that He is over the church, all the same names are applied to the Pope. - from On the Authority of the Councils II:17.

"Hence the Pope is crowned with a triple crown, as king of heaven and of earth and of the lower regions." - from Ferraris, Prompta Bibliotheca VI:26, Papa II, 1763.

"This is our last lesson to you: receive it, engrave it in your minds, all of you: by God's commandment salvation is to be found nowhere but in the [Roman] Church; the strong and effective instrument of salvation is none other than the Roman Pontificate." - Pope Leo XIII, Allocution 25th Anniversary of his election, February 20, 1903.

"The Pope is of such great authority and power that he can modify, explain, or interpret even divine laws... The Pope can modify divine law, since his power is not of man, but of God, and he acts as vicegerent of God upon earth." - Lucius Ferraris, Prompta Ribliotheca, Papa.

How about a few more to beat the horse to death:

"The Pope takes the place of Jesus Christ on earth... by divine right the Pope has supreme and full power in faith,... He is the true vicar, the head of the entire church, the father and teacher of all Christians. He is the infallible ruler, the founder of dogmas, the author of and the judge of councils; the universal ruler of truth, the arbiter of the world, the supreme judge of heaven and earth, the judge of all, being judged by no one, God himself on earth." - New York Catechism.

"God himself is obliged to abide by the judgment of his priest [the Pope]." - Liguori, Duties and Dignities of the Priest, p.27.

"The poor sinner kneels at his confessor's feet. He KNOWS he is not speaking to an ordinary man but to ANOTHER CHRIST. - William Doyle, Shall I be a Priest, p. 14.

"It is error to believe that Every man is free to embrace and profess that religion which, guided by the light of reason, he shall consider true." -Pope Pius IX, The Syllabus, 1864, Section III.

"No man has a right to choose his religion." - Catholic Bishop Hughes, Jan 26th 1852.

"Protestantism has not, and never can have, any right where Catholicity has triumphed." - Catholic Review, June 1875.

"It is error to believe that hence it has been wisely decided by law, in some Catholic countries, that persons coming to reside therein shall enjoy the public exercise of their own peculiar worship." - Pope Pius IX, The Syllabus 1864, Section X.

"Not the Creator of Universe, in Genesis 2:1-3,-but the Catholic Church can claim the honor of having granted man a pause to his work every seven days." - S. C. Mosna, Storia della Domenica, 1969, pp. 366-367.

"The Pope has the power to change times, to abrogate laws, and to dispense with all things, even the precepts of Christ. The Pope has the authority and often exercised it, to dispense with the command of Christ." - Decretal, de Tranlatic Episcop. Cap. Ferraris's Ecclesiastical Dictionary.

"The penetration of the religion of Babylon became so general and well known that Rome was called the New Babylon." - Cardinal Gibbons, Faith of our fathers 1917 ed., p. 106.

"In order to attach to Christianity great attraction in the eyes of the nobility, the priests adopted the outer garments and adornments which were used in pagan cults." - *Eusabius, Life of Constantine.*

"The popes filled the place of the vacant emperors at Rome, inheriting their power, their prestige, and their titles from Paganism." - *Stanley's History, p. 40.*

The decree set forth in the year 1229 A.D. by the Catholic Council of Valencia... places Bible on *The Index of Forbidden Books.* The doctrine withholds 'it is forbidden for laymen (that's you) to read the Old and New Testaments. - We forbid them most severely to have the above books in the popular vernacular. The lords of the districts shall carefully seek out the heretics in dwellings, hovels, and forests, and even their underground retreats shall be entirely wiped out.' - *Pope Gregory IX, Council Tolosanum, Anno. Chr. 1229.*

Pope Francis (born: Jorge Mario Bergogilo) sitting within the body of Christ, claiming to be God upon a white throne flanked by golden cherubs, exalting himself in the place of Christ. He is pope #266, and the first Jesuit to so sit.

Appendix D

Revelation as an
Old Testament Book

*The Old Testament is the New Testament concealed,
the New Testament is the Old Testament revealed.*
— *Sunday School saying*

There are more than 500 references to the *Old Testament* in the *Book of Revelation*.[142] The list here is therefore not a complete one. It is clear from these that John was both well read in regards to the scriptures of his day and that the Lord was using this book as a summation of all of the Law and the Prophets to date.

Cross referencing these will definitely add to your understanding of how scripture answers scripture. I have also included some of the Scriptures of the Restoration as well. This is how feasting is done. Add your own as you discover them.

Revelation 1:1: Daniel 2:28-29; D&C 88:79; v3: D&C34:7; v4: Isaiah 11:2; v5: Genesis 49:11, Psalm 89:27; D&C 77:5; v6: Exodus 19:6, Isaiah 61:6; D&C 76:50-60; v7: Daniel 7:13, Zechariah 12:10-14; D&C 45:49, 53; v8: Isaiah 41:4; v10: D&C 29:4; v12: Exodus 25:37, 37:23; v13: Daniel 7:13, 10:5,16; D&C 35:1, 38:1; v14: Daniel 7:9, 10:6; D&C 110:3; v15: Ezekiel 1:7, 24, 43:2, Daniel 10:6; D&C 110:3; 133:22; v16: Judges 5:31; Isaiah 49:2; v17: Isaiah 41:4; 44:6, 48:12, Daniel 8:17-18;10:9, 10, 12, 15, 19; v18: Job 3:17, Hosea 13:14.

Revelation 2:2: D&C 64:38-39; v4: Jeremiah 2:2; D&C 4:1-7; v7: Genesis 2:9, 3:22-24, Proverbs 11:30, 13:12, Ezekiel 31:8; v8: 1 Nephi 8:10-12; v10: D&C 6:13; 31:13; 20:14; v12: Isaiah 49:2; v14: Numbers 25:1-3; v17: Exodus 16:33-34, Isaiah 62:2, 65:15; D&C 130:10-11; v18: Dan 10:6; v20: I Kings 16:31-32, II Kings 9:7, 22; v23: Psalm 7:9, 26:2, 28:4; Jer 11:20, 17:10; v27: Psalm 2:7-9, Isaiah 30:14, Jeremiah 19:11; D&C 110:2-3.

Revelation 3:4: Ecclesiastes 9:8; v5: Exodus 32:32-33; v7: Isaiah 22:22; v9:Isaiah 43:4, 49:23, 60:14; v11: D&C 87:8; v12: Isaiah 62:2, Ezekiel 48:35; v14: Genesis 49:3, Deuteronomy 21:17; v18: Isaiah 55:1; v19: Proverbs 3:12; v20: 88:63; v21: D&C 6:30.

Revelation 4:1: Ezekiel 1:1; v4: D&C 77:5; v2: Isaiah 6:1, Ezekiel 1:26-28, Daniel 7:9; v3: Ezekiel 1:26, 28, 10:1; v5: Exodus 19:16, 25:37, Isaiah 11:2, Ezekiel 1:13; v6: Ezekiel 1:5, 18, 22, 26, 10:1, 12; D&C 77:1-2; v7: Ezekiel 1:10, 10:14; v8: Isaiah 6:2-3, Ezekiel 1:18; 10:12; v9: Deuteronomy 32:40, Daniel 4:34, 6:26, 12:7; v11: Genesis 1:1.

Revelation 5:1: Ezekiel 2:9-10; Daniel 12:4; D&C 77:6; v5: Genesis 49:9-10, Isaiah 11:1, 10; v6: Isaiah 11:2, Zechariah 3:8-9, 4:10; v8: Psalm 111:2, v9: Psalm 40:3, 98:1, 144:9, 149:1, Isaiah 42:10, Daniel 5:19; v10: Exodus 19:6, Isaiah 61:6; v11: Daniel 7:10.

Revelation 6:2: Zechariah 1:8, 6:3; v3: D&C 77:7; v4: Zech 1:8, 6:2; D&C 1:35; v5: Zech 6:2; v8: Jer 15:2-3, 24:10, 29:17, Ezekiel 14:21, Hosea 13:14, Zech 6:3; v9: D&C 135:7; v12: Isaiah 50:3, Joel 2:10; D&C 77:10; D&C 45:42; D&C 1:35; D&C 88:87; v13: Isaiah 34:4; v14: Isaiah 34:4, Nahum 1:5; v15: Psalm 48:4-6, Isaiah 2:10-12, 19; D&C 34:4; v16: Hosea 10:8; v17: Psalm 76:7, Jer 30:7, Nahum 1:6, Zephaniah 1:14-18, Malachi 3:2.

Revelation 7:1: Isaiah 11:2, Jeremiah 49:36, Ezekiel 7:2, 37:9, Daniel 7:2, Zechariah 6:5; D&C 77:8; v2: D&C 77:9; v3: Ezekiel 9:4-6; v4: Genesis 49:1-28; D&C 77:9-11; v9: Leviticus 23:40; v10: Psalm 3:8; v14: Genesis 49:11; 3 Nephi 27:19; v15: Leviticus 26:11; D&C 88:13; v16: Psalm 121:5-6, Isaiah 49:10; v17: Psalm 23:1-2; Ezekiel 34:23.

Revelation 8:1: D&C 77:13; v2: D&C 77:12; v3: Ps 141:2; v4: Ps 141:2; v5: Ezek 10:2,5-6; Ex 19:16; D&C 88:90; v7: Ex 9:23-24, Ps 18:13, Isa 28:2; D&C 77:12; v8: Ex 7:17-19; v10: Isaiah 14:12; v11: Jer 9:15, 23:15; v12: Isaiah 13:10; v13: D&C 88:92, 5:5.

Revelation 9:1: Isaiah 14:12-14; v2: Genesis 19:28, Exodus 19:8; v3: Exodus 10:12-15; v4: Ezekiel 9:4; v6: Job 3:21; v8: Joel 1:6; v9: Joel 2:5; v11: Job 26:6, 28:22, 31:12, Psalm 88:11, Proverbs 15:11; v14: Genesis 15:18, Deuteronomy 1:7, Joshua 1:4.

Revelation 10:1:Ezekiel 1:26-28; v4: Daniel 8:26, 12:4-9; v5: Deuteronomy 32:40, Daniel 12:7; D&C 88:110; v6: Genesis 1:1, Deuteronomy 32:40, Nehemiah 9:6, Daniel 12:17; v7: Amos 3:7; v9: Jeremiah 15:16, Ezekiel 2:8-33; v10: D&C 77:14; v11: Ezekiel 37:4, 9.

Revelation 11:1: Ezekiel 40:3-4, Zechariah 2:1-2; v2: Ezekiel 40:17-20; v4: Zechariah 4:1-3, 11-14; v5: Numbers 16:35, II Kings 1:10-12; v6: Exodus 7:19-25, I Kings 17:1; v:7: Exodus 7:3, 7, 8, 21; v8: Isaiah 1:9-10, 3:9, Jeremiah 23:14, Ezekiel 16:49, Ezekiel 23:3, 8, 19, 27; v9: Psalm 79:2-3; v11: Ezekiel 37:9-10; v15: Exodus 15:18, Daniel 2:44-45, 7:13-14, 27; v18: Psalm 2:1-3, 46:6, 115:13.

Revelation 12:1: Genesis 37:9-11; v2: Isaiah 26:17, 66:7, Micah 4:9-10; v3: Isaiah 27:1, Daniel 7:7, 20, 24; v4: Daniel 8:10; v5: Psalm 2:8-9, Isaiah 66:7; v7: Daniel 10:13, 21, 12:1; v9: Genesis 3:1, Job 1:6, 2:1, Zechariah 3:1; v10: Job 1:9-11, 2:4-5, Zechariah 3:1; v14: Exodus 19:4, Deuteronomy 32:11, Isaiah 40:31, Daniel 7:25, 12:7, Hosea 2:14-15, v15: Hosea 15:10; v17: Genesis 3:15.

Revelation 13:1: Daniel 7:3, 7, 8; v2: Daniel 7:4-6, 8; v3: Daniel 7:8; v4: Daniel 8:24; v5: Daniel 7:8, 11, 20, 25, 11:36; v7: Daniel 7:21; v8: Daniel 12:1; v10: Jeremiah 15:2, 43:11; v11: Daniel 8:3; v13: I Kings 1:9-12.

Revelation 14:1: Psalm 2:6, Ezekiel 9:4; v2: Ezekiel 1:24, 43:2; v3: Psalm 144:9; v7: Exodus 20:11; v8: Isaiah 21:9, Jeremiah 51:7-8; v10: Genesis 19:24, Psalm 75:8, Isaiah 51:17; v11: Isaiah 34:10, 66:24; v14: Daniel 7:13; v18: Joel 3:13; v19: Isaiah 63:1-6; v20: Joel 3:13.

Revelation 15:1: Leviticus 26:21; v3: Exodus 15:1-18, Deuteronomy 31:30-32:44, Psalm 92:5, Psalm 111:2, 139:14; v4: Psalm 86:9, Isaiah 66:23, Jeremiah 10:7; v5: Exodus

38:21; v6: Leviticus 26:21; v7: Jeremiah 25:15; v8: Exodus 40:34-35; Leviticus 26:21, I Kings 8:10-11, II Chronicles. 5:13-14; Isaiah 6:1-4.

Revelation 16:1 Psalm 79:6, Jeremiah 10:25, Ezekiel 22:31; v2: Exodus 9:9-11; Deuteronomy 28:35; v3: Exodus 7:17-25; v4: Exodus 7:17-21, Psalm 78:44; v5: Psalms 145:17; v6: Isaiah 49:26; v7: Psalms 19:9, 145:17; v10: Exodus 10:21-23; v12: Isaiah 11:15-16, 41:2, 25, 46:11, Jeremiah 51:36; v13: Exodus 8:6; v14: I Kings 22:21-23; v16: Judges 5:19, II Kings 23:29-30, II Chronicles 35:22, Zechariah 12:11; v19: Jeremiah 25:15; v21: Exodus 9:18-25.

Revelation 17:1: Jeremiah 51:13, Nahum 3:4; v2: Isaiah 23:17; v3: Daniel 7:7; v4: Jeremiah 51:7, Ezekiel 28:13; v8: Exodus 32:32-33, Daniel 12:1; v12: Daniel 7:24-25; v16: Leviticus 21:9.

Revelation 18:1: Ezekiel 43:2; v2: Isaiah 21:9, 34:13-15, Jeremiah 50:30, 51:37; v3: Jeremiah 51:7; v4: Isaiah 52:11, Jeremiah 50:8, 51:6, 45; v5: Jeremiah 41:9; v6: Psalm 137:8, Jeremiah 50:15, 29; v7: Isaiah 47:7-8, Zephaniah 2:15; v8: Isaiah 47:9, Jeremiah 50:31-32; v9-19: Ezekiel 26:16-18, 27:26-31; v9: Jeremiah 50:46; v10: Isaiah 13:1; v12: Ezekiel 27:12-25; v20: Jeremiah 51:48; v21: Jeremiah 51:63-64; v22: Isaiah 24:8, Jeremiah 25:10, Ezekiel 26:13; v23: Jeremiah 7:34, 16:9, 25:10, Nahum 3:4.

Revelation 19:2: Deuteronomy 32:43, Psalm 119:137, Jeremiah 51:48; v3: Isaiah 34:9-10, Jeremiah 51:48; v5: Psalms 22:23; 134:1; 135:1; v6: Psalms 93:1, 97:1, Ezekiel 1:24, 43:2, Daniel 10:6; v11: Psalm 18:10, 45:3-4, Isaiah 11:4-5, Ezekiel 1:1; v13: Isaiah 63:3; v15: Psalm 2:8-9, Isaiah 11:4, 63:3-6; v16: Deuteronomy 10:17; v17: Isaiah 34:6-7, Ezekiel 39:17; v18: Isaiah 34:6-7, Ezekiel 39:18; v19: Psalms 2:2, Joel 3:9-11; v20: Isaiah 30:33, Daniel 7:11; v21: Ezekiel 39:19-20.

Revelation 20:2: Genesis 3:1, 13-14, Isaiah 24:21-22; v4: Daniel 7:9, 22, 27; 12:2; v5: Isaiah 26:14; v6: Exodus 19:6, Isaiah 26:19; v8: Ezekiel 38:2, 39:1, 6; v9: Deuteronomy 23:14, II Kings 1:9-12, Ezekiel 38:22, 39:6; v11: Daniel 2:35; v12: Exodus 32:32-33, Psalms 62:12, 69:28, Daniel 7:10; v15: Exodus 32:32-33, Daniel 12:1.

Revelation 21:1: Isaiah 65:17, 66:22; v3: Leviticus 26:11-12, Ezekiel 37:27; v4: Isaiah 25:8, 35:10, 51:11, 65:19; v9: Leviticus 26:21; v10: Ezekiel 40:2; v11: Isaiah 60:1-2, Ezekiel 43:2; v12-13: Ezekiel 48:31-34; v15: Ezekiel 40:3, 5; v19-20: Exodus 28:17-20, Isaiah 54:11-12; v23: Isaiah 60:19-20; v24: Isaiah 60:3-5, 16; v25: Isaiah 60:11, Zechariah 14:7; v26: Isaiah 60:5, 16; v27: Isaiah 52:1, Ezekiel 44:9, Zechariah 14:21.

Revelation 22:1: Psalm 46:4, Ezekiel 47:1, Zechariah 14:8; v2: Genesis 2:9, 3:22-24, Ezekiel 47:12; v3: Genesis 3:17-19, Zechariah 14:11; v4: Psalm 17:15, Ezekiel 9:4; v5: Isaiah 60:19, Daniel 7:18, 22, 27, Zechariah 14:7 22:10, Daniel 8:26, 12:4, 9 v11: Ezekiel 3:27, Daniel 12:10; v12: Psalm 62:12, Isaiah 40:10, 62:11; v13: Isaiah 44:6; v14: Genesis 2:9, 3:22-24, Proverbs 11:30; v15: Deuteronomy 23:18; v18-19: Deuteronomy 4:2, 12:32; v19: Deuteronomy 29:19-20.

About this Series

If you would like to be notified when future volumes are available, send an email to Randallco@mac.com and let us know. Don't worry we'll keep your contact information private.

Volume 1: Daniel & The Last Days

Volume 2: Jonah and the Great Plan of Happiness

Volume 3: Ruth & the Saviours on Mount Zion

Volume 4: Zechariah & the Teachers of Righteousness

Volume 5: Ezekiel & the Millennial Reign of Christ

This is Volume 6: Revelation & the Mark of the Beast

Volume 7 will be Genesis & the Sons of the Morning (part 1)

Volume 8 will be Genesis & the Everlasting Covenant (part 2)

Volume 9 will be Genesis & the House Divided (part 3)

Volume 10 will be Genesis (part 4)

Supplemental Feasts include:

Ezra & the Great Assembly

Gad the Seer & the Corruption of the Covenant

The Testimonies of the Sons of Israel & the Message of the Plates of Brass

Available at GospelFeastBooks.com.

Additional Books by the Author:

Tell Me the Story of Joseph (Standard & Deluxe Editions)

Photograph Found: A Concise History of the Joseph Smith Daguerreotype

The Atonement of Jesus Christ (illustrated)

American History Stories you Never Read in School (Vols. 1&2)

Dore's Wandering Jew. Legend speaks of an ancient Jew who witnessed the death of the Lord Jesus and still wanders the Earth until the end. We know that one great Jew, John the Belovéd, is doing just that! I want to meet him.

Notes

[1] see *Joseph Smith's Inspired Version* of these verses for more.

[2] They had a third sister named Anna as well. We don't know of any brothers in the family.

[3] This was most likely a comet, called one of the "hosts of heaven" by the Lord.

[4] Mary, John's aunt went into hiding with Elisabeth. It's impossible that her sister Salome didn't know this.

[5] Satan would use this same tactic of utilizing the State and money to infiltrate Christianity after the death of the Apostles. Much of the New Testament warns that the pseudo-christs were on the rise. The Herods were of Esau, as were the Caesars through the blood of Zepho, the son of Eliphaz, the son of Esau. In our day Satan is using the Luciferiains (who call themselves the Illuminati) to do the same. They are part of the clan of Edom through "Chief Magdiel." see *Genesis 36:43* and *1 Chronicles 1:54*. They took over Italy in the days of Joseph of Egypt under Zepho. We are going to see more and more of them soon.

[6] Many suspect that this wedding was actually Jesus's wedding. It has been suggested that He was married to both Martha and Mary of Bethany, so this may have been His marriage to one or both of these ladies. The Catholic desire to make Jesus unmarried poses a problem. In Jewry this would have labeled Him as both a sinner and unfit to minister. He was never accused of this by His countrymen and He would have been if they could have used it against Him.

[7] Some still question that John was referring to himself when he used the term the "disciple whom Jesus loved." They are wrong. He was. They miss John's closing words where he defines the term as belonging to him. See *John 21:20-25*. Sometimes this confusion is done to try and suggest that there was a secret 13th woman apostle. There wasn't.

[8] Irenaeus (/aɪrə'niːəs/; Greek: Εἰρηναῖος) (late 2nd century – died c. A.D. 202), also referred to as Saint Irenaeus, was Bishop of Lugdunum in Gaul, then a part of the Roman Empire (now Lyon, France). He was an early Church Father and apologist, and his writings were formative in the early development of Christian theology. A resident of Smyrna, he heard the preaching of St. Polycarp, a disciple of St. John the Evangelist.

[9] Eusebius, *Ecclesiastical History* 23:104-107.

[10] The matter relating to the Three Nephites was this: The morning that the Army of Governor Boggs attempted to come into Far West and exterminate the Mormons, Joseph the Prophet stood with the brethren behind the breast works so hastily thrown up in the night and remarked, as they were sweeping and swarming towards the beloved city, that if they came beyond a certain place, we would open fire upon them. The army did come on to near the spot designated, when on a sudden, they all turned and ran pell-mell back to their camp, in great fright, declaring they saw too many thousands of soldiers to think of attacking the city. Joseph told Brother James Bird, "that he saw between them and the mob one of the Three Nephites, with a drawn sword, before he made the remark about opening fire upon them. When the mob had returned he saw the Three Nephites near the same place armed for battle." Joseph Smith said "...I am willing to state that the names of the Three Nephites who do not sleep in the earth are Jeremiah, Zedekiah and Kumenonhi." see *History of Oliver B. Hungtinton, p.5 and Oliver B. Huntington's Diaries and Journals Vol. 2 pg. 20*

[11] On July 14th 1777, an Act of the Continental Congress endorsed its adoption; thus our second flag (sometimes called the "Betsy Ross" flag) took its place. He said that the adopted "5 pointed star represented the promise of greater spiritual power yet to come." This flag is today a much beloved ensign of the American People. The American Flag is the only national flag in the world which the people own the copyright. Not incidentally, a 5-pointed star is considered "the star of Jehovah's Grace" in Jewish mystical thinking. Grace is indeed a promise of greater things to come.

[12] The original article is entitled: "Who was the Mystery Man in Independence Hall?"

[13] Quoted from the learned Manly P. Hall "The Secret Destiny of America," pp. 147-172 First Ed.

[14] The Continental Congress at Philadelphia, so far as records go, had nothing to do with the destinies of the original flag. The flag unfurled at Cambridge, Massachusetts on January 2nd 1776 symbolized the Union of the Colonies. It was called the "Grand Union Flag." This Union Jack and thirteen stripe flag was also hoisted over our navy by John Paul Jones on December 3rd 1775. Prior to January 2nd 1776, Washington had prepared a very high flag staff at Cambridge, Massachusetts. On this date Washington in person hoisted this "Grand Union," or "Cambridge flag." The English army standing at a distance observed that it was "English still," and they too, with the American Army, saluted it with thirteen guns.

[15] There is a peak just north of Salt Lake City that holds important meaning to members of the Church. This is how it came by its name. After the death of Joseph Smith, when it seemed as if every trouble and calamity had come upon the Saints, Brigham Young, who was President of the Twelve, then the presiding Quorum of the Church, sought the Lord to know what they should do, and where they should lead the people for safety. While they were fasting and praying daily on this subject, President Young had a vision of Joseph Smith, who showed him the mountain that we now call Ensign Peak, immediately north of Salt Lake City. There was an ensign upon that peak, and Joseph said, "Build under the point where the colors fall and you will prosper and have peace." The Pioneers had no pilot or guide, none among them had ever been in the country or knew anything about it. However, they travelled under the direction of President Young until they reached this valley. When they entered it, President Young pointed to the point and said, "I want to go there." He went up to the point and said, "This is Ensign Peak. Now, brethren, organize your exploring parties, so as to be safe from Indians; go and explore where you will, and you will come back every time and say this is the best place." They accordingly started out exploring and visited what we now call Cache, Malad, Tooele, and Utah valleys, and other parts of the country in various directions, but all came back and declared this was the best spot. When Brigham Young climbed Ensign Peak, he took some of the brethren with him. Upon the same peak he raised a replica of the ensign that Joseph Smith held across the valley. Don Maguire, in his Diaries and Memoirs, described the flag that Brigham flew. "The so-called flag of the stars and stripes placed there (on Ensign Peak) was a flag having in its upper left-hand corner a blue field with a circle of twelve white stars and in the center a large white star. The stripes on that flag, instead of being red and white stripes, were blue and white stripes..." Brigham raised this flag for the world to know that the Saints of God had found the place where they could worship God as they pleased. Many over the years have accused Brigham of wanting to leave the United States and form his own nation. Although it is true that the Brethren left this option open, it was not their first choice. When President Young and the Saints established the Constitution of Deseret, the forerunner of the Utah State Constitution, they stated in the Preamble that the Deseret Constitution would function in the valley, "until the Congress of the United States should otherwise provide for the Government of the Territory hereinafter named and described by admitting us into the Union." People have commented on the striking similarities between the Flag of the United States and the Mormon Ensign. See *JD 13:85-86* too.

[16] see *Job 24 & 30* which describes some of these cave people in Job's day.

[17] Biblical Archeologist Ron Wyatt found evidence that Jesus was actually 6' 4" based on the Garden Tomb. A thanks to Fred Jepson for reminding me of this.

[18] The word chiasmus comes from the Greek letter chi (X). It symbolizes the top-to-bottom mirror image pattern of the poem.

[19] see *1 Nephi 19:23*.

[20] see the *History of the Church* 5:267 for more on this matter.

[21] see *Amos 3:7.*

[22] I am indebted to Mark Pedersen for first pointing this out to me.

[23] from a discourse by the Prophet as recorded by Thomas Bullock, as found in *Words of Joseph Smith*, pp. 378-381.

[24] As a side note for those interested in the Tsabim, one of the greatest, most visible feature of the Planet Jupiter is his swirling clouds. As one digs deeper, one continues to find these things holding together in surprising ways. Clouds also bring the thunder (a voice like a trumpet) and lightning (the arrows of Jah-Zeus). See what I mean? Interesting, no? See *Vol. 5: Ezekiel for more on this.*

[25] In celestial thinking, a girdle (really a slash or cord around the waist) is a sign of Heavenly Mother. In terms of our relationship to God the Father, who is the Father(s) of all things, the Elohim (plural) of all life, it is our connection to Him via Heavenly Mother that makes us special. It is she that makes you and me (and Jesus Christ) God's *children*, as opposed to His *creation*. A man's chest is his El Shaddai. Gold is glory. So here the picture is of the Son of God, born of the Chosen Mother, filled with great strength and glory.

[26] see *Job 38.*

[27] Wait a minute! Until Pluto was, and then wasn't, a planet again, the Earth sat among Mercury, Venus, Mars, Jupiter, Saturn, Uranus and Neptune. That is 7 planets? How could the ancients have possibly known this? *See Vol. 5: Ezekiel.*

[28] As well as *pineal gland-sodomy*, symbolized in antiquity by the pine cone from which the gland is named, this type of ritual was believed *to force a rebirth into the family* of whatever flavor of the month Lucifer was using at the time.

[29] Saint Antipas was ordained bishop of Pergamum by John around 92 A.D. He was cooked alive by order of Emperor Domitian in a brass, bull-shaped, altar-cauldron. He had dared to cast out several powerful demons who were worshipped in the city by the power of the priesthood. The Eastern Orthodox Church still honors him on April 11th every year.

[30] The ancients felt that the reins, specifically the kidneys (but also the broader region of the loins) were the seat of human strength, prowess, power, desire and affection. Today we assign these to the heart, but consider the logic here: A man in fear might "wet" himself. A man in love might feel a stirring in his loins. A man preparing for battle will strap a gun or sword to his waist. One's heart today only really pounds in fear. Satan teaches that the heart is the seat of man's *manna*. Luciferians eat hearts or cut them out to own a victim's soul.

[31] see *Acts 16:14-15.* She is considered the first documented convert to Christianity in Europe. The Greek Orthodox honor the site of her baptism with a garden chapel.

[32] In this they are as the *Mark of the Beast*, determining who can buy and sell. Buying and selling is a right given of God not man. Thus these types of restrictions are inherently luciferian.

[33] from *The Evening and Morning Star*, March 1834, p. 144.

[34] So many secular-christians are hypocrites. They scoff and mock Joseph Smith and his teachings of the Restoration, but note here carefully, the Lord Himself uses *Amen, Amun, Amon* as one of His ancient names. Joseph taught that once all these ancient faiths had the truth but corrupted it. When you see some similarities of ancient truths in Mormonism, you had better know that they are there because they have been restored in their truth. God had them first!

[35] Translation of *Colossians 4:17*.

[36] see *D&C 88*.

[37] There are other lists too, but Michael, Gabriel, Raphael and Uriel are almost always on the list, in that order.

[38] It was one of the elders who testified of this. We have just such a gift every 6 months in General Conference with our special witnesses.

[39] Joseph Smith would say that these 7 eyes and horns should have been written *12 eyes and horns* and were symbols of the Lord's Apostles who function as His special witnesses and eyes on earth. Seven works in this case because it matches the 7 heads of the dispensations, one for each seal. But as I learned long ago, "When in doubt, go with Joseph." He always ends up being right in the end.

[40] see *Psalms 22:30*.

[41] from a discourse by the Prophet on April 7th 1844 as remembered by Thomas Bullock, William Clayton, Willard Richards and Wilford Woodruff who were all in attendance. I have combined their various recollections here.

[42] see *Teachings of the Prophet Joseph Smith*, pg. 291.

[43] from a discourse of the Prophet as recorded by William Clayton, Franklin D. Richards and Willard Richards on April 8th 1843.

[44] from a discourse of the Prophet as recorded by Willard Richards on April 2nd 1843.

[45] from a discourse of the Prophet as recorded by Thomas Bullock on June 16th 1844.

[46] see *Gospel Feast Vol. 3: Ruth & the Saviours on Mount Zion*.

[47] Hence the importance (and blessing) of a priesthood declaration on one's behalf *that you have been freed from the blood and sins of your generation*.

⁴⁸ Eight was all that was worthy! When the granddaughters of Noah chose Mahanistic husbands over the priesthood sons of God, the Lord was done with the Old World.

⁴⁹ Now you understand why Joseph Smith would say that it was his "testimony last of all." It is my opinion that had Oliver Cowdery stayed firm through the Nauvoo years he would have been offered up at Carthage as well, instead of Hyrum. For the importance of these statements see *Vol. 1: Daniel.*

⁵⁰ The original name of the Dome of the Rock during the early Muslim era was, Qubbat al-Sakhrah, and "Beit al Maqdis" بيت المقدس — or "Beit Hamikdash" in Hebrew, in English "the Jewish Temple". Many early documents and a dedicatory plaque above a mihrab-prayer niche inside an active mosque in the village of Nuba, located 7 miles north-west of Hebron, confirm this. An increasing amount of researchers are discovering that in the early Muslim era the Dome of the Rock was the site of worship services that were influenced by the ceremonies of the Jerusalem Temple: cleansing, incense, anointing the Foundation Stone with oil and surrounding it with curtains inspired by the divine parochet. The current shrine, built around the Foundation Stone, just like the two Jewish Temples, was completed in 691 A.D., by an architect named Yazid Ibn Salam, who was either Jewish himself or had Jewish aides. Evidence is suggesting that Umayyad Caliph Abd al-Malik originally had the Dome of the Rock built as a shrine for the Jews, while Al Aqsa, the mosque on the southern end of the Temple Mount, was built for Muslims. These two buildings being a sign of peace between them. However, today's trend is for the Muslims to refer to the entire Temple Mount compound, the al-Haram ash-Sharif ("The Noble Compound"), as Al Aqsa, saying that the whole was always just for them.

⁵¹ see http://www.nature.com/articles/srep01655 (as of this publication date.)

⁵² see *Annals of Geophysics,* Vol. 48, No. 3, June 2005. *The historical earthquakes of Syria: an analysis of large and moderate earthquakes from 1365 B.C. to 1900 A.D.* by Mohamed Reda Sbeinati, Ryad Darawcheh and Mikhail Mouty of the Department of Geology, Atomic Energy Commission of Syria, Damascus, Syria and The Department of Geology, Faculty of Science, Damascus University, Damascus, Syria.

⁵³ Scholars of that generation say that the Chicago Fire was actually caused by the tail of a comet. What is less well known is there were fires all throughout the midwest that night, but Chicago suffered the worst of it.

⁵⁴ Jewish tradition suspects that this is Gabriel. See *Ezekiel & the Millennial Reign of Christ* for more. I think Mormons would lean more to Elijah (aka Raphael).

⁵⁵ from a discourse by the Prophet as witnessed by William Clayton, Martha Jane Coray and Franklin D. Richards on August 13th 1843.

⁵⁶ Remember that it is God's right alone to count His children. King David got into terrible trouble when he took a census without the Lord's permission. See *Gad the Seer*, a supplemental feast in our series.

⁵⁷ Joseph was heir for three reasons. First, Jacob had contracted to marry Rachel but got Leah by chicanery. Joseph was Rachel's firstborn son. Second, Reuben lost his place as eldest through adultery. But the third reason is the most important, the birthright was Jacob's to give. Just as Isaac gave it to Jacob over Esau and Abraham gave it to Isaac over Ishmael. Jacob gave it to Joseph.

⁵⁸ This commentary is not precisely accurate but will suffice for this study. See the *Gospel Feast Supplemental Book: The Testimony of the Sons of Israel* for a more accurate study.

⁵⁹ Hence Moses's veil and the addition of the Red Heifer into Levitical Temple worship. You will also note that when the Lord tells Moses about the orgy on the valley below, He says, "YOUR people have sinned." God offers to kill them all and start the Tribes over under Moses. Moses intercedes on their behalf and thus becomes a model of our future advocate with the Father, our Jesus Christ. Our feast on *Exodus* with explore this and the Aaronic verses Levitical Priesthood too. See *The Testimony of the Sons of Israel* for more as well.

⁶⁰ Some have confused this term silence to mean that the heavens would be shut. It does not mean this. It means that the wrath of the heavens, the promised judgement which should have opened the Millennial Day, would not occur with the opening of the calendar. The much awaited ripping apart of the sky, so to speak, by the angels waiting to do it, would not happen until 1/2 hour into the Millennium had transpired.

⁶¹ It is our understanding that Enoch's City will return and be placed into the *Gulf of Mexico*. This will force the ocean water into the *Louisiana Purchase lands*.

⁶² https://science.nasa.gov/science-news/science-at-nasa/2009/04feb_greencomet/

⁶³ How's your water storage? Also store a gallon of bleach. 8 drops of bleach can sanitize 1 gallon of clear water for drinking in an emergency.

⁶⁴ Luciferians worship the sun as a sign of the lightbringer, one of the names of Satan. You will remember that he drew away 1/3 of the sons of God in the War of Heaven. This punishment of the sun by 1/3 is most likely a pre-warning of what is coming for all the cults of Satan in the world today.

⁶⁵ *Helel ben Shaḥar* means *day-star*, or *son of the dawn*. It is associated with the planet **Venus**, one of the brightest celestial bodies at night. It can also be seen in the early morning when no other star can be seen. It appears to hang as *though thrown from heaven* in the sky. It vanishes when the sun, the real light, rises. It was seen as a sign of Lucifer, who fell in the night and will be completely out matched by the light of the Son of God - Jesus Christ. *See the next footnote.*

[66] This name is a bit of an enigma. I believe that it is an Angelization of *apollymi* which actually means *to destroy* in Greek. Christian Greeks liked to call Apollo (the lightbringer) as in the pagan god of the sun. This then is a worldplay that the great lightbringer of pagan praise was actually a destroyer. Lucifer wants to be the source of light but he is actually the one who ruins everything he touches. *See the previous footnote.*

[67] see *Ezekiel and the Millennial Reign of Christ*, Vol. 5 of the *Gospel Feast Series* for a lengthy discussion of this topic.

[68] This may be Prince David foretold. David Ben Gurion was the first great leader of the newly established State of Israel. He led them in their first war. His last name means; "Son of the lion" or "the lion's cub." The lion is the royal emblem of David's tribe and house. It is possible to read David Ben Gurion's name as the *little royal David*. A man that is royal but smaller than the King is a prince, thus Prince David.

[69] These demons are known as "strong men" and they enter humans in extreme moments of fear brought on through ritual and ritualistic torture. Only the enmity of Elohim keeps them in check. Without even this, they will rage!

[70] The secular-christian answer to these questions is tied up in the apocryphal *Book of Enoch* and the story of the *Watchers*. It strongly appears that Joseph Smith didn't believe the story, although in general, only Mormonism's doctrine can accommodate it. We will explore the Watchers when we study *Genesis part 1* together in Volume 7 of our series.

[71] as recalled by O. B. Huntington in his private journal.

[72] You should know this by now. Go back and look it up in *Daniel & the Last Days*, if you don't remember.

[73] I owe a debt to Mark Pedersen who first pointed out this angel's connection to Noah. It makes a lot of sense for a variety of reasons. One in particular is *D&C 77:9*. Noah and Elijah are always connected in some way that is not particularly clear but of which I will offer this opinion; Noah is Elias.

[74] *Godly Mysteries* always refer to the gifts of the Temple. I suspect this verse is saying what Elder McConkie taught: Once you reach a certain point on the straight and narrow path of Christ, you reach your calling and election made sure. There is no falling off the path when you reach a certain milestone.

[75] Not all of these tales are faltering. Many say this wandering Jew was forced to endure the pains of life as a punishment. I suspect that these are later inventions made up by Catholics and Muslims to believe that their churches are destined to replace the mission of the Jews. I suspect that the greater truth lies in the sources and stories herein quoted.

[76] Perhaps we would say "through the right side" if we spoke Hebrew.

⁷⁷ see *Zechariah 2:1-5*. Our John is often symbolically "the beloved young man" since he was a teenager when he was called to be the Lord's apostle.

⁷⁸ Remember that Nephi also was given a glimpse of John the Beloved and his Latter-day mission when he received his amazing vision recored for us in *1 Nephi 14:27*.

⁷⁹ I am aware of D&C 77:15 *Q. What is to be understood by the two witnesses, in the eleventh chapter of Revelation? A. They are two prophets that are to be raised up to the Jewish nation in the last days, at the time of the restoration, and to prophesy to the Jews after they are gathered and have built the city of Jerusalem in the land of their fathers.* I always say, "When in doubt, go with Joseph Smith." My question to those who read this to say that these two prophets are modern men and not Moses & Elijah is this. Are you sure that the term raised up here means that they were born in modern times? What if this raising up means being prepared for a mission or saved for such a purpose? Also what does it mean "at the time of the restoration?" If we assume it means the Restoration of the Gospel then when did it happen? The Jews have rebuilt the city of Jerusalem, not the Temple, but the city. No, I suspect that there is more going on here than simple words allow. I think this is one of those instances where the Lord is purposefully being vague for a wise purpose which will some day be clear to us. But, either way is fine.

⁸⁰ Joseph Smith explained that Moses did not die as the *Bible* says but that he said his goodbyes to the children of Israel and walked away from them. They assumed that he died because he was never seen again. This is why the scripture says that the Lord buried him, "but no man knoweth of his sepulchre unto this day." When the Lord buries you, you are taken like Elijah was. It is amazing to me that Joseph Smith said this and we discover that the Jews also have such a tradition but don't know how to sync it up with *Deuteronomy 34:6*.

⁸¹ Current Luciferians teach that they will beat Jesus and take the Earth for theirs. Lucifer knows he is lying to them, they will discover it too late.

⁸² This is not a typo and it is plural. A *Basileus* is a Greek term and title that means *king* or *emperor*. It was used by the Byzantine emperors, and has a long history of use by sovereigns and other persons of authority in Greece.

⁸³ When the city of Zion fled, and hung above the Earth for a time, as it slowly ascended in the heavens, it was bright like our moon is today. This was the start of our earthly notion that the moon is feminine. Zion is the bride. She was the first moon we knew, just as Saturn was our first sun.

⁸⁴ When one of the Lord's Holy Temples are thus adorned, in sunstones, moonstones, and starstones, it is symbolic of Lady Zion. see *Genesis part 1*.

⁸⁵ see the *Gospel Feast Vol. 1: Daniel & the Last Days* for an extensive exploration of these topics.

[86] Hebraic tradition holds that none of God's daughters fought against Him in the War of Heaven. While not official doctrine, it is said that at the creation of our spirits, God made an equal number of Sons and Daughters. When 1/3 of the Sons of God were cast out with Satan for rebellion, this left an imbalance in the family. Too many daughters and not enough sons. Since the man is not without the woman and vice versa, the institution of polygamy was permitted under the priesthood to save God's daughters from reproach and ruin. We will know for sure some day if this is true or not, but at least you know what the ancients thought about it.

[87] The KJV reads *days*, but Joseph Smith said that *days* here should be translated as *years*.

[88] Satan means *Enemy*. It is a truthful title and Satan being a liar doesn't like to be exposed. His real name in heaven was Helel, but when he fell he lost his -el ending. This is where we get the name "Hell" for him. Lucifer is Hel in Latin. Both mean "light-bringer." Apparently his job in heaven was the same as Hermes, the winged foot messenger of God. We might call him the former Executive Secretary of the Godhead.

[89] There are inhabiters in the sea? What? For those of you who have read Vol 2: *Jonah and the Great Plan of Happiness*, you know what I'm talking about. Didn't I tell you, "once you see it, it's everywhere."

[90] They have a Luciferian General Conference every 27 years. At that time Lucifer appears as an angel of light, accepts their sacrifices, rants and rails, and gives them their next set of marching orders for total World Domination. *Sieg Heil, comrade, dude (or whatever is the stupid new one this month.)*

[91] We will soon see that the Lord will be dressed in red at His coming battle. The Luciferians, who have everything screwed up, will attempt to call our Red adorned Lord on His war chariot, the red dragon who has come to attack their Great White Brotherhood, but they have the roles reversed. The Red here is the Lord dressed for righteous war, while their white are the sepulchers filled with dead men's bones.

[92] But they could not protect us from what the Lord called "the hearts of men in our own land." When the books are opened, and we see the traitors, we will be astonished.

[93] In the year 1820 A.D. — the same year the Joseph Smith received the First Vision — Thomas Jefferson wrote this astonishing statement in a letter to his friend, Mr. F. A. van der Kemp. Mormons love the Founding Fathers of America, seeing them as inspired leaders, despite their human foibles. Later when Joseph Smith needed a word to call the subdivisions of a *Stake* in Mormondom, he chose *ward* in honor of Thomas Jefferson. Jefferson had said that in America we needed a new word for congregations that showed the world that we were not the Old World with her old ways but the New World. He suggested *wards*. We needed a word and so Joseph used it. Now you know.

⁹⁴ As a curiosity, make a study of how many times *devil, Satan* and *Lucifer* appear in the *Bible*. It will become shockingly apparent that considering he is our greatest enemy, he has been almost completely removed from the *Bible*. Why? You will discover with a little searching that he was removed on purpose.

⁹⁵ from a discourse by the Prophet on April 8th 1843 as remembered by William Clayton.

⁹⁶ If you are starting to get the Eastern Thinking lessons I keep shoving on you, you will understand it. Priesthood is the male force of motion and protection. A male animal protects his own and carves out his space with his horns. Thus, here they are a sign of his authority and priesthood. It's a paradigm shift I understand, but it's a richly rewarding one if you are willing to shift there. Wait until you read Isaiah and understand him!

⁹⁷ This is nothing new. The Jews cried for a sign and Isaiah said, "Here is one then: a virgin shall give birth to the Son of God and He will dwell among us." They didn't want that sign, so they went back to worshiping idols. Today secular-christians cry the same and the Lord said, "I will give you a book from the dust!" And they won't read it, but instead go back to their modern idols and football leagues. Adulterers seek after signs. To the Lord adulterers are also idol worshipers. Here we see that's true.

⁹⁸ Note: Although Rev. William Miller was convinced of his Second Coming calculations by 1818, he continued to study privately until 1823 to ensure the correctness of his interpretation. In September 1822, Miller formally stated his conclusions in a twenty-point document, saying: "I believe that the second coming of Jesus Christ is near, even at the door, even within twenty-one years, — on or before 1843." Miller did not, however, begin his public lecturing until the first Sunday of August 1831. In 1832 he submitted 16 articles to the *Vermont Telegraph*, a Baptist newspaper. Soon Miller was " flooded with letters of inquiry respecting my views; and visitors flocked to converse with me on the subject." In 1834, unable to personally comply with many of the urgent requests for information and the invitations to come in person, he published a synopsis of his teachings in a 64-page tract called, *Evidence from Scripture and History of the Second Coming of Christ, about the Year 1844: Exhibited in a Course of Lectures*. The Saints in Joseph's day became aware of Miller's views and had questions. See *Gospel Feast Vol 1: Daniel & the Last Days* for a lengthy discussion of Miller and what it all meant to Mormons.

⁹⁹ see *D&C 77*.

¹⁰⁰ Hilarious! How many are really saved then? If these are not really saved by their own logic, are any of them really saved? Easy for me to answer that one for them. This is why they search for signs, get it? They have no comforter.

¹⁰¹ Now you know why the Gift of the Holy Ghost is also called a confirmation. The companionship of the Holy Ghost confirms the covenant within your soul (the peace of his presence) and in heaven since he alone can dwell both in you and above. His stamp of approval is as a *seal*, confirming the covenant.

¹⁰² We can take this one decree further and state symbolically that Satan's beguiling of Eve to bite the apple of death is the same as the poison of Satan's lie infecting the body. It was the bite of the forbidden fruit that started the seed of death, the poison or the blood, to enter our human parents. Thus symbolically they were bitten by the serpent's venom. Think eastern and it works. John, the mystic poet, would have loved it!

¹⁰³ Study the traitor Woodrow Wilson, Jacob Schiff and the founding of America's Federal Reserve Banking System. You will learn way more than you want to about Lucifer and evil banking schemas.

¹⁰⁴ The *Book of Ezekiel* contains an amazing threshing event, starting literally at the Lord's House. It is well worth your restudy as it is a model for a global event which we may soon see in the flesh.

¹⁰⁵ There are some old texts which say that the Number of the Beast is really 616. This typo began while John was still alive. He and men like Polycarp worked to correct it during their lifetimes, so we know that 616 is wrong. It is 666.

¹⁰⁶ Again, I owe this insight to Mark Pedersen who went further than I dared. He suspects that these boys who had died before the age of eight, or were murdered in the womb by their mothers, make up the Lord's personal guard, protecting Him and attending Him until the day they can be resurrected and gain most of what was lost to them in the Millennium. Joseph Smith taught that righteous parents would be given their lost children back to raise. It is also inferred that many other willing and worthy parents will be given other children to raise in joy and love during the Millennial peace of Christ. It will be a grand time of happiness and family for those willing to embrace it.

¹⁰⁷ from a discourse by the Prophet on October 5th 1840 as remembered by Robert B. Thompson.

¹⁰⁸ from a discourse by the Prophet on March 20th 1842 as remembered by Wilford Woodruff.

¹⁰⁹ see *Zechariah 14:9-11.*

¹¹⁰ The Prophet Joseph's full quote reads: *We understand that the work of gathering together of the wheat into barns, or garners, is to take place while the tares are being bound over, and preparing for the day of burning; that after the day of burnings, the righteous shall shine forth like the sun, in the Kingdom of their Father. Who hath ears to hear, let him hear.*

¹¹¹ Go back and read Vol 3: *Ruth & the Saviours on Mount Zion*, because I am not going to tell you. You're a good eastern student now. You can do this. A Jewish trumpet is an animal's horn and a vial is nothing but a bowl by another name. If we were playing charades, how would you make a horn sign? If you wanted to make a bowl, what would it look like? What do you get when you put a male horn and a female bowl together? (*1 Corinthians 11:12-12*). *Oh, I guess I ended up telling you after all. Read Ruth anyway. It's good stuff.*

[112] by Henry U. Onderdonk, (1789-1858) and Joseph Martin Kraus, (1756-1792). 1985 LDS Hymnal.

[113] See the supplemental *Gospel Feast: Gad the Seer* for this story.

[114] Symbolically, Whore Babylon has pretended to be Lady Zion. A whore is a poisoned bride, so these symbols are more than appropriate here.

[115] see *Exodus 7:20*.

[116] re-read *Vol 5: Ezekiel & the Millennial Reign of Christ, chapter 6.*

[117] Rabbi Eliezer Ben Jacob said, *They once found my mother's son asleep on duty, and they burnt his clothes as a punishment.* see *Hebrew and Talmudical Exercitations.* see also *Matthew 22:1-14.*

[118] Joseph Smith said that the Jews would not actually change the name of the city but that this would be the city's cry, *Jehovah is Here!*

[119] Luciferians use sex, and the embarrassment of sex, to trap men and women into silence or obedience. What is so odd about it is that the very sexual acts that trap them by shame at first, become the *common treat* they are given for following orders later. Where repentance and shame could set them free, silence and the future lack of shame becomes their shackles. Pretty clever, very demonic. *Sit, Heel, Good Boy! It's a dog's price in the end.*

[120] The scripture reads, *I wondered with great admiration.* I would bet serious time in a nursery class filled with ADD children, that this word was altered by the Church of the Devil anciently. John did *not* admire her. He was deeply *astonished* at what had become of her. The Lord's Lady Zion became the Whore.

[121] The Vatican Hill lying northwest of the Tiber River, the Pincian Hill lying to the north, and the Janiculum Hill, lying to the west, are not counted among the traditional Seven Hills. Tradition holds that Romulus founded the original city on the Palatine Hill on April 21st 753 B.C., and that the seven hills were first occupied by small settlements that were not grouped nor recognized as a city called Rome. The denizens of the seven hills began to participate in a series of religious games which began to bond the groups. The city of Rome thus came into being as these separate settlements acted as a group, draining the marshy valleys between them, and turning them into markets (fora in Latin). *I suspect this is how, over time, Tuscany fell to the Latins.* Later, in the early 4th century B.C., the Servian Walls were constructed to protect the seven hills. Of the seven hills of current Rome, five (the Aventine, Caelian, Esquiline, Quirinal, and Viminal Hills) are populated with monuments, buildings, and parks. The Capitoline Hill now hosts Rome's city hall, and the Palatine Hill is a main archaeological area. Constantinople is claimed to have been built on its own seven hills, following the example of Rome. *See Wikipedia for more.*

[122] Khubla (also Kublai) was born on September 23rd, 1215 A.D., to Tolui (youngest son of Genghis Khan) and his wife Sorkhotani, a Nestorian Christian princess of the Kereyid Confederacy. Khubla was the couple's fourth son. Khubla's daughter Khutugh-beki married King Chungnyeol of Goryeo and became Queen of Korea. Christianity was once much stronger among the children of the fallen houses of Shem than it is today.

[123] In our own annuals the *Mountain Meadows Massacre* was born out of fear and revenge. It never ends and Satan is there to push the buttons every time.

[124] This does not mean that they weren't evil.

[125] I believe the story of Moses asking the name of God in *Exodus* (and if you read it carefully you will see that he wasn't told it) harkens back to this story and is echoed here by John.

[126] Historians say that upper and lower Egypt were the upper and lower run of the Nile Valley, but I disagree. I believe that Upper Egypt (the white crown) was heaven and that Lower Egypt (the red crown) was earth. We'll explore the evidence that this is true in another feast. Lower Egypt is "Deshret" in the Egypt tongue, according to Egyptologists who think they can mostly speak Ancient Egyptian but admit they don't know where to put the vowels. Joseph Smith, who actually could read Ancient Egyptian via the *Urim & Thummim*, said the word was *Deseret*. Deseret, Deshret, Desheret, Deseret? And this was 80 years before man could read any Egyptian. The world mocks Joseph Smith at their own peril.

[127] I suspect that His war chariot, which we will see in the heavens above, is the planet Jupiter or a comet which Joseph Smith told us He would be riding. It (and He) will be blood red as well. The wicked will say it is only a flying red dragon, but it will be the Lord of Sabaoth with one of his Tsabim-children! Read *Vol. 5: Ezekiel & the Millennial Reign of Christ* if you want more.

[128] see my favorite scripture story *Gen. 32:24-32* and also Abraham: *Gen. 24:1-6*.

[129] Consider the man in the Nauvoo Sunstone and read *Gad the Seer* for more.

[130] It is from this verse that Alfred Hitchcock and Daphene DeMoriete, took their inspiration for the movie the *Birds* in 1963. Hitchcock was a faithful Catholic and was actually very afraid of birds.

[131] see *Times & Seasons,* July 15th 1842, p. 857.

[132] from a discourse by the Prophet remembered by William P. McIntire, March 16th 1841.

[133] see *Times & Seasons*, October 1st 1842, p. 934.

[134] see *Messenger & Advocate*, November 1835, p. 209

[135] see *Messenger & Advocate*, November 1835, p. 210.

[136] No sun? Remember that. When we feast on *Genesis* together we will talk about mighty ringed Khima and how it is said that "he" was our sun until after the days of Noah's flood.

[137] Joseph Smith noted that, "The angel that appeared to John on the Isle of Patmos [had] a translated or resurrected body."

[138] Mormonism has no traditional hell of fire and pitchforks and serpent tongued demons torturing humanity and unbaptized babies for eternity. Instead we believe that a God of Love would never torture people forever for sins done in the limited here and now. Instead we believe in *damnation* in the dictionary sense of the word; that the greatest punishment of all is being "stopped" or "damned-up" in your forward progression of eternal life. The Lord has said that He is living water. Living Water in Judaism is moving water. Stagnant water is dead. Water that is damned, in an eastern sense, is dead water because it, like the male priesthood of God, must move to have eternal life. Priesthood is motion. Motion is life. Life is increase and Eternal life is eternal increase. Those that love and make a lie are those who give birth to, or further Satan's will. He is the father of all the lies on Earth. If we love his lies more than reality, we become the stagnant water of death.

[139] See *D&C 76:82-112* for more information but remember that only God can make a final judgement as to where a person will end up on Judgement Day. In order that all final judgements be fair, it is necessary that some knowledge as to what merits a judgement be available to all, but none can see into the heart and mind of another like Jesus Christ can. It is my conviction that His final judgement will be padded with abundant mercy as well as tempered justice. Men over-judge each other. (So I thought you should read it twice.)

[140] There are examples in the scriptures of the Lord requiring the original teacher of a sin to pay for the sins of his or her students. How horrible this must be! How can one properly repent of another's sin? Time and circumstance would naturally cause the teacher to drift away from the particulars and if the student continued teaching said sin to others, where would it end? Study the lives of Cain, Laman, and Lemuel for examples of this. I for one don't want to pay for anyone's sins but my own. Frankly, I don't want to pay for my own either. I want the love (and blood) of my Saviour Jesus Christ to pay for them.

[141] *Sacred Hymns & Spiritual Songs for the Church of Jesus Christ of Latter-Day Saints*, #386, 1871, 14th Edition; *Faith like the Ancients*, N.B. Lundwall; *The Diary of Charles L. Walker*, p. 691; also private collection of the author.

[142] Also, several events including: Joshua's conquering of the Holy Land; Ezekiel's witness of the angelic marking of men from the Temple Mount; and the Lord's appearance in the Americans, are all types of the events recorded there. Careful study of these verses can add clues to events yet to come.

Made in the USA
Columbia, SC
01 December 2018